Henry Watson Fox

A BRIEF MEMOIR

OF THE

REV. HENRY WATSON FOX, B.A.

OF WADHAM COLLEGE, OXFORD;

MISSIONARY TO THE TELOOGOO PEOPLE, SOUTH INDIA.

PHILADELPHIA:
AMERICAN SUNDAY-SCHOOL UNION,
No. 316 CHESTNUT STREET.
NEW YORK: No. 147 NASSAU ST......*BOSTON:* No. 9 CORNHILL:
LOUISVILLE: No. 103 FOURTH ST.

☞ *No books are published by the* AMERICAN SUNDAY-SCHOOL UNION *without the sanction of the Committee of Publication, consisting of fourteen members, from the following denominations of Christians, viz. Baptist, Methodist, Congregationalist, Episcopal, Presbyterian, Lutheran, and Reformed Dutch. Not more than three of the members can be of the same denomination, and no book can be published to which any member of the Committee shall object.*

CONTENTS.

NOTE.

THE following Memoir has been abridged from the larger work of the Rev. GEORGE TOWNSHEND FOX, B. A. This valuable service has been kindly and gratuitously rendered by a valued clerical friend, who is anxious, with us, that so bright an example of missionary zeal and devotion should be presented to the youth of the United States, through Sunday-schools and Bible-classes.

Rugby School. p. 5.

A MEMOIR.

CHAPTER I.

BIRTH—EARLY EDUCATION—REMOVAL TO RUGBY—CORRESPONDENCE WHILE THERE.

HENRY WATSON FOX, son of the late George Townshend Fox, Esq., of the city of Durham, England, was born at Westoe, in the county of Durham, on the 1st October, 1817.

His early education was conducted under his parent's roof, where he was surrounded by a sweet atmosphere of piety; and at the age of eleven he went to the Durham Grammar School, where he continued till February, 1831, at which time he was thirteen years old.

The remainder of his education he received at Rugby School, where he continued for six years, until his removal to Oxford, and thus enjoyed the benefit of Dr. Arnold's instruction and example, during the most vigorous period of his valuable life. That instruction was not thrown away, nor that example without its influence. During his residence at Rugby School, and especially toward the latter part of it, when he had the privilege of coming into closer contact with Dr. Arnold, he contracted the greatest affection and reverence for his character; while the simple Christian instruction, which he so faithfully delivered in the school-chapel, produced a strong and abiding impression upon his heart; so that it may truly be said, that the classical knowledge and intellectual development which he acquired at school were the least of the blessings he there received: for though other influences were co-operating during that period, yet the controlling power of Dr. Arnold's mind in forming his Christian character was of the highest value, and to the end of his days was ever remembered by him with affection and gratitude.

I may here mention that my brother enjoyed the advantages of a careful education at home, as well as those which have been referred to as arising from his connection with Rugby School. Much seed had been sown in days of childhood, and thus a good foundation of religious knowledge had been laid. And no influence was so happy, or proved of such lasting benefit, as that which his eldest sister exercised over him during his holidays, when he was in the habit of reading with her regularly, and of receiving instruction, which, though for a season it lay dormant, yet in due season sprang up and brought forth fruit.

The first communication of a religious character which I can remember having held with him, took place in the year 1833, and is still vividly impressed upon my memory. I well remember the discouragement which I felt at finding, as I imagined, no response, after having read to him, one Sunday, and conversed with him about the value of his soul and the duty of serving God. He appeared uninterested, and made no reply; but, as the following letter afterward informed me, his countenance had not been a fair index of his heart.

Rugby, Nov. 10, 1833.

MY DEAR GEORGE,

As you wish me to write to you before I go home, and as I have both opportunity and will to do so now, I shall set about it. * * * Perhaps you recollect a conversation you had with me one Sunday at Durham; that conversation did me most inestimable good, for which I have to thank you; for before that, I had become, I may say, callous, or at least lukewarm in religious matters. But that first roused me, and it being followed by reading with Isabella at Cullercoats, I have become alive to my situation: I see how great is sin, and to what extent I have sinned, and hope that God will now forgive me; but still I feel myself constantly led away by temptation, in one shape or another, and still have a great repugnance to looking back on the actions of the day. I now follow a practice which —— advised me to, and from which I feel great benefit, that is, before I leave my room in order to go to the bedroom, to pray heartily to God, instead of, as I used before to do, merely saying my prayers before I got into bed; and if in these I was disturbed by other boys talking, I used to go to bed and to sleep, without offering up any prayers from my heart, and without having even asked forgiveness for the sins of the past day. I have been this evening reading one of Dr. Whately's Essays, on comparing the life of a Christian with that of children, wherein he shows how little we know of God, and in how confined a sphere; what low and earthly ideas our very best must be concerning the Divine being. We have lectures from Mr. Price on a Sunday evening, and partly from what he said, and partly from my own thoughts, the following idea arose, which, though new to me, has undoubtedly occurred to most persons, namely—that an additional reason for turning to God early in life is, that as the faculties of the body are more developed by exercise, even to the last period of one's life, so a person, the longer he lives in the fear and love of God, the more righteous and more fit for heaven he becomes. I must leave off now, for want of time: which though generally an idle excuse, is not so in this case, as it is now nearly bed-time, and I shall have no time to finish this letter next week, so now—Good-night! I remain, Your affectionate brother,

H. W. Fox.

Some religious impressions had been made upon his mind, however, at an earlier period, as the following letter to a school-fellow will show. It seems that being confined to the sick-room, this boy had spoken to him seriously; but at that time, as too often happens under similar circumstances, the counsel, instead of being gratefully received, was unthankfully rejected, and caused rather a breach of friendship. His friend having removed to Harrow, it led to a correspondence, of which the following letter forms a part.

TO M. BUCKINGHAM, ESQ., DR. LONGLEY'S, HARROW.

Rugby, Oct. 30, 1834.

My dear Buckingham,

You will, no doubt, be much astonished at receiving a letter from me so long after our correspondence had closed; and especially as I was the party who put an end to it. I now write to ask your pardon for so doing, and to express my sincere sorrow for it. Do not think these expressions are feigned or exaggerated; for though our acquaintance was but very short, yet it was blessed by the hand of God, and you were made by him the first instrument to call me to him: at first, as you may remember, I obeyed the call, but after you left, I fell away again, and on your writing to me—as religion was *then* a disagreeable subject to me—I did not answer your letters, and so the correspondence broke off. I now beg of you, that if you can forgive me, you will be so good as to renew it. I recollect you told me that you were brought to the knowledge of God by an elder sister, and this has been my case. About a year ago my eldest sister and brother took great care of my religion, and have, by God's blessing, bestowed on me the best gift they could have given me; or rather not they, but God. I have often thought of you since you left, but more especially lately, and have intended for some time to write to you, but have had no opportunity before this; and now though later, I hope you will not reject this letter. Since you went away from here, nearly three years ago, great changes have taken place in myself, my friends, and the school. From the "shell" I am now advanced to a high place in the "sixth," and my mind and faculties have had a great change; but this is too egotistical and boasting. Again and again, as I go on writing, I constantly think how you will receive this, and am afraid that you will not take it well: but pardon what is amiss, and believe me Your affectionate Friend,

HENRY W. FOX.

It may seem to require an apology for publishing the letters of so young a person, at a time when his mind was imperfectly developed, and his Christian experience of the most juvenile character; but I have ventured to do so under the impression that more instruction may be derived to those who are of like age, and under similar circumstances, by tracing the early workings of God's Spirit upon a school-boy's heart, than by having the character of a mature and experienced Christian presented to them. The feelings, the sympathies, the affections of a school-boy are more likely to be enlisted by a record of the trials, temptations, and spiritual progress of another school-boy, than by the example of an older person, with whom he can have no fellow-feeling and few sentiments in common.

Rugby, Wednesday, Feb. 19, 1834.

MY DEAR ISABELLA,

I received your kind letter by Robert, for which I am much obliged to you. Now that I have come here, I have fallen into such a vortex of temptation, that I scarcely know what to do; and they chiefly come on so insinuatingly, that I can scarcely perceive them at first. The two greatest are, I think, pride of heart, in thinking myself better than others, in comparing myself with others; and though in my understanding I see how wicked I am, yet my heart is so sinful that it is with difficulty I find means of repressing such thoughts. The other temptation is, wasting time, which comes on by little and little, but which I hope soon to be able with God's assistance to overcome. I find myself so sinful, that were it not for Christ's blessed promises, I could scarcely fancy he would hear me; but he has felt the infirmities and temptations of man, and from thence I derive great comfort. And on account of the very temptations I meet with here I ought to rejoice and be thankful to God, that he has given me such opportunities of becoming more perfect and patient than I could otherwise hope to be; but I as well as you, am anxious and fear greatly lest I should fall. During the day I feel myself clinging to this world far too much, and, if it were not for my devotions evening and morning, I feel I should quite forget my Maker. I intend therefore to read the Bible several times during the day, for there is such a blessing in the Holy Scriptures, that they always inspire one with good thoughts, and set me forward afresh to follow the precepts laid down in them. Oh, if they were taken away, how could man exist? I often follow the plan of Wilberforce Richmond, of reading the Psalms and praying over them. I find them so full of beauty and comfort, so full of holiness, that they quite refresh my soul. I constantly wish I was with you, but God's will be done: if he wills it, we shall meet again, when I shall be able to talk to you and learn from you so many good things! I pray for you continually.

There is a very interesting case here. There is a little boy about fourteen years old, in other respects a nice little boy, and one whom I was rather fond of: but, the other day, in talking with him, I discovered he never read his Bible; in short, he knew nothing of the Christian religion. I have been endeavouring to impress on him the awfulness of his state, but he seems scarcely to care whether he is lost or saved. He understands neither heaven or hell, nor that he is born for any other state than this,—that is to say, he does not *feel* it to be the case: he has apparently been completely neglected at home with respect to religious matters. Now I want to know how to proceed with him—how to open his mind—for I think when he once perceives in his heart how wicked he together with all others are, that he will be more able and willing to understand the truths of the gospel. When I have got him to do any thing right rather than what is wrong, I generally discover it is done merely because I asked him; and this doing what he thinks I wish, together with other points, shows that he has naturally a good heart, but that it wants cultivation. Oh, how thankful I ought to be to God that he has given me such good and kind parents, and brothers and sisters; for, as Sumner says, we should be thankful that we were not born in any heathen country, and that we are placed in a land where the gospel is preached, for it is by no merit of our own that we were not condemned to darkness and ignorance. Dr. Arnold, in his sermon on Sunday, used a simile I thought particularly beautiful. In talking of those who seek God in this world, they are, he said, like those foreign plants which we see here flourishing, but not having flowers nor fruit; we see that this is not their proper place, and that they must have some other place where they come to full ripeness. Both Robert and I constantly make use of the books you wrote out for us, in which we find great use. That God may requite to you the good you have done us, is the constant prayer of

Your affectionate brother,

HENRY W. FOX.

Rugby, March 1st, 1834.

MY DEAR GEORGE,

When I returned to school this half I was wofully disappointed. I had a great friend here; and though I had spoken but little on religious points with him, yet I expected that on that subject our hearts would be knit together. But alas! I find that he is little actuated by Christian principle; not that he is a bad boy in the eye of the world, but it is almost only when duty and pleasure run together that he follows the former. The following verse struck me the other day on this point: "Yea, mine own familiar friend in whom I trusted, hath lifted up his heel against me." Ps. xii. 9. Not that I mean he is no longer an acquaintance, but I find that I can no longer make him my friend; our two grand pursuits being so different. So that, besides my own family, there is not a human being who is my *intimate* friend. It is in this situation that I find how kind God is to me—He is my all to me. I remain, Your affectionate brother,

H. W. Fox.

Rugby, Thursday, March 6, 1834.

My dear Isabella,

* * * I am glad to be able to say that I was partly deceived in my old friend who is here, for I thought he was far too fond of the world; but on talking with him lately, I have discovered he is more willing to turn to God than I had expected; in fact I have great hopes of him. I am however disappointed in another point, namely, a boy who was once a great friend of mine, but who, for various reasons, has not been such a one for the last half-year, and whom I was endeavouring to assist, has put an almost insurmountable bar to *my* progress with him. I have in this instance particularly felt what you mentioned in your letter, "That God alone giveth the increase, and without that, how useless

are the efforts of man!" Whenever lately I have spoken with this boy on religious subjects, he has refused to answer questions; will not say a word on the subject, and does not attend to what I am saying. He fancies that he can serve God and mammon; he used to answer my exhortations to him, *that I was going "too far,"* and that he did not think it necessary to avoid *small faults,* but because they were small, (though he could not deny they were faults,) he quite neglected attending to them. I have therefore, since he refuses to listen to a conversation, determined to write out different things for him, to the best of my power, which I hope with God's holy assistance may be to his advantage. I have already written out one paper for him, pointing out the chief points of the Christian religion, yet without immediately applying them to him. I intend next to remark on several of the faults I have observed in him lately, which he does not feel to be faults. I was the more disappointed in him, as I had before found him willing in the general; but when I came to particulars, and he saw he must give up certain pleasures if he would give himself entirely to God, then he thought he had gone far enough, and I had gone too far—for God tells us to go as far as we can.

But this last-mentioned boy is not the one I told you of before; he is improving; he *feels* what it is to be endeavouring to do one's best, but yet he is scarce strong enough to resist temptations; which I point out to him as wrong, yet which he has all his lifetime believed to be perfectly innocent. I find it is very difficult to persuade him, and some others, that any common amusement is wrong; all the world, they say, do such and such a thing, and certainly all the world will not go to hell. But with God's grace, all will I hope go well with him.

While I am thus talking to and thinking of these three, I am often afraid, lest I should, by seeing their faults, fancy mine own smaller; humility is, I find, a very difficult thing to attain, and doing good from the motive of pleasing God, still harder. I have to struggle very hard for this last, for when I do any thing right, I do it too often for my own sake, that is, falsely thinking at the moment that it will advance my salvation; but of late God has had mercy on me, and I have been able to discover the system of faith. I was much obliged to you for your kind letter. Give my love to all. I remain,

Your affectionate brother,

H. W. Fox.

Rugby, March 17, 1834.

My dear Isabella,

I received your letter dated the 10th, yesterday morning. I am very much obliged to you for it; it will do me a great deal of good, and it has warned me from doing a great injury: for, on Saturday evening, I induced the "silent boy" to talk, and he informed me he had been silent because I had so constantly been speaking to him on religion. During the conversation, he told me he intended to serve God wholly, (which I thought a great point gained;) and next he confessed he was not so doing at the time. He asked me then, whether I thought it wrong to read light books, and do lessons on a Sunday. I was quite struck with astonishment at the question, and I answered that I certainly did. He said he thought the contrary, and his only argument was, that if he was not so doing, he would be thinking of something wrong, and therefore it was *right* to do lessons on a Sunday; he perfectly *understood* what keeping Sunday holy was, viz. endeavouring to think on God only; but he could not get it out of his head, that because he would (or rather thought he would) be doing worse, that therefore the end justified the means. He acknowledged he had *never* tried to keep, for one whole Sunday, his heart on God, yet because he had tried for one hour, he thought it was impossible that man could help thinking of things wicked in themselves on a Sunday. But I cannot help thinking that those reasons were put forward for an excuse, and that in his heart he felt it to be wrong. I urged him to try the very next day. But I have not yet learned whether he did so or not. With respect to "amusements," I believe I used the word in too general a sense when I wrote to you, but your observations on that subject are very true and just. I may perhaps, and I believe I have often spoken of religion to these boys as leading to other pleasures besides what they now enjoy, and have perhaps made them view it in a gloomy light, as they did not understand nor feel how great the new pleasures would be. For my little pupil, I have constantly changing hopes and fears: at one moment I see outwardly no hope of him, and again shortly I am quite rejoiced. I trust however that Christ will not let him fall back again after he has now been once called.

I have been particularly happy lately; I read over again the account of Wilberforce Richmond's latter end and death. I was struck, still more than I was the first time, with the beauty and simplicity of it; with his sincere faith and trust in God: since then I have been able to keep God continually in my heart, which I was not able to do before; I have therefore derived such comfort and happiness, that I hope never to lose that gift. But still sin clogs me greatly. I get proud, and fancy I do *any thing good* of my own self; at least I feel it to be so, though I know full well that I am exceedingly sinful, and that the very thought I had just been indulging in (viz. of pride) was very wicked in itself.

I derive very great comfort from reading the Bible every day. I understand it better and better, and see the meaning of the various passages in it, in a more forcible light. I always find the Sunday too short for what I want to do on it. Many others here think as I used to do formerly, that Sunday is too long, and therefore spend two or three hours in bed longer than usual, and spend the rest of the day in listlessness, or perhaps worse, never thinking what a blessing they are throwing away. I feel now, as you told me you did, that the Sabbath is quite a rest from the worldly thoughts of the other parts of the week. Last Sunday was a most beautiful day, and I took a walk by myself into the country, and never felt so happy before. I continued for more than an hour, praising and praying to God, and thanking him. I shall never neglect it again. I felt it as a preparation for heaven. I remain,

Your affectionate brother,

HENRY W. FOX.

Rugby, April 7th, 1834.

MY DEAR ISABELLA,

I have in truth spent a very bad Easter, very lazy I was all the time, and I have just returned to working again. I had intended to have read several books during the holidays, but I neglected them, and have not kept half my resolutions. All this shows how very weak I am, and how unable I am to resist extraordinary temptations. I can manage to resist, and often to overcome, my every-day trials, because I have experience of them and am aware of their approach; but when those come which I am not so much accustomed to, or if my old ones come on me in a new shape, then I fall a victim to them. When I know and have determined in myself that any thing is wrong, then I generally overcome it; but my greatest difficulty lies in making out whether the thing is wrong or not. I have of late been able to see all my sins so clearly (that is, all I consider sins) that I scarcely could dare to look up to God, or to pray to him, were it not for his gracious promises. I have given over all hopes of persuading the "formerly silent boy" by speaking to him, for he over and over again says, he is convinced of what he holds to be true, and that he will not change his opinion; or if he does enter into conversation about keeping the Sabbath holy, he merely repeats his foolish arguments over again, and will not attend patiently to what I say in answer to them. In this case he seems unable to connect what I say to him, though in general he is clear-headed enough. He is evidently not affected by my arguments, for every Sunday he continues to do his lessons, &c. Instead therefore of talking to him on the subject, I am writing out for him the best arguments I can think of, which I shall have finished in about a week. * * * I was thinking to-day, what an inducement there is to convert any one who wanders from the truth, to convert him from the error of his ways, for we are told that God and the angels in heaven rejoice when one sinner turns to heaven; and how great must be the honour and glory for him who is the instrument of joy in the heart of our Heavenly Father. The same reasoning applies, indeed, in every case where we do good from a right motive; but this case struck me to be so much stronger than most others.

Rugby, April 19, 1834.

MY DEAR ISABELLA,

* * * I have not yet been able to finish my paper for the boy I mentioned in my last letter, for I have been very busy this last week, but I hope to finish soon. I feel I have no hope from arguments, it is God that must open his heart; no argument I fear can do so: it shows me still more strongly how truly Paul says, "Apollos planteth, Paul watereth, but *God giveth the increase.*"

Rugby, May 13, 1834.

MY DEAR GEORGE,

* * * I am sorry we shall be unable to see each other for a long time; but though far distant, we may yet constantly communicate with one another, and it will be a great consolation to think that our thoughts are constantly on one and the same great object. What I have always till now found my greatest difficulty has been prayer. I could offer up words, but as I could have no idea of God, I felt I could not offer up my heart to him: but lately, on thinking, and at last feeling, that God is always present in my inmost soul, I can heartily ask for what I need, and often, and continually throughout the day, keep my thoughts on him, which I used to find almost impossible. I derive the very greatest advantage from this, for while I am continually keeping my heart with God, it is contrary to my

very nature to commit sin against him; that is, at least, known sin. I feel and know that all this has not been through my own means, but through the grace of God alone. I also have had my eyes opened, to view my wickedness and depravity, and God's purity and holinesss. I was before, as it were, covered with darkness; I could not see any thing though I tried. But now these things stand before me in glaring colours, and I almost wonder God has not yet cut me off, or even now allows me to live on in the many sins I daily commit; for notwithstanding the greatest care, I am constantly falling into, and often yielding to temptation: the greatest is lying in bed in a morning; it is of all the most difficult to overcome. It thus appears how vain and futile are all men's endeavours, unless they be assisted by God's grace. I often find that those temptations which outwardly appear very small, and which one would almost pass by unperceived, are the very strongest which attack me. There is the continual whispering in my ear—this is but a small sin, it maketh no matter to commit it; and thus I sometimes yield. But I find my only true test of right or wrong is to ask myself whether I do it from a motive of pleasing God. I find, as you mention in your letter, the great advantage of reading the Bible, with an earnest desire and prayer to understand it: often the meaning of a before-hidden passage breaks in upon me in a way which quite astonishes me. I have got, therefore, a very small pocket edition of the New Testament, to carry about with me always, that I may use it whenever I have opportunity. I remain,

Your affectionate brother,

HENRY W. FOX.

Rugby, June 5, 1834.

MY DEAR ISABELLA,

* * * I lately discoursed again on the Sabbath question with the boy I before mentioned, and he seemed, though he did not acknowledge it, to be somewhat convinced. He candidly confessed that it was not for God's glory that he did his lessons, &c. on a Sunday. He seemed not to understand that we must "do all things for the glory of God." This is a matter I have found very difficult in myself to feel thoroughly, for I am unable to see, individually, how each little action I may do, is to the glory of God; for many seem to be perfectly indifferent to do, or to be left undone. However here, as elsewhere, faith must come in and lead me at last to understand what I am as yet too blind to see. I still feel great difficulty in the evening, in examining my motives for various actions during the day. I cannot often recall them: often perhaps, because I had done them from no particular motive. I am glad to say, that the friend I before mentioned in this letter, has been persuaded to leave off several wrong things, and I have more hopes of him than of any others here. His conscience seems to be touched, and he feels it, though he does not confess it. But H—— is no better than before, if not worse. He has no steadiness nor strength, nor does what I say to him have any weight: he does not think, or I am convinced he would not say or do what he does. Believe me

Your affectionate brother,

H. W. FOX.

Rugby, August 23, 1834.

My dear George,

I have come to the end of a very unsettled vacation, in which my mind has been very wandering, and at times worldly; for the many new sights, and the travelling which I have had, have often turned my thoughts from better subjects to the objects immediately before me, and therefore, I am returning with joy to the quiet and peace of Rugby, and yet I find in this, as in every thing else, no good is without evil, nor evil without good; for though the unsettled way in which my holidays have been spent, has been in some degree of injury to me, yet that evil has been tempered by the good advice and conversation of my dear Isabella, from whom I have learned many new and important truths, for the first time, and in like manner, notwithstanding the quiet of Rugby, the want of her presence will fall heavy on me. For, at Rugby, I have no one (except Robert) to converse with on religious subjects; if I begin to do so with any, they either show a complete reluctance, or a great coldness to it. I however feel that it is for the best, for it leads me to rest on God as my only friend, and to open my heart to him more. I believe I mentioned to you in one of my last letters, that I found such great assistance in prayer, by considering that God is intimately present to me, and I am thankful to be able to say, that I have in it a constant source of grace to me; for it brings me to a more constant feeling of his presence. * * * I feel my greatest want at present to be a deficiency in my love toward God. I look on him too much as an angry rather than a merciful Judge, and do good or ill from fear. I also find a difficulty in keeping my thoughts on God throughout the day, for my customary occupations and lessons drive them out of my head; at Rugby I tried a method to assist me, viz. with certain actions and at certain times, to make it a rule to turn my thoughts to heavenly objects; but I found this only of partial use, as it served only for particular times. I pray to God daily to assist me in this, yet I know not how to direct my efforts. Believe me,

Your affectionate brother,

H. W. Fox.

Rugby, Sept. 2, 1834

My dear Isabella,

I received your letter on Sunday, as you expected, and return you many thanks for it. Though I have found less difficulty, than I usually have found, in returning to my school duties, yet I feel the change still irksome and difficult to be borne up against. I have got settled to my work, but not quite to my habits, and not having got again accustomed to a regular rule for spending the day, I frequently waste some part; not however in absolutely doing nothing, but time slips away in getting ready and beginning. On looking back to the holidays, I find much of my time has been lost in the same way, for though I was *busy* at my lessons almost all the day, yet on the whole I have done but little; I have, however, acquired a habit of doing something at least, for hitherto during former holidays I have never done any thing worth mentioning. I have already begun what you advise in your letter, namely, selecting some prayers; but I have done it from Bishop Ken rather than from Wilson; as I thought those in the former better suited and more applicable than those in the latter. I have now a matter to talk about, which it would have been better I had mentioned to you during the holidays, but I have such a great dislike to converse personally on such subjects; it is, I now think, a foolish and perhaps wrong dislike, but I could not then overcome it, and I therefore now mention it in writing. It is, how to be sure that I am in the way to heaven, not inquiring of the truth of the Bible, but how to find it out in my own heart. For I believe that not what I do of myself, but the death of Christ, brings me to heaven: at the same time I have some love of God, (but very little I fear,) and *some* of my actions are done for his sake, and I try to do all so by his assistance; now, is this the beginning of what is requisite? Is not faith a junction of belief and works springing from love to God? I am, as you may well suppose, very anxious on the question; and on examining myself on the point, I fear I do not do enough for God's sake, and thereby have not sufficient faith. I find it is so difficult to separate in my head faith and works; for as the former is more than belief, and in part consists of the latter, they seem to approach each other's nature. I wish you would be so good as to set me right on this subject in your next letter. Believe me,

Your affectionate brother,

HENRY W. FOX.

Rugby, Sept. 7, 1834.

MY DEAR ISABELLA,

I received your most excellent letter this morning, and was exceedingly comforted and strengthened by it; for being, I thank God, able to answer most of the questions in the affirmative, I received assurance that I have at least *some* faith. Since the time of reading it, my happiness has been growing greater and greater, and I have passed one of the happiest days I have as yet spent; though I have not been blessed with that exquisite joy, and as it were foretaste of heaven which I have sometimes met with, yet my happiness has been deep, though quiet and continued; and I know no better way of employing a few minutes this evening, than in returning thanks to you, and through you to God. For, my dear sister, I always consider you as one of my greatest blessings, for you have been God's instrument in recalling me from the deadness and corruption of sin to newness of life, and to a firm hope in Christ. I have been this day examining myself in the most doubtful points of my faith; for strange it is, the most doubtful parts have been the most vital parts; for I have never till to-day had a clear conception and firm belief that my salvation is from Christ alone and entirely; and that my own good deeds are worth nothing in God's sight. My chief difficulty is now, praying to God, for his Son's sake; for I do not feel at the moment of praying the necessity of so doing: deceiving myself by thinking God will hear me because he is merciful, and not *merely* for Christ's sake. This one day has been of more benefit to me than many days, for I have considered and learned many things which I understood not before. We had a most excellent sermon from Dr. Arnold this evening, explaining the duty of obedience to masters; that it was only then truly shown, when in some matter indifferent in itself, we obey them because they command us, and not because of any servile hope or fear from them. He took his text from the first lesson of the evening, and referred to that in the morning; also saying, that the two afforded examples of the greatest obedience and disobedience. I feel great advantage from his sermons, for he addresses us practically, as well as generally on doctrinal points. Believe me,

Your affectionate brother,

HENRY W. FOX.

Rugby, Oct. 20, 1834.

MY DEAR GEORGE,

* * * I have been living here free from all worldly anxieties, in prosperity, with all the pleasures of youth around me; and seeing the brightest side of a worldly life, I have been led away from the true service of God. Not, as you may expect, suddenly or violently, but day after day I have been declining faster and faster from the love of God, from the love of serving him, and inclining rapidly to the love of the world. I have become proud, trusting in my own means, *careless* of the *Sabbath*, and opposing the workings of conscience. But, oh! the unspeakable and never-failing mercies of God; He has called me back from this wicked way, by the means he has so often used toward me and others, viz. the Sabbath, and an excellent sermon; in the latter, Dr. Arnold spoke as though he had written for me—taking the text from Gal. v.: "Ye did run well, who did hinder you, that ye should not obey the truth." After explaining the text, and showing the danger of trusting in being once justified, he added: "And if any one has ever fallen away from God, trusting in being safe, there is but one course for him; let him return again, and, repenting of his sins, trust in Jesus who came into

the world to save sinners." Now this was my case exactly, I had been lately trusting in part to having been once justified. I had even drawn poison from the bread of life. For I had been lately learning the verse in the Romans—"Whom he foreknew, them he also justified, and whom he justified, them he also glorified." And mistaking the true state of the case, I supposed I was safe. Which case, which verse, and the danger arising from taking it in a wrong light, Dr. A. particularly mentioned, and was thus a striking and warning means of grace to me. I can never sufficiently thank God for his great mercies to me, when I consider the difference between us;—he the great Almighty and only God, who made heaven and all the stars; who rules all things, who of his infinite love came down to earth and *died* for us wretched beings that we were; while I am the least of all his creatures, worse than the brutes who never corrupted their own nature, who never sinned wilfully against their Maker, ever loving evil and avoiding good. And while I do this, while I am fleeing God, he mercifully calls me to him; he looks on me with pity, and pardons me. Surely to one who loves him, his ways are the ways of peace and happiness. Every day as I am raised and more freed from the bonds of this world, I see and observe the wickedness, the deeply-steeped wickedness of those around me, of all England, of all the world: while only a remnant are left to serve God. * * *

Your affectionate brother,

H. W. Fox.

Rugby, March 24, 1835.

My dear Buckingham,

* * * I have this morning been reading the Dairyman's Daughter, in Richmond's Annals of the Poor: a book you have probably read before, but which I have been reading for the first time. I shall always think of it as an especial means of grace to me, for it has been so blessed to me, as to open my eyes to many of my secret and besetting sins—as self-confidence and deadness of faith—which are hard to discover and to root out: yet God has now in his mercy assisted me, or rather, I should say, done the work wholly himself, of restoring me to a better knowledge of him; for I do not think, on looking back, that I have ever had true faith: I have always had some trust or hope in my own works. I have often, or rather generally, endeavoured to do good, in order that *I might be saved thereby*, instead of acting on the true motive of love and thankfulness, and trusting implicitly to God that he would take me to his heavenly kingdom for his *Son's sake*. And even now, I find it difficult completely to eradicate this evil motive and self-confidence from my heart. * * * Dr. Arnold has just instituted a new practice, which I think was much needed, and it is to be hoped that it will extend further than at present. In addition to the prayers in the big school, we now have a prayer before beginning our first lesson, in order that we should begin the day by asking God's blessing on our endeavours. I only trust that it may be a means of making many of us pray more than we do; for I cannot help thinking that, especially in the higher part of the school, a very great deal of irreligion, if not infidelity, exists. * * * I find it a very difficult

point to manage in my duty as præpostor, namely, to draw the line between "official" and "personal" offences—to discover where I feel revenge, and where I do any thing to enforce the power which properly belongs to me. I think I may learn from this not to desire earthly power, as it only increases our difficulties and temptations: God alone can teach me aright. To him therefore I pray, and do you also pray for me, that I may have wisdom and strength to execute judgment rightly. And believe me,

Your affectionate friend,

HENRY W. FOX.

Rugby, April 13, 1835.

MY DEAR ISABELLA,

* * * I feel every day an increasing desire of becoming a clergyman. I desire to be always employed in more immediately serving God, and of bringing many souls unto salvation. I am aware that we can do our duty and a great deal of good in every station of life; but I think that a clergyman is more particularly appointed to do good, being a light set upon a hill. I have hitherto, and I know you have at home also, looked forward to my going to the Bar, but it is not so now,—it can scarcely ever be too late to change my prospects. If it is particularly the wish of my father and mother and you all that I should fulfil the original proposition, I willingly acquiesce; but if it is indifferent, or of no great importance to you, I should prefer very much to enter the service of the Church. However, whichever profession I may hereafter follow, my present and future (for some years at least) studies will suit both; I wished however to mention this desire of mine to you. Dr. Arnold has made a great

improvement in the public prayers; for besides the prayers which are read when we first assemble in the morning, (to which I fear few attend,) we have now immediately before our first lesson a prayer to ask God's blessing on us for the day. * * * Believe me, Your affectionate brother,

H. W. Fox.

Rugby, May 16, 1835.

My dear Isabella,

* * * I trust I shall not disappoint your hopes and mine also, that I shall continue a Christian unto the end, for though I have often feared that I should not continue struggling for so long a period as my life may be, I now feel so confident that God having once brought me to a knowledge of him, will keep me safe till he takes me to his kingdom, that I have little fear, but still I labour anxiously, knowing the difficulty I shall have ever to wrestle with, and the dangerous possibility of relaxing into a state of utter wickedness. I have just been reading Guthrie, which you gave me last year, and have found it of very great use in strengthening and establishing my faith; which is however still weak. Your affectionate brother,

H. W. Fox.

Rugby, August 30, 1835.

My dearest Isabella,

I cannot refrain from writing to you now to express my happiness, my great and exceeding joy, which I have received from the Lord. During the holidays indeed, I was constantly led astray by the pleasures and amusements of the world, and though frequently called again by God to return to him, as often as I turned I fell, for I did not enough trust in him; nor was I able to turn more steadfastly to the way of salvation, till the very last day I was at home: which day was to me the beginning again of serving the Lord: and during my journey, especially during the first night, I had leisure and opportunity, and God gave me grace to pray fervently to him for grace and strength to resist my temptations; and I have most mercifully been heard, so that this week has been to me one of very great joy and growth in grace; but this afternoon during the service, I experienced more happiness and a greater foretaste of heaven than ever before, especially during the singing of the hymn, "From Egypt's bondage come," and particularly of the words, "We are on our way to God." Oh, then I felt the great mercy of our Saviour in leading us to himself, and the greatness and majesty of him to whom we are led. I have been reading the life of Henry Martyn, (for which I have to thank George, as being a means both of great profit and pleasure,) and I have derived the most instructing lessons from it. I found how much the enjoyment of things of this world have hold on me, and when I considered his state of giving himself up to be a missionary, and asked myself, Could I give up home, and the pleasures and happiness I enjoy from worldly objects, to do this laborious work for the Lord's sake? I found the weakness of my love to God, and my need of constant prayer that I may set my affections on things above and not things below; that I may confide my present as well as my future happiness to my heavenly Father, and make God my all in all, my desire, my happiness, and my hope.

Wednesday, Sept. 3.—Though at the beginning of the half, I am in the middle of an exceedingly busy week, for my lessons of course occupy a large portion of my time, indeed larger than before, for we have had some additional ones imposed, and I have received a sudden call for articles for the Rugby Magazine. I am appointed also one of the committee for the examination of the articles; and these things together have kept me so busy, that since Saturday morning (Sunday excepted) to the present moment, I have been as hard at work as possible all day, with the exception of an hour's walk each day, and I shall have similar occupations for the remainder of the week. But in the midst of all my business, I trust I do not forget the end and aim of it all, namely, that I may the more glorify God; still I find it a very great difficulty and temptation, to be able to give up so little time daily to the immediate service of Christ. I have begun searching the Scriptures for a settlement of the various articles of faith, and I find it an excellent plan for acquiring an accurate knowledge of the Bible and the situation of various passages, and I each time discover more and more how our religion must be sought for through many indirect passages, and from the whole tenor of the book; for instance, I have found no passage *exactly* defining faith, but collating several, I have gained my end.

Believe me, Your affectionate brother,

H. W. Fox.

Rugby, Sept. 10, 1835.

My dear George,

* * * Baxter has done well in laying out so very plainly how that we must not seek our rest here, and I feel it every day more and more, for as I pass through this vale of tears (well may it be called so) my natural man lays hold of every thing it meets

with, and clings to them eagerly; and often have I to thank God for showing me that this is not our abiding-place, by showing me the folly, the weakness, and sad deformity of all worldly things: how even the most innocent (otherwise) pleasures must be used —not abused—must be made means to lead us on our way to God, and not to merely delight ourselves in them; home, for instance, and the holidays, though they ought to be a time of great spiritual advancement, become to me a snare and a temptation, and the half-year at school a *comparatively* lighter time. Yet here I have a large stock of temptations and difficulties which need constant struggling with: and they too show that a state of warfare, such as a Christian life must always be, cannot be "our rest." I often long to leave this sinful world (I mean one in which *my* sins are so many) and be at rest; but I am reconciled to do God's will and remain here as long as he shall ordain: as Baxter says,

> If life be long, I will be glad,
>   That I may long obey;
> If short, yet why should I be sad?
>   That shall have the same pay.

One of the most difficult *outward* causes of temptation is my great quantity of business, which is at present so large, that merely doing the work of the school leaves me scarcely any time for devotional exercises; yet as this is not of my own ordering, I believe it will work for my good, by making me more constantly resting on God for grace and assistance, and teaching me to make use of even the shortest periods, for the purpose of prayer and meditation. * * * I have to thank you very much, my dear George, for the Life of Henry Martyn, which you gave me; for I think from no book did I ever experience so much good, so much urging to be more diligent and zealous in God's service, and knowledge of how much I fall short of even what a good *man* can acquire. I like the book the more as giving Henry Martyn's *own* thoughts and feelings, and showing us an example of the inner man, that we may derive good in that part of ourselves, and such improvement in the heart more especially. Believe me Your affectionate brother,

HENRY.

SUBJECTS FOR SELF-EXAMINATION.

1. Did I perform my devotions last night, and were my last thoughts on God?
2. When I awoke, were my first thoughts on God, and what was my state of mind while dressing?
3. How did I perform my devotions, private and public?
4. Did I rise when first called?
5. How did I do my lessons?
6. Have I wasted any time?
7. Have I obeyed all that are placed over me?
8. Have I spent my money in the best way I could?
9. Have I in any case behaved uncharitably?
10. Have I loved God with my whole heart, not allowing any other object to interfere?
11. Have I, in all I have done, sought to do his will?
12. Have I been humble toward God and toward man?
13. Have I, in conversation, sought to do good?
14. Have I yielded to temptation?

15. Has my conduct been influenced by the opinion of the world?

16. Have my thoughts been constantly heavenward?

17. Have I at all trusted in myself, either for salvation or strength?

18. Have I been thankful?

19. How did I read the Scriptures?

20. Am I cherishing any idol in my heart?

Rugby, Oct. 25, 1835.

MY DEAREST ISABELLA,

I take up my pen to write to you in a very mixed state of mind, partly mourning for the weight of my sins, partly rejoicing for the mercy God has shown me. I am just come to the end of a Sunday, one of the most unhappy, but I trust, not unprofitable I have had for long past: for I have just finished a week with more than usual backsliding and coldness toward God—chiefly the immediate effect of a neglect of my daily devotions and self-examinations, and have been passing to-day, weighed down by the weight of my sins, unable through my wickedness and hardness of heart to look up unto God, and feeling all the bonds of sin upon me. But it is good that I have been thus troubled and brought low, for I am thus taught the hateful and miserable nature of sin; and again and again I am forced to see, spite of myself, my own wickedness of heart, and to feel my own weakness, and thus to throw myself entirely on God. And he this evening has raised me somewhat from my low and dark state to some perception of him; yet how thick and dim is the glass we still see him through, and how much need have I to come closer to him. Yet whither else can I go? No one but he hath the words of eternal life, and that alone is worth living for. Oh! how unspeakable are the riches of his mercy, and how eternal is his love: to bring us back again and again when we fall away from him, and again to teach us how gracious he is. In truth, eternity itself cannot be too long to praise him in; and yet this life must also be spent in that same service of praise and love, though these be mingled oftentimes with troubles, and groanings, and tears; and be often hid from us by some earth-born idol of our own creation. (Tuesday, Oct. 27.) To-day again I have been blessed by great peace of mind and by strength to continue aright: this I feel more than I have generally felt before, for it has always happened that my days of coldness toward God and unwillingness to serve him have been some of the week-days, and my days of greatest peace have been the Sundays: on which days (the Sundays) I have often looked forward to the coming week with great fear and almost horror, expecting to be again swallowed up by the world; but now I am going on with my usual avocations, yet feeling in me that peace of God which passeth understanding, and a firm hope of eternal salvation through Christ; and feeling also that between to-day and to-morrow there is no great and marked difference to break in upon my comfort. I thank you very much for your advice about my anxiety for the Exhibition; and I think I fully feel how much I must humble myself, and how much there is still in me of self, which must be rendered up wholly unto God. This anxiety has been exercising very bad effects on me, by leading me to work for the Exhibition, and hiding God from me in all my daily school-work; but I pray daily that I may be led more and more "to do *all* things for Christ's sake." * * * My dearest Isabel,

I am your affectionate brother,

HENRY.

Durham, January 30th, 1836.

MY DEAR GEORGE,

I am just coming to the end of a period of great trial and temptation, and one which I have always to lament over, for the many failings and errors which I have made during it. For though during the holidays my earthly means and assistances are very much greater, being surrounded by Christian friends, yet I have as yet always found myself during the holidays in a very cold and dead state toward God, and only relieved at times by being brought to him again; and yet after this revival, as it were, in my heart, in a day or two, or even less, I fall back again;—not into open and wilful sin, but into carelessness and forgetfulness, and with this backsliding, or rather as its effect, there comes on me a great spiritual blindness, fulfilling those words: "If we do his will we shall know of the doctrine." The chief cause of all this sin is my trusting partly in my own strength, and not watching unto prayer. The immediate cause of the temptation which besets me is the broken-up state of my studies, and my mind at home, and the too many earthly enjoyments I there meet with. But yet all these backslidings are, and I trust will be, very useful to me, teaching me by frequent experience to put my whole trust, not merely for salvation, but for strength and support as well, on Christ only. * * * I can in some degree sympathize with you, with respect to the peace and happiness of the Sunday; at least, at school, I have every opportunity of being quiet, and am able to spend almost the whole of the day in communion with God. But latterly I have given up two hours on the Sunday evening to teach some of my younger school-fellows. I have found it an advantage even to myself, to begin to teach; it makes me learn more and more clearly the doctrines of Christianity, and prepares me for teaching hereafter. It is a great consolation to me also, to have around me Christian friends; two have come to a knowledge of religion since I knew it myself, and the others have become friends since then; it seemed best to God, and I now perceive the advantage, that when my eyes were first opened, I should be left without any Christian companions; but all around me were in this light strangers. It made me trust more to heavenly assistance, and prevented me from falling into carelessness, by surrounding me with those whose conversation and conduct showed me what state to avoid. I am now on my way to Cambridge, where I shall stay a few days on my road to Rugby; and I expect to see there, perhaps to hear, Mr. Simeon, Henry Martyn's friend; I will write to you again soon, and tell you respecting him, for old as he is, he preaches nearly every Sunday at his church. Believe me, my dear George,

Your affectionate brother,

HENRY W. FOX.

Rugby, April 17, 1836.

MY DEAREST ISABELLA,

* * * I have just returned from visiting a poor sick woman, who is, and apparently has long

been, a sincere Christian; and though she was unable from weakness to say much, yet I have received much good from witnessing how a Christian is supported in the most trying hour, and in again viewing how transitory and empty is this world and its goods, and I find that this last especially is a lesson which I have constantly to learn afresh; for I live in a state to see the best and most desirable parts of this world; in boyhood, free from most outward cares and troubles, and with many pleasing and exciting things in prospect; all this naturally draws me down to the level of the things of this world, and I need constantly to see poverty, weakness, and misery, in order to call to mind that all present things are quickly passing away, and that my affections must be more and more set on things above. I feel a very great temptation attacking me now, in the form of a love of this world, which has come upon me from the prospect of the examinations at the end of this half-year; for these are constantly before my eyes, on account of my preparations for them, and I am led to look forward to them as the end to which all my present labours are to be directed, instead of doing all things directly for God's sake;—this necessarily brings a great darkness over me, since I am tempted to have another object in view instead of Christ; but yet with the temptation God gives a way to escape, and I trust and pray, that by his grace I may not only come out of this trial unhurt, but improved by it. I read in Dr. Arnold's sermons to-day, that "if we have truly tasted that the Lord is gracious, our only reason for wishing to remain on earth must be to further his kingdom," and I thought how very true, and yet how many other motives do we allow to come in the way;—how many other ties to earth do we make for ourselves! Oh, how very weak and inconsistent are we, and how very sinful, and how thankful should we daily be, that it is not on our own works that our salvation rests! And yet even, though we ought to be, and perhaps are thankful that such is the case, how fain would we try to seek our salvation by our works, and put our trust in them, if we were not constantly checked, and called to remember how sinful they are, and how weak we are! * * *

HENRY.

Rugby, May 20, 1836.

MY DEAR FATHER,

Though I begin this letter so soon, yet as I intend it to reach you on your birth-day, I must begin it by wishing you many happy returns of the day, and I pray God that they may be also both happy and blessed. However the event of the examination may turn out, I know that it will be by God's guidance, and I trust I may not only be content, but glad to receive that allotment which he knows to be best. I have had some severe struggles with myself; but God has given me his strength, and has enabled me to be willing to commit myself and all my concerns to him. I should very much like to succeed, according to your wish, but it may be best for us all that I should not; and then we shall all have need to be thankful that matters have not gone according to our short-sighted wishes, but have been under the direction of Him, who looks not only on our worldly benefit, but on what most forwards us in our approach to his holiness. As my time draws to a close here, I feel a great deal of pain at parting with old scenes, and leaving school seems to be like leaving the world, for though one rejoices to go away and be at rest, and enjoy the presence of Christ eternally, and would not return for worlds, yet there is a feeling of pain at parting with what has been so dear on earth; and the leaving my study for ever will be painful, for it has been the place of my joy and sorrow for the five years, and has also been the scene of my first opening views of religion, and where for two years and a half I have offered up my daily prayers, and have received so many tokens of God's grace, and mercy, and love. And yet it is better that these ties should be broken, for it teaches me more manifestly that our rest is not here. To-morrow I shall receive the sacrament the last time while I am at Rugby, and much need have I to be exceedingly thankful to my God and Redeemer, for his having so often vouchsafed me the means of attending at his table, and of enjoying the blessed promises of his word; for if it were not for his grace, and his only, I might be now entirely ignorant of him, and be one of those who go away from his table careless of his goodness. Believe me, my lear father,

Your very affectionate son,

HENRY W. FOX.

Rugby, June 13, 1836.

MY DEAR ISABELLA,

Though I have not been able to manage that you should receive a letter from me to-day, yet I have found time to begin one, and I have not thought the less of you; but when you will receive this one I cannot tell, perhaps scarcely before the end of the half. I am heartily wishing that time was come, for I am quite tired out with school-work for the present, and wish to be at home among you again, and have some rest and quiet; and besides the weariness of merely finishing one labour to take up another, I often feel tired of having nothing but boys' company. * * * But my weariness of school is a very partial feeling; and who can be unhappy, who is a Christian? It is enough to know that our present situation is of God's appointment to make us content and happy in it, and as I know that it is only the feeling of his presence which can in any circumstances confer happiness, it is rather a mark of weakness of faith to be always looking forward to some future part of this life, as being happier than the present. I am sure you will rejoice in my joy at having at last found a person sincerely desirous of becoming a Christian; he is a boy about fifteen years old, and I first became acquainted with his state by his coming to me about a month ago, and inquiring whether I thought he could go to the sacrament, considering his state; by this he meant, that he was so sinful. I found that God had been working in him for some time, but he was yet dark with respect to the knowledge of many necessary things:—since then we have met every Sunday evening, and I have endeavoured to teach him from the Scriptures, and explain them to him; he appears very sincere, and has gained more knowledge since I first spoke to him, and though the time we shall have been together will be short, yet I pray and believe that it has been made a means of strengthening his faith; and in leaving him I shall have little fear (I mean humanly speaking) of his relapsing, for God has truly called him, and will uphold him. We had a very nice meeting here about a week ago, for the Church Missionary Society; Baptist Noel was present, and gave a very interesting account of the Missions in the East, especially of an entrance into China; he made me remember Henry Martyn. The assembly was addressed by several other clergymen, and it was very delightful to retire for a while from the bustle and worldly-mindedness of my general scenes and companions, to be among those whose only aim was to advance their Saviour's kingdom, and who were talking of him alone; it was very refreshing and useful to me, and may perhaps be the cause of still more good; for what Mr. Noel spoke so earnestly about,—the want, not of funds merely, but of missionaries,—has much more than even before led me to think seriously of so employing the talents which God has given me: but of this I wish to speak more fully during the holidays. Believe me to be

Your affectionate brother,

HENRY.

Liverpool, July 7, 1836.

MY DEAR GEORGE,

* * * I have just gained an Exhibition, and am going to lie by for a time in seeing Scotland. * * * The little sickness I had, put an end to the plan in view, of my standing for a Wadham scholarship, by coming just at the time I was to have gone up; at first I was somewhat disappointed, but it was God's own working which prevented me, and he also taught me to be content; it brought much fresher to my mind how I was to work for his glory, and made me depend on him much more for every result; yet still I constantly find myself seeking my own will, instead of looking only on what is his. I have felt a good deal on leaving Rugby, and seeing each spot,

not perhaps for the last time, but for the last as a school-boy, and many of them will be sadly altered before I shall be able to see them again;—it was in the case of inanimate objects that I felt most; parting with my study was by far most severe, and I could scarcely resolve to take my last look at the place, where for five years I have sat in joy and sorrow, where day after day I have knelt in prayer, and week after week I have spent many happy Sundays; it was a breaking up of all the physical ties which I have had since I was a mere child. And yet it is strange I would not have returned next half for any thing; it is like leaving life altogether; there is a pang and a pain in parting with so many endeared objects, but not for worlds would I return to them; in the midst of sorrow we are in joy at the prospect before us. I have several plans in my head at present respecting my future employment, but the chief one is to go out to some quarter of the world as a missionary: young men are needed for that course, and I feel myself in some respects fitted for it, as having a strong constitution, and a fondness for learning languages. * * *

Your affectionate brother,

HENRY W. FOX.

Durham, August 29, 1836.

MY DEAR GEORGE,

I thank you for your letter of June 7th, which I received a few days ago: the subject you have spoken of in it has been for a long time, I assure you, a matter of consideration with me, but I do not think that, till very lately, I have entered upon it with a single heart. It is with shame and sorrow that I have to say, that from the time I was first brought to a knowledge of God, I have scarcely ever walked with a single and entire devotedness to his service; there may have been short times, perhaps for a few hours or days, in which God has been the only object of my desire, but for three years I have had a snare in my path, and have been endeavouring to unite a love of God with a love of the world: and of course the latter has been too frequently gaining the ascendancy. When I look back on this period, I have more and more need to render thanks to God that he has not cut me off for my hardness of heart. But, praised be his name, he has at last, I believe, brought me to love him alone, and given me strength to cast away the sins that beset me; so that now, though my spirit is constantly attacked by, and too often yields to, the enticements of the world, yet I am enabled to set my heart on him only. And now that I am freed from having a worldly object constantly before me, I have much greater peace and comfort in Christ—much, very much more—than I have enjoyed for many months, or I may say, than I have ever had: now I feel that I can do all things through him that strengtheneth me; but only *through Him.* Hitherto my holidays have been to me a constant source of trial, and of sorrow afterward; this year (I know not why; I have not deserved it, and it is through his great mercy alone) God has granted that they should be to me a season of great joy and comfort, and I trust I may be enabled to make them a useful time of preparation, for the change in my scene of life which I am just about to enter upon. To return to the subject of your letter, I believe that now I am seeking sincerely how I may best glorify God by my choice of a profession, and that is the sole object I have; but it was some time before I could entirely cast away earthly advantages from my view. As far as I can judge at present, my views agree with your's. I seem to be rather fit for the ministry than the bar; and physic, though opening very many means of doing good, has never occupied my attention. My own desires are certainly for the first of the three, and my attention is frequently drawn to view its peculiar duties, so that I should in some respects be more prepared beforehand for it than for the others. But I have still some years before I need make a definite determination, and I trust that God will hear my prayers to the effect that I may be guided aright in my choice. I thank you deeply for your letter, which has been of very great use to me; for your assuming in it that the glory of God was my only object, made me feel guilty and aware that such was not the case; it has been the beginning of my throwing myself entirely on Him. It is indeed an exceeding great mercy to be enabled to have an abiding sense of our acceptance with God through Jesus Christ's merits, not by our own. There is the point;—we are so sinful and so weak, that when once our eyes are opened, we must despair of salvation by our own means. And how great is the peace and comfort to feel that our sins, however heinous they may have been, are blotted out by Christ's sacrifice, and that our imperfect prayers are heard, and our works of love accepted through him, and for his sake; it is indeed a joy unspeakable, and a peace which the world cannot give nor take away. The chief danger I feel now is lest I should become proud, and fancy it is my own doing, or my own merits, which have brought me to so happy a state; for if we avoid one error, it is difficult to keep in the straight path; but we are tempted to fall into the opposite one, and humility is only to be learned after frequent backslidings. How strange it is that such beings as we, who have most cause of all created things to feel shame, since we alone are fallen creatures, should ever be in danger of becoming proud of our good things, which even are not our's, nor of our doing. * * * Believe me, my dear George,

Your affectionate brother,

HENRY W. FOX.

CHAPTER II.

REMOVAL TO OXFORD—SPIRITUAL TRIALS DURING HIS UNIVERSITY CAREER.

MY brother left Rugby at midsummer, 1836, and began his residence at Wadham College, Oxford, in October of the same year.

His correspondence during his career at Rugby has shown a steady development of mind, and a healthful progress in divine knowledge and grace. I cannot refrain from observing, how much more happy was his course than that of many enjoying similar privileges, who neglect opportunities, waste time, and worse than all, quench the impressions which the grace of God is making on their hearts, instead of cultivating and carefully improving them.

My brother went up to Oxford fortified by the grace of God, and better prepared to withstand the temptations of University life than most at his age; yet, for all that, it proved a season of peculiar trial, during which, though he lost not his foothold entirely, though he was graciously preserved from vice, nay further, maintained to a certain degree his Christian character and his Christian warfare, yet he received a check; his course for a time was no longer onward, but backward, and he became the victim of that enemy so destructive to the Christian life, a spirit of backsliding.

1. The first error, by no means an uncommon one, into which he fell, was that of not being sufficiently choice in the selection of his companions; associating with many who had no sympathy with him in divine things, and whose influence could only be that of deteriorating his better impressions.

2. He contracted a violent passion for boating, in the pursuit of which amusement he found it difficult to stop at that point which yields healthful exercise; but became so enamoured of the sport as to spend on it many precious hours to which study was properly entitled.

3. A want of regular habits and of fixed times, both for study and devotional purposes, were consequences very likely to supervene from such associations, and such was the case;—but beyond this, my brother's decline, at its worst point, went not. The grace of God had been too deeply rooted, and his conscience was too sensitive, to allow of his falling away entirely from Him to whom he had early consecrated his heart. Besides this, he had other healthful and corrective influences acting upon him; among which may be mentioned his connection with the Sunday-school of St. Ebbe's, and his acquaintance with Mr. Champneys, at that time the valuable curate of the parish; he had also had a district for visiting the poor;—to which must be added the healthful influence of domestic affections, and a frequent corre-

spondence with his sister. Thus therefore, though to the eye of the world there was not much to complain of,—nay, if he had not previously been the subject of deeper impressions, and a more vigorous piety, one would have rejoiced even at that measure which still remained, when most palsied by lukewarmness; nevertheless, the disadvantages which he experienced from the causes already detailed, were serious and permanent. He was not prevented from reaping to a certain extent the advantages of mental culture and intellectual development; but he did fail, as he himself often afterward lamented, of obtaining the full benefit which he might have derived from his residence at Oxford; and it was mainly owing to this cause, that the expectations of his friends were not realized, and the standing he had gained at Rugby not maintained, so that, though he took a respectable degree, those higher honours of which he at one time gave promise were not obtained.

Writing to a friend shortly after he had taken his degree, he expressed himself as follows:—"I trust your course at Cambridge may be a more steadfast and Christian one, than mine was at Oxford. If I may be allowed a word of advice, I should say, consider the object of the University, viz. the education of the mind, and formation of habits, and set yourself to fulfil it; and consider in, and for whom you are to do it, and be much in communion with Him, who is the highest blessing."

The altered circumstances in which my brother was placed, no doubt added greatly to his temptations on entering upon his university career.

While at Rugby, he had enjoyed the advantage of discipline, that "pressure from without," which was greatly serviceable in helping the conscientious workings of his own mind; so that habits of study, and a system of living by rule, were more easily attained. Now the great advantage of this to the spiritual life, need hardly be pointed out. Early rising, with a period of healthful prayer and study of God's word, before entering on the duties of the day, gives vigour and nerve to the soul, enabling it to discharge its duties with energy and perseverance.

Again at Rugby, during the latter period of his course, he had the advantage of being in the Sixth Form, which gave him the office of Præpostor; and it is curious to observe what a control this sense of "office" seems to have exercised even upon boys who were not governed by higher motives; they felt, that upon them rested in a great degree, the discipline, the credit of Rugby; they were strongly impressed with a sense of their importance in the exercise of their præpostorial duties, and very high notions were entertained of "the dignity of the Sixth."

No doubt some self-conceit and self-sufficiency were infused by such feelings, but the standard of conduct was elevated by it decidedly. I speak more especially of those who had not higher motives to govern them, but even those who had, would feel assistance from such external influences.

At Oxford these advantages were lost, and what would be more injurious, perhaps without being perceived. In the place of discipline came perfect freedom—no external helps toward regular habits—so that except the warning voice of conscience, there was nothing to check self-indulgence, lying in bed, waste of time, and unprofitable lounging companions.

The following extract from his letters will illustrate his progress.

Wadham College, Nov. 4, 1836.

MY DEAREST ISABELLA,

* * * I have entered a Sunday-school, which contains 160 boys, and is conducted in a very able way by Mr. Champneys, the clergyman, who is a most excellent person. On Sundays, except for morning and evening chapel, I am free all day, as far as regards the college, and thus am perfectly able to give two hours to the school. I have found this change of life a very great trial indeed; for independently of the broken-up state in which my time has till now been, (I hope that in a few days more I shall be done with all invitations,) I have been frequently tempted and yielded to the temptation of foregoing my mid-day devotions; and thus when the morning has been spent in continual application of my mind to classics, and the afternoon and evening been frequently spent in others' company, you will know that when my devotions have been neglected, I have been worldly-minded in the extreme; this has kept me in a very low state of love to God, till the last few days, when I have been enabled by his grace to resist more successfully the inclinations of my heart. I have all along found the morning and evening service in chapel of great benefit; and instead of growing weary from the constant repetition of the same service, I grow more and more to like it. How daily does one's experience of the wickedness of the heart of man increase! I find mine continually drawing me back to the world, and always at variance with God; and every season of backsliding feeds afresh the half-extinguished flame of sin in it, and the fight has to be fought again. But still, notwithstanding all this knowledge, I am ever yielding to some temptation: I

often think of that line of the hymn, "Cleanse me from its guilt and power!" And the days are fast passing away, and the time will soon be at hand, in which the weary shall be at rest, and not only so, but rejoicing in the glory of God. I have already, in spite of the unfavourable weather, become a great waterman. On my third-day of rowing, I went down to Abingdon in a four-oar, during which, I rowed rather more than eleven miles, and yesterday the same crew of us went above eight miles, of which the first four was in the rain, and for above a quarter of an hour in the heaviest storm of rain and hail I ever felt; but we pulled through it, and none of us have taken any harm from it. * * *

HENRY W. FOX.

Louth, Jan. 9, 1837.

MY DEAREST ISABELLA,

I spent rather a lonely three weeks at Oxford, but did not make so much use of it for reading as I might have done. Perhaps you will be rather astonished to hear that I am now strongly tempted to be idle, and it has been one of my besetting sins during the last term; I have always had this as a temptation, but at Rugby I was generally enabled to resist it, and I trust I shall again be able to do so when I return. * * * I am not astonished at your being anxious respecting me at College, for it is indeed a place full of temptations of every kind, both outward and inward: I am tempted on the one hand to be idle by a hundred different temptations; and then when I work I am tempted to do so for the sake of worldly honours and rewards, and the very work itself is always leading me away to be worldly-minded. But next term I expect to have a great assistance, by visiting the poor regularly: for as far as I have hitherto done so, I have found great benefit from its spiritualizing my mind. I have not yet overcome my old habit of laziness in rising, and I feel it to be a constant source of ill to my soul, either causing me to hurry my devotions, or to neglect some of my daily work. Believe me

Your very affectionate brother,

HENRY.

Wadham College, Feb. 2, 1837.

MY DEAR BUCKINGHAM,

* * * I have now been up here about three months, and much as I expected to like Oxford, my expectations have fallen short of the reality. I had before I came up, one or two religious friends, and I expected to be able to form one or two other friendships which should have for their foundation the love of Christ; but instead of one or two, I at present know above a dozen such persons, with several of whom I am very intimate. This has been a great blessing, but I have put it to very little use, for last term I was very idle, which being itself sinful, led into a cold and worldly state; and even now I can scarcely dare to say that I am out of it. The morning service in chapel ought to be a great advantage to me, but through my laziness I seldom use it: however, by Christ's assistance—for it is by his grace alone that we stand—I trust to be able to overcome this bad habit. Many, too, of the blessings, I have turned to evils by neglecting and abusing them. I waste time in vain conversation with my friends. I allow my reading to take away my heart and thoughts from heavenly subjects, and my heart to fix on those objects which were given me only for

refreshment or assistance. Very soon after I came up, I was able to become teacher at a Sunday-school, under Mr. Champneys, who is a most excellent and delightful man; and I am just about to take a district in his parish for visiting. I have hitherto had very little of this; but whenever I have had it, I have felt its great benefit. All this will be a preparation for the time when I shall have a parish myself; or, as I often look forward to it, for teaching the heathen in foreign lands. * * * Believe me,

Your very affectionate friend,

HENRY W. FOX.

Wadham College, June 10, 1838.

MY DEAREST ISABELLA,

* * * I never knew so much wickedness in myself, so much innate sin, growing apace and overrunning all things, the moment it was unchecked by the grace of Christ. My dear sister, you can no doubt feel for me, but you can scarcely know the extremity of my sin, and the blackness of my heart; the frequent entire neglect of God in private, which made its appearance, even before men, in the form of carelessness, and the laying hold of the world again, and its pleasures; the dimness of the spiritual light: so that these things which before had been plainly sinful and hateful, were now become doubtful, and many which before had been disallowed, were admitted; nay, even *now* I scarcely dare say, that I am out of this slough, so often and often do I fall back, even when I have been somewhat brought back to God, and then to think that this is the case with one who has had committed unto him, not five, but ten talents, for here am I surrounded, as it were, by every means of grace, if I choose to make use of

them;—daily prayers, outward assistances for regularity of mind and habits, good sermons, truly Christian and wise friends, Sunday-schools, visiting, and every assistance which books can give—all this, and yet so neglected; and I, who am here placed in a most responsible situation, as a light upon a hill, have become darkness;—how much evil I have done, not to speak of the absence of good to those around, I dread to think of; but Christ, who loves us better than we know,—deigns to call us brethren. * * *

HENRY.

St. Bees, August 23, 1838.

MY DEAR ISABELLA,

* * * I often find myself deceiving myself by fancying utility in some pleasure which has perhaps nothing but the pleasure to recommend it in reality; thus I am not always careful about my society, apologizing to myself, that to mix in this or that sort, it may be rather lower than my rank, or less moral than ought to be, is useful, in order, both in endeavour to raise those who form it, and to learn men's manners and minds under every form. I have been passing by no means a happy time at Ambleside, as far as regards my state of mind, and I have been in a situation in which I do not recollect to have been before, though I have known of it from the writings of others. During my moving about, I was generally in so unsettled a state, my attention so constantly caught by some novelty or amusement, that I fell into a very careless and godless state. I cannot tell you how low my heart sank in forgetfulness of God, even though I continued my forms of devotion:—on my arrival at the Lakes, my quiet situation and sudden change of habits from idleness

and irregularity to steady reading, gave me every opportunity for returning to God; but here he has used punishment for my sins, and after having a thousand times used mercy, shown in immediate reception after fallings away, he has now hid his face from me; I feel as if I could not come near him, and my prayers are full of darkness and want of faith. I know that even my present coldness is an additional cause of this state, but it is more than usual. I desire to bow myself under this trial too, and oh! I desire to struggle after Christ; I know that he has not altogether given me over to my own wickedness, or else he would not have left this desire after him in my heart, and I can trust that he will receive me again, nay, does now receive me through his own blood, but that he is using correction to warn me against my sins, and to show me more plainly what are the fruits of following the world;—I have gone many steps backward, I find myself ever looking forward to some earthly place of rest, and I seem not to realize Christ's kingdom. Oh! what a miserable sinner I am, to be but now entering into God's service, so long after he has called me, and after so many great and manifest mercies to me. I sometimes look forward, that probably in two years, or a little more, I shall be a clergyman, and if I am no more advanced during that time, than I have been during the last two years, how shall I teach, who shall need teaching in the very elements myself? * * *

Believe me,

Your affectionate brother,

HENRY.

JOURNAL.

Newcastle-upon-Tyne.—*Sunday, August* 27, 1837.—A very joyful day: God mercifully heard my prayers for the Sunday-school children, and they were more attentive and inclined to learn. He was very graciously present with me during morning service. Mr. Clayton preached on "With desire have I desired to eat this passover with you," showing the great love of Christ, in caring only for his disciples, even just before his suffering. I received the sacrament with more joy than I have ever before done, feeling perfect assurance in Christ's redeeming love,—but the afternoon was wasted in sleep; thus neglecting my almost only time for reading. Before evening service I studied Ephesians iii., which set forth the love of God as shown in our salvation, and the freeness of his gift. In the evening I was again blessed by a very excellent sermon from Mr. Hopper. While walking to Gateshead, I was enabled to return thanks to God for his numerous and full temporal blessings to me, for his having so mercifully and patiently brought me so far, with an assurance of continuing me to the end. Oh! the glory of the thought, that I am now an heir of salvation. "We are now on our way to God," not a thing to be hereafter attained; we are now heirs, waiting merely till the time of our inheriting comes:—"Even so, Lord Jesus, come quickly." "Thanks be to God for his unspeakable gift."

Monday, September 11.—On Saturday I accompanied E. C—— to Cullercoats; the day was spent in sauntering, in sailing, fishing, and chatting in the evening;—truly to be in the society of friends, gentlemen, and persons capable of affording continual amusement, and where the train of kindly feeling is never so much as wounded—this is a great pleasure; but it is an entirely worldly one, and independent of its indulgence, it had its bad effects on me, of deadening my spirit of love and adoration. On the Sunday morning I was somewhat refreshed by prayer in my own room, but the continual interruptions and worldly conversation of the day were a snare by which I was entangled. I was under a continual feeling of guilt, save during the afternoon and evening service.

In the evening I had a solitary walk on the beach, "where the tide was gently flowing," and one little rippling wave after another made sweet music on the shore; under the calm and silent light of the full and mist-embosomed moon,—was enabled to thank God for all this, and to feel his love and mercy by giving us these enjoyments of his works.

Sunday, October 1, 1837.—Yesterday I was nineteen,—to-day, I am twenty years of age. I desire to record some particular mercies of God to me during the past year:—First of all, his daily preservation of me in health and strength, and the grace which he has given me for spiritual advancement. I think, that now, all striking outward objects which would tie me down to the world are removed. God has placed me in situations of great usefulness and responsibility at Oxford;—in the Sunday-school, the district visiting and lecture, besides my influence upon individual friends—these, especially the last, have been sadly neglected on my part, which I pray may be corrected henceforth. I have been, during much of the last year, in great spiritual coldness; from my first residence in college, to my present vacation, I was wrapt up in worldly things, many had hold on my heart, and more entangled me in daily business: at times, especially on Sundays, and during the Easter vacation, I arose by the Lord's assistance and shook off the world, but yet was there always one worldly tie holding me down; another evil was, my engagement in boat-racing, whereby I was much associated, for two hours daily, with persons entirely worldly, and never had any quiet solitary walks to lead me back to God—this same thing was the cause of a great deal of idleness, of weariness at night, to the injury of evening devotions, and of laziness in the mornings, hurting my hours of prayer, and altogether forming a weight of sin on my soul. Periods of travels, as that to Louth in the winter, and to London and home in the summer, were scenes of utter ungodliness, when at night I felt afraid to kneel down to ask forgiveness. I thank God, that after my return home he called me more to him; living quietly at Newcastle, early rising, regular habits, were the means he used. For two or three weeks immediately following, I was enabled to live more closely to Christ than ever before—since, I have varied much; at times had seasons of prayer, and looking closely to God;—at others I have fallen into wilful sin, and consequently worldly-mindedness.

Friday, October 20th.—OXFORD.—On Saturday, S. H—— and I travelled through pretty hedge-woodlands to Newark, where we stopped to see the Castle. Proceeded solus in a fly to Rugby, and as I approached that dear place, all glad thoughts stirred within me, and my heart leaped to recognise in the moonlight each scene of my boyhood. How kindly too was I received by Mr. and Mrs. Price, and was there not cause for giving of thanks in all this happiness? Next morning I went to chapel, and entering that place of worship where I first and so often enjoyed in fulness, the presence of God's spirit, and hearing that same beloved voice, and seeing those well-remembered faces, filled me with such an unearthly ecstasy, that I trembled and could scarcely stand—for years had I been looking forward to that moment, and the reality surpassed the expectation. And here I desire to record my intense and heartfelt respect, admiration, and love for Dr. Arnold, and I wish always to praise God for his great kindness in having placed me under him, as from him as a means, is derived all that I have of use or pleasure. Again did I receive from his hands the Lord's Supper,—again did I see him ascend the pulpit, and hear his words of wisdom and of truth. The weather at Rugby was lovely;—during one calm evening's walk to the mushroom-field, I was struck with the change that had taken place in my perception of beauty during the last year. Each day at Rugby was ended by a different but a lovely sunset. I wish to repeat what delight it was to return to old scenes, and places, and friends. Rugby is my polar star, and I think of it daily. Oh! dear beloved place.

Durham, Sunday, Jan. 14, 1838.—Lord, do thou occupy that place in my heart which has been emptied of its former possessors, and which is indeed thy seat by right. I desire to love my Saviour, but I do so very little. I am about to enter on some severe trials at Oxford, by leading a different life, and endeavouring to make all things subservient to the will and glory of God; (alas! how I have hitherto conformed to the world, and led an inconsistent life!) but to do this, my hope is in Christ, who is my Redeemer. Oh! may he be also my exceeding joy.

Oxford, Feb. 2, 1838.—I live much more by myself, and am able to mingle much more in religious conversation. I begin again, after the lapse of a year and a half, to take a great delight in reading, and begin to read more steadily.

April 30.—I have read something, but not much —my old sin of idleness and dawdling still besets me hard. I have been neglectful of prayer, and have been in a dead state.

September, 1838.—During my stay at Frome my life was inconsistent with my profession, and I laid a great stumbling-block in the way of ——, who was quite irreligious herself, and observing how ill my conduct agreed with my language, took, as she told me, a greater objection than ever to religious people.

I desire to bewail my sins and backslidings. As a general fault, my want of love to God is chief; I can love men enough, but feel little of a similar love to God. As to means of grace, I am careless and sluggish. I know that prayer, thanksgiving, and Scripture-reading are the very life of the Christian; and he lives and dies according as he uses those. And I oftentimes propose to continue more instant in prayer, but I am ever neglecting: in the morning I am frequently hurried by late rising, at mid-day my heart is cold, and I generally put off, and thus neglect prayer. At evening, I too often lie down in unrepented sin, braving God's wrath, or at most spending a few cold moments in prayer, and I accept the most paltry excuses for neglecting to read God's word. My Sundays are cold and worldly: I sometimes enjoy the public services very much, but I misspend in idle conversation, sleep, or foolish thought, much of the afternoon and evening; so that I go to bed cold-hearted and godless, and have no strength for the coming week.

In particular offences I am very guilty. I am inactive and indolent, and give way to temptations, even when known as such. Nor am I watchful to avoid and resist them; nor do I fly to Christ for assistance when under them. And so in outward words and acts, I am inconsistent with my professions, and I fear I was a great snare to many during my visit in the summer, and at Kirk Michael: in fact, in outward things, what difference is there between me and any moral person? How do I let my light be seen? How do I fight against Satan in the hearts of others? O Lord, forgive me my great falling short in this point; for I am set on a hill, yet show no light. How many will there be who, from the depths of hell, will accuse me of not having warned them, or of having encouraged them by my example in their evil courses.

So passed the two first years of his University life; a better day seems to have dawned upon him with the third; and though there are few records remaining of that period, it is evident that the struggle of which he complained had produced a more vigorous renewal of the warfare; and that instead of sitting still and complaining, he had been led into the heat of the battle, and there gained a victory over his own heart.

And with this revival of God's work in his heart returned those early thoughts of devoting himself to a missionary life, which had engaged his mind as far back as his school-boy days. There is an intimate connection between love to God and to man: where the former decays, the latter will not long remain—at least, the heart will refuse to respond to all calls which involve self-denial, and require the exercise of a spiritual mind. To look out upon a world dead in trespasses and sins, ignorant of a Saviour's love; to feel their misery, to be willing to hasten to their rescue—this, no man ever yet has done, in whose heart the love of God has not established itself, with great vigour, and much power.

Should any youthful reader of these pages be conscious of a decline like that which Henry Fox so condemned and lamented in himself, let him not despair, if he but desires, like him, to strengthen the things which remain, and is ready to rise and strive with deeper humility than before. It was after such experience that Henry Fox became what the remainder of this book will show him, "shining more and more unto the perfect day."

CHAPTER III.

TAKES HIS DEGREE—OFFERS HIMSELF AS A MISSIONARY TO THE CHURCH MISSIONARY SOCIETY—FIELD OF LABOUR CHOSEN, THE TELOOGOO PEOPLE IN SOUTH INDIA—ORDINATION AND MARRIAGE—DEPARTURE FROM ENGLAND, AND ARRIVAL AT MADRAS.

MY brother took his degree on the 4th of December, 1839, but resided for some months after at Wadham College.

He was ordained 21st December, 1840, and married at Bagborough, Somersetshire, on the 30th December, to Miss Elizabeth James, daughter of the late G. H. James, Esq. of Wolverhampton.

Previous to these events, he had come to the decision of devoting his life to the Missionary cause: he offered himself to the Church Missionary Society, and the field of labour to which his attention had been directed was that of the Teloogoo people, or Northern Circars, who inhabit a district of South India, north of Madras, numbering ten millions, to whom, though subject to British rule for eighty years, no clergyman of the Church of England had ever been sent.

By a singular coincidence, the Rev. Robert T. Noble, of Sidney Sussex College, Cambridge, had had his attention drawn in the same direction, and they both offered their services for the same people, unknown to each other, at the same time.

One of the most painful trials of the Missionary career, or at least that which is first encountered, is the separation from friends and home which it involves. But surely this ought not to be a sufficient reason to justify parents in refusing their children, or children in refusing to go, when called of God on so high and holy an errand. We find parents ready to give up their children for secular pursuits, gladly sending them to the same country, and submitting to the same separation, for worldly considerations; while those who profess and call themselves Christians are not willing to do that for Christ which every one rejoices to do for the world. Many a young man, with a heart beating high for God's glory, has been prevented from carrying out his purposes of love to the heathen, by the selfish love of parents, who are only willing to permit their children's separation when worldly honour and wealth are the price paid.

Such obstacles, by the blessing of God, stood not

in the way of my brother's course; both his parents assented to his plans, and so entered into the spirit of them as to rejoice in the privilege of having a son willing to consecrate himself to so noble a work. The separation about to be made was at that time looked upon as final, and my brother's character was so endearing, that it seemed to all as if we had given up the choicest member, him whom our hearts could least afford to spare: yet surely when making an offering to God, it should not be the maimed or the lame, but the choicest of the flock.

At the time of his departure, nearly the whole family happened to be assembled in London, and it was there that the painful separation took place, on Saturday, the 6th of March, 1841; whence he and his wife proceeded to Gravesend, but were detained contrary to expectation, until the 8th, when they embarked in the ship "Robarts" for Madras.

The contrast between the plans which have the glory of God for their end, and those which have not, is most striking in their results. There is a security against disappointment in the one, which is nowhere else to be found in this world of change and chance. For, however the Christian's plans may fail, however his hopes be disappointed, there is to himself no loss, his life has not been thrown away, his time has not been squandered, and his soul is in peace. The letters which follow will give a most interesting view of the heart of Henry Fox, while he was engaged in the inquiry, "Lord, what wilt thou have me to do?" How clearly does he anticipate all! How humbly does he think of his own qualifications, while yet, like a brave soldier, he is ready for the post of danger and difficulty, because it is avoided by so many! He loves dearly his friends, his home, and even the villages and green lanes, the flowers and birds of his own land; but the love of Christ prevails, and he is relieved from that hardest trial, the resistance of those who are most beloved.

TO JOHN EMERIS, ESQ.

2 Oriental Palace, Brighton, Jan. 9, 1840.

MY DEAREST JOHN,

* * * My next subject is regarding poor me. I have been casting about an old question, which I have long put off, as out of season, but now presses upon me in full force, because now is the time for decision. I mean the question:—"Must I be a minister in England, or among the heathen?" I am not aware that I have any new reasons on the subject, nor that I see them more strongly than before, but in times past I had to say to myself, "This is not a question to be at present decided, while I am yet in education for the ministry generally." Now, however, when each day tends to fix my situation in life, and a decision either way would alter my plans, even for the morrow, I am obliged to give a definite answer to the ever intruding question; and I see not what answer I can give than this:—"I must be a missionary." My reasons are, as I dare say you know, simply these: that there is an overwhelming call for missionaries to the heathen, and we, the Church of England, have been bringing down punishments on our heads, by our neglect in not hearing the call: and thus some one *must* go, and if no one else will go, he who hears the call, (peculiarly adapted for the service or no,) *must* go; I hear the call, for indeed God has brought it before

me on every side, and go I must. My external qualifications of health, strength, and spirits are rather in favour of my aptness, and my internal qualifications are my only drawback; for so great, so honourable, so important a charge is it to be entered upon, that I shrink to think that a being so worthless, so wicked, so very wicked and faithless, should presume to offer himself for it. But better be it filled by the weakest of the weak, than by none at all, and God can give me strength. As often as I turn the question in my mind, I can only arrive at the same conclusion, and weak and earthly as are many of my present motives for going, (for I am full of romantic fancies,) yet I see reasons far beyond these motives, and pray that my heart may be filled by more worthy motives, and a pure and single love of men in Christ; and I know that when I enter on my labours, such fancies will be driven away like chaff:—nay, I accept them rather than nothing, to be a sort of temporary balance to the contrary feeling of pain, in the thoughts of separation from home and friends. My brother Charles has all along urged me to take this course, and within these last few days I laid my case before Mr. Elliott, (you know whom I mean,) whose advice I felt confident I could receive; for he knows my situation in the family, in life, &c., and is a man of excellent judgment, and considerable experience;—he strongly confirms me in the view I take of it, and he has shown me an extract from a letter of the Rev. Mr. Tucker, in Madras, on the subject of a new mission in India where all is ready, people, scholars, house, chapel, school, funds, &c.:—all except a man to fill the place of missionary. I have not yet FIXED, I believe I shall do so before many weeks are passed.

Now, my dear John, I write all this to you, to ask you for your prayers on my behalf, that I may be guided by Christ's Spirit in my decision, and supported by him under all trials. Oh! I do so dread my inconsistent life—an intended missionary, and yet a careless liver. Do pray for me, that I may walk more firmly in my conversation with others. Also I wish for your straight-forward advice; what do you think to be my duty? I do not feel any tie to country, family, or friends, which might not equally apply to every Missionary who ever left this land. * * * Believe me,

Your affectionate friend,

HENRY W. FOX.

Wadham College, Feb. 21, 1840.

MY DEAR ISABELLA,

* * * My letter to Dr. Arnold contained the substance of what you will see in the accompanying paper, his answer you will see. I might say much upon it, for it has given new thoughts to my mind, but not altered my original views: for still I *feel* it impossible to say that no one, or that only a few are to go abroad as missionaries, or that a fair proportion to the demand are ready to go; and whether it be to the English colonists in Australia, or to the English at Calcutta, or to the natives in India, or elsewhere, is all one to me; these are after-questions, the prior one is more general, and regards the two stiuations of *at home* and *abroad:* however, Dr. Arnold's letter puts several points in a new light. I intend to devote the season of Lent, which is fast coming on, peculiarly to prayer for guidance in my choice, and a single heart to decide purely and without bias for God's glory. I feel each day more and

more, how that this is a scene of turmoil, and must be one of hard fighting and struggling, and often I long to be back again among you all, which is to me the scene of peaceful life, as well of all soft and gentle happiness; but I remember that the victory is to him who struggles, and the crown of glory is to him, who having worked in the heat of the day, has not fainted: but oh! pray for me, that I faint not, for temptations beset me on this side and on that. This term I am mercifully and unexpectedly preserved from trials of my belief and doctrinal faith; my struggle is one more practical, (so to speak,) and I am beset by deadness of heart to God; want of sincere, humble faith and love; by idleness and neglect of my daily duties. * * *

Wadham College, March 8, 1840.

MY DEAR ISABELLA,

As I draw nearer to the time when my final decision must be made, it rises up before me in a more awful form, and it appears to be a thing scarcely credible, that I should have in a few weeks to make so important a decision, affecting my future life and the interest of thousands. I feel vividly, that as far as man is concerned, the weight of the decision rests upon myself, and myself only; that no man can aid in lifting it by so much as their little finger,—all that other men can do is, to lay before me advice; with me rests the choice of such advice. I am thankful to have had opportunities of obtaining what seem to me the highest human authorities as my advisers. But it is indeed with God that the decision rests, and it must be according as he puts his wisdom into my heart, that I must give my answer: so that I have indeed much need of earnest prayer for his grace, and I earnestly desire the prayers of all my friends at this important moment. Would that I felt all this more; it is easier to express such feelings on paper, than really and warmly to entertain them. I have secluded myself from a good deal of distraction during the present season, and I am endeavouring to fast, not as a good work, but as a means for drawing off from the senses to the mental sight of God. I have not acted rashly in so doing, but I thank you for your cautions on the subject, which express what I had already thought about it, and can find many ways of denying myself without going near to injure my health. I have this evening been reading that part of H. Martyn's life, which records his embarkation and voyage to India, and each page has filled me with shame, and a sense of unworthiness, and of my present deadness and coldness of spirit, instead of the lively faith and love which should be in one who is looking forward to be a worker in God's vineyard, and who is aspiring to an honourable place therein. Oh! I do so fear, lest there be nothing but worldly-mindedness in my desires to be a missionary; and if so, how can I expect God to guide me aright? Were I more sure that this was not the case, it would remove many difficulties out of my way. I have great cause to thank God for the following circumstances:—A gownsman whom I have known a few months, and who has joined me in my district-visiting, came to me a few days ago, and informing me that a society had been formed in Wadham for the encouragement of missionary objects,—requested me to be president of it, to which, after a short consideration, I acceded:—at present we are but a small body, not more than six or seven, but we shall soon add a few more to our number; we intend to meet for the purpose of praying that God would pour out his Spirit on the missionaries already at work, and would add many more to their number, and we shall endeavour to obtain what information we can. I thank God for thus permitting me already to take a hand in furthering these objects, and for putting it into the hearts of others to do so too. But while doing all this, while thus actively exerting myself in aid of missions, it frequently occurs to me, "If I do all this and am justified in doing it, what can prevent me from answering the prayers offered to God and saying to him, 'Here am I, send me?' Should I go abroad, it will be a great comfort to think that my companions and successors will be offering up prayers on my behalf, and that I may have been instrumental in leading others to follow me.

My dear sister, pray for me, that I may think upon it with holy and humble thoughts, and seek truly to know God's will about it. I often look on spots of earth, and view them with regret as seen for the last time; when I think of leaving Oxford, to return to it *never* again—of Rugby to be seen no more—no more speaking to Dr. Arnold and P——; and again, when each friend passes before my eyes in review, as to be seen and spoken to for the last time, some perchance for the last time *for ever*, I see that I have in prospect a mournful and painful trial yet to pass through: yet none so grievous as the last moment I shall see you. * * *

EXTRACTS FROM JOURNAL.

Brighton Jan. 9, 1840.—This morning I had a note from Mr. Elliott, enclosing part of Mr. Tucker's letter from India, which contained the following information:—"They are contemplating a mission among the Teloogoo country, which for eighty years has been under British government: the population, above ten millions, living in towns and large villages on the coast to the north of Madras. Among them there are only six Protestant missionaries—*not one* of the Church of England. For eighty years we have neglected it utterly. This is the last attempt that will be made; every thing is ready except the missionary."

Brighton, Jan. 13.—I still feel bound to be a missionary, chiefly because I hear and am ready, while none others, so to say, will attend to the call made; and I feel the call abroad to be stronger than at home: 1st. Because the want numerically is a thousandfold greater.—2dly. Because here the seed is sown—we have ten thousand clergy, and many are daily pressing into orders, but abroad the seed is yet unsown, and of course no fruit can be expected if we wait till doomsday.—3d. Our colonies and our trade can be given us for no purpose but to spread the gospel, and where are the ministers?—Though some of the apostles stayed in Judea, yet Paul, Mark, Silas, and many others travelled abroad.

Brighton, Jan. 21, 1840.—I have been very happy; all the early part of the vacation my mind was in a state of very great activity, so that almost every sentence I heard made a train of thought arise, often even to a painful extent. I soon felt the happy effects of living nearer to God—peace and content. I then too read somewhat, and wrote a good deal.

Oxford, Feb. 16, 1840.—On January 23d I proceeded to London and stayed till the following Monday: one of my chief objects was to gain a sense, as far as I could, of the evil and wicked state of that great Babylon, which in some degree I did. The poor fallen women whom I met by night, and the weak men too, the busy, godless, unloving faces, whom I met in multitudes by day, all oppressed my spirit. I spent the Sunday at Whitechapel with S——, and there again entered, in another way, into a perception of the want of spiritual instruction in the metropolis. I did all this with the object of giving as much weight as possible to the home demands, in order to make my decision more candid; but all these sensible sights did not outweigh my former sense of the needs abroad.

Oxford, March 16, 1840.—How small the finite! How incapable of containing or satisfying the infinite! I have been raised above and beyond the world, and felt how all around is but a vesture, and God, the Infinite, the Eternal, has been very present and visible to my soul; and thanks and glory be to him, that he has revealed himself to me, in his Son, by his Spirit, and I am able to cast myself, my sinful, helpless soul, on Jesus Christ: yea, thanks to him, he has received and upheld me; I can look on God as my Redeemer. After many vicissitudes, many risings and fallings, he has brought me still closer to himself; praise be to him!

Friday, March 27, 1840.—This is a day much to be remembered in my household; for to-day I have come to my final decision to be a missionary; I am well satisfied and convinced as to this being my true course of duty, and I thank God for so making it plain to me. Emeris sat with me during the evening, and we prayed together for guidance and help, and comfort in our absence. It has been a formal decision, because I have for some time felt it could not be otherwise. I am willing and thankful to be permitted to give myself up to do God service, by preaching to the heathen and leaving father and mother, brothers and sisters, home and friends; yea, and if it please him, life itself. It is an honour too great for me. Oh! may grace be given me to serve him in it.

I have of late been able to feel more sure of my salvation in Christ—to lay hold on his cross with more confidence: would that I took up my own cross more diligently. I can love Jesus more, for I know him more as my Saviour; and I am well content to be cut off from social ties and joys, and to give myself up entirely to promote his kingdom, for it is he who has called me to it, who has given me grace to devote myself, who is indeed my all in all. I sometimes feel great consolation in the thought, "This God is our God for ever and ever."

A second letter from Dr. Arnold concurs with my plan as a missionary. Thus has God opened my way on every side: praise be to his name!

TO G. M. MESSITER, ESQ., OXFORD.

Clifton, May 6, 1840.

* * * Well, I must tell you a little regarding my time in London. On arriving there on Monday afternoon, after a delightful drive, I put your letter in the post and went to St. Bride's Church, where the annual sermon for the Church Missionary Society is preached—the church was full, holding about 2000 people. The sermon was

preached by Mr. Raikes, the Chancellor of Chester. He took a text which has been ringing in my ears many a time:—"The harvest truly is plenteous, but the labourers are few; pray ye therefore the Lord of the harvest that he would send more labourers into the harvest." He traced the great deficiency of labourers since the days of the apostles themselves, through rise and fall, to the present day—the want of prayer for such, and spirit in the labourers themselves, and the divisions and party ends which have ever been made instruments of Satan, for turning the attention of the world away from the grand object of the conversion of souls. Next morning, at eight o'clock, I was at Exeter Hall, where there is a breakfast for the "clerical friends of the Society." I found an American clergyman, an intimate friend of both my brothers, who I knew was in England, and whom I discovered by hearing him addressed; so we being strangers to the rest of the party, sat down together, and had a good deal of conversation. As soon as breakfast was over, Mr. Jowett, one of the secretaries, addressed the assembled party, (we were about 150 in number, chiefly clergy,) for half an hour, on the subject of praying for "all men;" and after this, Mr. Stewart of Liverpool, a fine old clergyman, prayed for about the same space of time. Mr. Jowett had spoken of the "blessing it would be, if but one of those present should be led to be a missionary;" and I could not help thanking God in my heart that he had so inclined me. At ten o'clock we ascended into the great room, and occupied the platform, which held from 200 to 300 men, chiefly clergy;—the hall was filled by about 3000 people; it was a striking sight in every way, first, as a *coup d'œil*, for it is a splendid room, and was quite full, then, as an assembly gathered together to hear of so glorious a work, and some perhaps, I hope many, really anxious on the subject; and I hoped that I saw before me many a sister or mother of companions in my labours, who might be first led to think of their duty toward the heathen, by what they were then to hear. The meeting was begun with prayer. Lord Chichester, the president of the society, then spoke a few minutes, and the annual report of considerable length was read by Jowett and Vores, the two clerical secretaries; the other speakers were the Bishop of Chester, who took a most firm and noble view of the earnest working of individuals and parties not separated from, nor in opposition to, but as forerunners of the limited working of the church, Dr. Gilly of Durham, Mr. Cunningham of Harrow, Mr. Shirley, Archdeacon Wilberforce, and Hugh Stowell of Manchester. Wilberforce had a motion regarding the Slave Trade, and his name and relationship had no small effect, joined to an exceedingly good, and eloquent, and energetic speech, in rousing me beyond what I have before felt from oratory—for I felt his reasoning to be good. I knew the truth and eternal importance of his subject, which are so often wanting, where eloquence of language and voice are present. I tried to avoid being over-excited; but found it difficult to do so; the scene, the subject, and the merely bodily sensations, and the long attention all assisted to excite, and I arrived at the conclusion, that valuable as those meetings are, they must be taken in moderation, as even a small dose may be too much for an excitable person. The weather here has broken at last, and we have hailed with delight the south-west wind and the heavy showers of rain:—this afternoon we had a very heavy rain; but about five, it cleared up, and there was an hour or two of "clear shining after rain" peculiarly brilliant in its lights, and what scenes the light fell on;—all over to Bath was still overshadowed by the storm, the air thick up Ashton Vale; to the west all was brilliant. I walked out on the Downs, and sat on the look-out point for half an hour, to the influences of shapes and sounds, and shifting elements, surrendering my whole spirit. The air was soft and balmy, and perfectly calm; the smell was as of fresh grass; the sounds were of "two or three thrushes" and the shouting of the cuckoo; the sights were the lovely Lea Woods and Nightingale Valley, all in the tenderest, softest green, half hid in dazzling light, half lying in quiet shade, and the gray rock shining through and against them. I must leave them all; the green woods, the balmy air, the birds' song, the English homes and green lanes, the little cottages and their gardens, the children with blue eyes and flaxen hair, are all soon to be seen for the last time; but I am thankful to say, I never so much as feel a wish to stay, though I feel a regret at going. We need much strength which is not in ourselves, to bear our trials, and not repine or shrink from going through them; it is truly through much suffering that we must enter into the kingdom of heaven; but it bears its fruit even at present, for God has promised spiritual blessings which shall more than compensate for the loss of relations, and friends, and home.

Your affectionate

HENRY W. FOX.

Keswick, Sunday, Aug. 2, 1840.

MY DEAR MOTHER,

I write to you because my heart and my head are full of many things; and it is to you that I wish to utter them. I have to thank both you and my father for giving consent to my plan of being a missionary; and a hundred times have I had cause to thank you in my heart for it, and to feel the comfort of it; but I wish, and it is for your own sake that I wish it, that you gave your consent, and now concurred more willingly and heartily; not merely *allowing* me to go, but with zeal *sending* me forth: and I wish this, not because you should destroy the feelings which cause pain at the prospect of my departure, nor because I think it a light thing that you should have given even a half-willing consent, but because our gifts to God should be given with the whole heart; for "God loveth a *cheerful* giver;" and if such be the spirit in which we should give our gold and silver, how much more should it be that in which we should give our own flesh and blood. Nor is it only a yielding to a fancy of mine, or to my judgment that the missionary sphere is the one most needing assistance, that I ask of you to give both liberally and cheerfully, but I ask of you heartily to acquiesce in the guidance of God's providence. I believe from the bottom of my heart, with that strong sense of certainty and assurance which is only given to us on important points, that the missionary course of life on which I am about to enter, is my peculiar mission and work for which I was brought into this world; and that, unless I was to follow the course so providentially and clearly pointed out to me in my heart, I might, so far as my peculiar work of life is concerned, as well be in my grave: and were I now to resist the light I have, or had I neglected to follow where the light (once not so clear) led me, it would have been in no wise inconsistent with God's providence and mode of dealing with us, to have taken me away from all work, either by lingering disease, by death, or other means. I do not ask you to rejoice because I am about to leave you; I know that you will have sorrow on that account—and for myself as great a sorrow is waiting, and is already besetting me—but I ask you to feel joy that I am about to enter on my great work, and that this work is one so honourable, and which even among those men who know what real honour is, receives so much estimation. For myself, I look on myself as entering (unworthy as I am) on an office which entails more glory on its holder than any bishopric or any civil situation could bestow on man. Were I seeking honour, and were I most ambitious, I could not, with the views I have now of temporal and spiritual things, desire a post more glorious than that of being a pioneer in a. land, in which I hope and believe the Christian church will hereafter be triumphant. I entreat you, my dear mother, to let the true view of my prospects, the joy which must thence arise, contend with, and put down the pain arising from the temporal view of parting. There is a pain, and there is a joy: the first is temporal, and though great, yet the smallest of the two: the latter spiritual and far exceeding the other; let it prevail. And while I write this for your sake, I write for my own also; for most desirous am I to have your sympathies with me in my course; and as I shall be but little thinking of turning back, but rather (I trust) in the midst of all pains and trials, rejoicing for the goodly heritage which God has bestowed on me, so I would have you working in spirit with me and rejoicing also. Do not fear from my language, that I am intending heedlessly to risk my life and strength; no, I hope to sell my life dearly, not throwing it away, without, if it please God, buying with it the lives of many souls. I remain,

Your affectionate son,

HENRY W. FOX.

Gravesend, Sunday night, March 7, 1841.

MY DEAR FATHER AND MOTHER AND SISTERS,

I cannot resist the desire of writing a few lines to you, before I leave England: we embark to-morrow morning at ten o'clock, and sail about midday. We have by this time had a quiet Sunday, and a more peaceable time for reflection. We have prayed, and do pray for you all, that the Comforter may be with you, and, supplying you with stronger faith, enable you to look even through your tears to the Lord, as a loving parent who afflicts us according to his good purposes. We have enjoyed too many mercies on late occasions to have any reason for doubting the love of God toward us, and doubtless we shall hereafter be able to look on this heavy trial of separation as one of the greatest of his mercies. May the blank which it has created in the daily habits of each, be supplied by a more intimate communion with Jesus Christ. For ourselves, we feel we are in a very solemn and responsible situation, for we are commissioned on God's service, and have many prayers poured out for us; so that no small spiritual advantages will be a fair interest for so many talents. My chief source of anxiety is, lest we fall by weakness of faith, by neglect of prayer, or yielding to indolence, or some other snare which Satan will lay before us to keep us from God. So long as we continue under the shelter of his wings, we are safe: our temptation is to leave that. We are quite well hitherto, except that Elizabeth is a good deal tired and worn; the delicious soft air and sunny sky of to-day have been very refreshing to us all. We walked to church about a mile off,—a quiet country church,—and just now I have been out and have heard the church-bells ringing for the last time. I cannot tell you what it has been to part with you; and I dare scarcely look back at it. I am thankful the bitter moment of actual separation is past: still there is much remaining; but it is through much tribulation that we must follow the Captain of our salvation. Again, farewell; I say it differently from what I have often before said it, for it is heavier, but let us remember, it is not for ever. The Lord keep you all and bless you.

Your affectionate son and brother,

HENRY.

Ship Robarts, Lat. 10° North of the Line.

MY DEAREST ISABELLA,

I do not know whether this will be a long letter or not, for it is uncertain when we shall meet a ship; for we are just drawing near the place where the course for the outward-bound ships crosses that of the homeward-bound vessels; and this will be our last opportunity of writing before we reach India. I promised you in my note which I sent from Madeira, a further account of our visit to that island. Well then, to lose no time, we arrived off there on the Wednesday in Passion Week, lay-to all night, and as day broke we were about two miles from the east part of it, which consists of a promontory of bold and craggy rocks broken into caves and arches, and of a very irregular and curved stratification: their colour is of a rich reddish hue, and as the morning light fell upon them, it showed them in great beauty against the background of hazy hills, the nearest of which gradually became unvailed, and presented a refreshing green contrast to the colour of the rocks. The sea was bright blue, and a fresh breeze made it sparkle with the white crests of the waves:—after running along the coast for a few miles, (which presents the side of a mountain about 2000 feet high, sloping to the sea, not much broken by ravines, and which resembles our English mountains, except in its richer and ruddier colouring,) which we did at the distance of about a mile and a half, we came to an anchor close off Funchal, the chief town of the island; it lies in a bay, and is built of white houses, which lying thick along the shore, become more scattered as they ascend the hill. Behind the town, and to the right and left, the ground rises at once pretty steeply, and after some minor hills, terminates in mountains of about 6000 feet high, but which from the clearness of the air did not *look* higher than Ben Nevis. Their character is more broken than that of our English hills—and from the numerous glens and separate hillocks among them, there are respectable horse-roads to their very summits. The colouring is the same as that at home, but richer;—it was a lovely sunny morning, and the white clouds were hanging and wheeling about the top of the highest mountains. All the lower part of the hills facing the sea—*i. e.* for four miles of ascent—are richly cultivated in gardens and vineyards;—every declivity is terraced, and every stream made use of in irrigation; this, though it takes off from the wildness of the scenery, adds indescribably to its richness. The whole place was so full of novelties, that I scarcely know how to describe them. All the buildings are formed for coolness, overhanging roofs shade the narrow streets, which are however beautifully clean and cheerful, in consequence of their being closely paved with small stones, (so that there is no dust, and of course no mud,) and of there being no carts or wheeled vehicles in the island. The air was delicious, the thermometer stood at 68 at 10 A. M. in a cool part of the house, but yet the sun was not in the least oppressive. I felt as if it was not possible to be unwell in such an atmosphere, and the universal appearance of health confirmed my own feelings. In the country the air was as balmy, and had the same scent (though less strongly) as in a green-house, and no wonder, for instead of daisies, there were geraniums, such as we highly prize for beauty; instead of dockens and such like, enormous aloes; instead of our dog-roses, lovely clustered and double pink roses; and instead of hawthorn, fuchsias and heliotrope, both lilac and scarlet. I am not in the least exaggerating: all these grew in the hedges, or rather on the vineyard walls, and the nosegays that our guides gathered for us as we rode along, would have shamed many a green-house bouquet. The path up to the English chapel was the most perfect thing I ever beheld—it was about thirty yards long, and three wide, of firm gravel, its sides were hedges so thick as to be impervious to sight, about ten feet high, and *entirely* composed of roses and heliotrope. Our first ride took us through gardens and vineyards; the up-hill ride reminded me of Balaam's position, when the ass bruised his knee, for our way led between the high walls of vineyards which did not admit much prospect, except looking backward to the sea, but which enchanted us by the flowers which hung over the wall. The English cemetery is a lovely little spot, enclosed in walls of ten feet high; one hundred yards square, with cypress-trees in it, and divided into small squares, though not stiffly, by thick geranium hedges in full blossom, about two and a half feet high; the tombstones are either on the walls, half hid by creeping plants, or else laid in different spots on the earth:—those in the latter place are nearly coffin-shaped, but rather smaller, and have simply the name, age, and date; every thing is simple and unaffected; passion-flowers, roses, and geraniums were planted on every grave. Being in Funchal at Easter time, we saw the Romish ceremonies in full, the altars adorned in lofty pyramids, with rich bouquets of roses and camelias, and lighted by lofty tapers, which were the only lights in the cathedral, of which the windows and door were all darkened by thick blinds; the mummery of the chanting by the priests, while the people looked on as at a raree-show, at the high mass, and the almost ludicrous "pride which apes humility" in the washing of twelve beggars' feet by the bishop in splendid robes, out of gold basins, with towels deeply fringed with lace, and attended by five or six priests and boys. On Good Friday a procession took place, carrying a full-sized representation of our Lord's body on a bier, and a gayly-adorned image of the Virgin.

On Saturday at twelve o'clock, the curtains of the cathedral were suddenly withdrawn, so as to admit the brilliant light of the sun, intended to represent the resurrection; but why on that day, and hour, I do not know. My heart was very heavy at the thought of the gross darkness of the people. I have never before seen Roman Catholicism rampant, as it is in Madeira, and a more distant pretence of imitating Christianity I cannot conceive. I was continually thinking of the worship of Baal and Ashtaroth by the Jews; surely in *practice* this is no whit better than the most barefaced idolatry. I was however much lightened in heart, by Mr. Noble bringing me an account of a Dr. Kalley who is acting as a Protestant missionary among the people. He is a physician, and has received ordination at the hands of the Independents, but has attached himself to no one church. He has the charge of the Hospital in Funchal, where he has been for two years.

On Easter Sunday we set sail from the island, with a fair breeze, and have been running from 150 to 200 knots a day ever since;—to-day, April 22, we are in north latitude 5°. We have not seen many tropical wonders yet; two or three sunsets have been superlatively magnificent, though very short, the brilliancy and translucency of the red and yellow lights have been almost beyond conception. I have seen more gay and varied colouring in English sunsets, but not the purity and depth of sky seen through the golden light. Some of Claude's pictures come nearest to it. We have had two short visits from a shoal of porpoises; they rushed and leaped alongside of the ship in great glee, and the pure water allowed us to see them as clearly as if in air. The deep (not dark) blue of the sea has been one of the most beautiful sights; in cloudy weather it is of rather a rich lead-colour. The flying-fish have delighted us much; they are very beautiful, and have a steady flight like a martin skimming along the surface of a river; their dark green backs and glittering white bellies make them very brilliant. A single shark seen by one of the party, a few Mother Carey's chickens, and some large dark brown sea-birds, complete the list, with the exception of a small boneto caught yesterday. * * *

Last Sunday we had the communion in the cuddy; there were thirteen present, including one of the cadets, a very nice youth of sixteen. He is very regular in attendance on daily service and our evening meetings, and is an inquirer after religion. I trust, and believe, God is working in him, to bring him to himself; among the rest we have seen no similar marks.

Madras, July 6, 1841.

My dear Father and Mother,

You shall have my first letter from this our new home, whither by God's providence we have been safely and quietly brought. We made land early on Sunday morning, July 4, with a very light wind. At daybreak we were off the Sadras hills, which are about thirty miles south of this place. We were about four miles from shore; the appearance of land was a long flat beach, behind which green wood closed the prospect at once—the land being the most perfect level that I ever saw—about five or ten miles inland rose the hills, very like the Malverns, but about half their height; we could not distinguish their colours: on the top of one peak was evidently a hill-fort. After an hour or two's sail we were off the seven Pagodas. These are the remains, I believe, of a great city in Hindoo days of glory: two

Madras. p. 86.

of them now stand in the sea, which has encroached on the land at that point; one of them I saw distinctly through a glass; it was just like Mr. Thomas's model. We lay becalmed almost all the day. In the morning, one "catamaran" came alongside; in the evening half a dozen or more sold fish to us: there were large ones, containing four men, and using a "lateen" sail. A catamaran of this size consists of four or five logs (*i. e.* rough trunks of trees) lashed together, about two feet wide at the front part, which is a little turned up so as to rise more easily over the water, and about six at the stern: it floats six inches above water, and lets the water through the interstices. The four men paddle along slowly, by means of rude paddles, which consist of a split bamboo five or six inches wide, quite straight, and without any blade. Several men came on board; their dress does not go so far as "shirt-collar, and straps," but consists of a cap and a piece of native cloth passed between their legs, and fastened before and behind with a string round their loins: to this string they attach their fishing-lines in a coil, and adroitly throw them out, at a single cast, the whole length. They are mahogany-coloured, and their method of speaking is, as Mr. Thomas says, like the rattling of pebbles in an iron pot. After morning service we had the communion, for the last time that many of us would join in religious worship before we meet in God's house above. We were favoured in being becalmed till sunset, otherwise landing would have broken up the Sunday. As it was, it was very warm, the thermometer standing at 88°, and no air to be felt. We anchored at eleven o'clock at night: nothing was visible but the light-house, the palace of the Nabob of the Carnatics, with thirty or forty windows, and the lights from a few houses along shore. We were up at daybreak, and there lay Madras before us, about sixteen large English ships, (an unusually large number,) and two or three times that number of "lonies," or small native sloops. There was nothing in the appearance of land at two miles' distance to distinguish it from England. To the right it was almost concealed by shipping; then appeared a row of houses, flat-roofed and chimneyless, about six hundred yards long, and not unlike the middle part of Brighton. Next was a sort of common of equal extent, with some tents pitched upon it; then came Fort St. George, skirting the shore for half a mile, and containing within its formidable walls several lofty houses, a church with a spire, (the oldest Protestant church in India,) and a flag-staff. Farther to the left still, was a line of trees as far as the eye reached, broken by the tops of a few houses, by one pagoda, and an *ice-house!* The morning was cool and refreshing, for though the sun shone clearly, which it had not done before for a fortnight, the land breeze blew cool and fresh. Immediately on landing we felt the heat to be scorching: we landed just before the row of houses which I mentioned as lying most to the right hand of Madras, and which contains the custom-house and merchants' and government offices. The sun was reflected from these, and from the pale red sand which composes the road, and was like a furnace.

Now I must begin to tell you of the novelties of this land: there is nothing like what we have seen before, except English faces, curs, (called Pariah dogs,) and sparrows. All is so new that I scarcely know where to begin. The country, as I said before, is a perfect level, and when riding through it you know no more of it than you would in riding along a road cut through a forest. The road is half overarched with luxuriant and bushy trees, not high; many of them are banians, which have suckers hanging from their branches, but I saw only one case where they had reached the ground and taken root. The cactus, which we prize so much in our green-houses, is much valued here as a hedge for a compound or garden, to keep snakes out: those which I have seen in blossom have been yellow or rose-coloured, pretty but not gorgeous. The soil is not so black as I expected; sometimes it is quite concealed by the thick foliage of plantains or young palmyra-trees. One of the most striking sights is the immense multitude of natives. Mount Road, which leads from the fort toward St. Thomas's Mount (ten miles off) is a fine broad road, with occasional bungalows at its side, and native villages (or pettahs) branching off from it. Each time that I have been in it, it has been crowded for two or three miles with fully as many pedestrians as you would find in Regent Street in the gayest hour of the day. To tell you the style of dress among the people, would be like telling you the shape of the clouds; they are endless in variety. The children amuse us much,—little mahogany creatures running about naked, generally with their heads bare, and shaven all but a tuft of the crown; the bigger boys and men have a roll of cotton-cloth round their loins, and a turban on their head. This is the case with some; others have fuller and more flowing costumes; some, a jacket and trousers, but quite unlike ours in appearance. The dress of a servant is a white wide turban, a long close shirt down to the waist and knees, and opening in front, and a roll of cloth wrapped round the thighs and loins like thick drawers, causing a protuberance in front. Almost every man, and many women, paint their foreheads; some have a round patch of the size of a sixpence between their eyes, others one, two or three diverging lines drawn upward from the top of the nose to the forehead, of white or yellow ochre. The men are moderately good-looking, the women and girls are immoderately ugly; they are always carrying heavier burdens than the men. They bore the lobe of the ear, and occasionally wear ear-rings in the form of a brass ball, as large as a turnip-radish; most commonly they enlarge the hole till you might pass your thumb through it, and then making a roll of betel-leaf, which is dark red, they place it in the hole, which looks very ugly. All living creatures (except the English) are thin; some men are bags of bones—all are slim: the cattle are also thin. All are thin like Pharaoh's kine, and the calves are quite amusing for the length of their legs. The fowls look like plants run to seed, as if their legs were the most important feature: they are all legs. I am obliged to conclude hastily, as this is last post-day. You shall have another long letter by next month's post.

Your affectionate son,

HENRY W. FOX.

Residence of Mr. Fox at Masulipatam. p. 91.

CHAPTER IV.

ENTRANCE UPON HIS MISSIONARY DUTIES AT MASULIPATAM —EXTRACTS FROM JOURNAL.

ARTER a short stay at Madras, Mr. Noble, my brother and his wife, proceeded to their post of destination, Masulipatam, (or Bunder, as it is called by the natives,) the chief town of the Teloogoo nation.

Masulipatam contains a population of 80,000, and lies on the coast, three hundred miles north of Madras, between the rivers Kistna and Godavery.

The first necessary object for both the missionaries was to acquire the native language. As soon as tolerable progress had been made in this, they directed their attention to different branches of missionary labour. Mr. Noble undertook the management of a school for the education of the upper ranks in Masulipatam, where a good English education is given and the Bible is made a text-book of instruction. This school has continued to prosper to the present day, and Mr. Noble, without intermission, and in the enjoyment of good health, has been able to superintend it. This branch of operations might have been greatly enlarged, could more suitable teachers have been engaged from England. My brother undertook the office of preaching to the natives, both in Masulipatam and the surrounding country, in other words, the work of an evangelist to a heathen nation. But when it is considered that the nation contained ten millions of people, the idea seems almost preposterous, that one individual should have been suffered to go out single-handed for such a work. Yet such must continue to be the case, while we at home remain insensible to the claims of the heathen.

Bunder, Sept. 5, 1841. (Sunday.)

MY DEAREST SISTER,

I like to give a short time on a Sunday to you. I used often to do so of old, and every old thing I like to renew or continue. It is no sinecure to be a missionary. I do not mean any thing regarding any work I have at present to do, for my present is just like the work I have had in past years—language-learning—and our movements and changes have hitherto prevented this from coming in any sufficient quantities to prove a weight to me; but I mean that a missionary life does not deliver one from spiritual trials, such as used to beset me of old. There are just the same temptations to indolence and love of ease, which have been my besetting sins all along; just the same reluctance to prayer and reading of the Scriptures; in fact, I see nothing but the grace of God to prevent a missionary from being as cold and dead a Christian as ever vegetated in an English parish. Perhaps there are more temptations of this kind, for all around is ungodly. Probably my work will be deadening to my spirit, up-hill work with the lowest, most corrupt, and darkened of any men that I ever met; but my Saviour is at my side, he can deliver me; but we do indeed need the prayers of fellow-Christians for ourselves as well as for our people. It is one thing to give up home, country, friends, &c.: to be a missionary is another,—to take up our cross, forsake all, and follow Christ. For that *all* which is to be forsaken has followed me here; it is not without but within: a man may travel and yet not bear his cross; all this I knew and expected; now I experience it. It does not dishearten me. I never expected that the being a missionary was to work any such wonderful change which belongs to the work of the Spirit alone. But I have great cause to thank the Spirit, for having made the circumstances of separation work for good in me. It is my own fault, my own sin that they have not worked more, yet I think I am not forejudging in saying that I have been led to see and know more of Christ and his kingdom during the last six months. Absence from home, without hope of ever seeing it again, of seeing you, my dearest Isabella, and all whom I have loved very, very much, is a daily trial; it is not a missionary trial, it is no more than every Englishman in this land is exposed to, yet it does teach one that there is no rest on earth for man. For if ever I feel inclined to look forward to some plan in the future, it is presently stopped: for I never plan any thing with the idea that it will be in India, but in England; and immediately a painful recollection comes across me that I shall never be there again, or if ever, it must be some years hence, and sorrows will have come and changes taken place, which will make each person and scene memorials of pain. We must rest only in the hope of heaven, our reward is not here: now is the time for work, and blessed be our Lord that he has given me such a sphere for it, and health and strength to labour. I feel that on me, humanly speaking, rest the souls of thousands yet unborn, for this will naturally be the fountain for spreading Christianity among the ten million Telugu, —in fact among all the centre of India, and according to our zeal, wisdom, and faith, will the event be. Pray for wisdom for us, especially pray for faith. * * *

Your affectionate brother,
HENRY.

Bunder, Oct. 19, 1841.

MY DEAR ROBERT,

* * * By the time you receive this, you will, I trust, have taken your degree. I can only hope that the months immediately succeeding it may be as much blessed to you as the corresponding ones were to me. The time for quiet meditation which I had at Brighton, and the assistances which I possessed there, were instrumental in bringing me out of a cold, inconsistent, and unhappy state, to a better knowledge and love of Jesus Christ. I can daily bear more sure witness that peace is to be found in him only, and I pray daily that you may soon find it there. Your residence in London will be to me a time of anxiety on your account, for it is a place, as you know, full to the brim of dangerous temptations and deadening influences. Should you settle there, let me beg of you to keep your Sundays to yourself as sacred days, and to attend some church where there is a clergyman whom you know to be a sincere Christian man. There is nothing in this life so joyful as a Sunday spent much alone in communion with God. My dear brother, forget not to pray often and much. You remember the verses,

> "And Satan trembles when he sees
> The weakest saint upon his knees."

Your affectionate brother,
HENRY W. FOX.

JOOURNAL.

Masulipatam, (Tuesday,) May 31, 1842.

To-day I have got a new moonshee, son of my old one; he is called Malampilly Subbaroydu; the first is his "house name," *i. e.* surname, and belongs to his family in common with himself; it is derived from the name of some village. The second is his personal name, answering to a Christian name: it is the name of the great serpent, which in some of their mythological books is said to be coiled round the world; like a similar reptile in the Scandinavian mythology. * * * I began reading Genesis in Teloogoo with him. On coming to the passage where man is said to be made in the image of God, I began to ask him what man was: "Was he mere body?" "Didn't know." "What was the difference between a man and a dog?" "A different shape." "If I was to make an artificial man, would he be the same as a living man?" "He would not speak." "But if by machinery I could make him speak, would there be any difference then?" "No." However, when I told him that man was a soul, a spirit, he generally acknowledged it. I next asked him if God had a body. He could not tell, but thought he had. I asked him where God was. Was he in the room? He laughed at this: but when I told him my body could not continue its functions without God was present to make it do so, he allowed his presence, and thence from his not being visible, that he had not a body. Again, on coming to the passage, "God sanctified the seventh day," I wanted to gather his notion of the Teloogoo expression, which is literally "to make clean or pure," and accordingly pressed him for his thoughts; he could get no farther than that it meant "making it clean;" but how a day could be made clean, he could not guess; when I pressed him to think, his answer was, "Well, it is enough, let it pass." At last he thought it meant, "made it a good day," which he explained as a "lucky day," "a day of good omen." On telling him how ill they treated their women, by utterly neglecting to give them any education (for none of them can read or write, or know any thing beyond menial household duties,) I was met by the general answer, "It is my people's custom;" which I believe is to them a stronger motive of action than any thing else, except a rupee.

Masulipatam, June 4, 1842.—To-day I have procured a new moonshee; a respectable Brahmin, who speaks no English: but like most of them he shouts his own language; he is a Neeyogee, which is one of the divisions of the Brahmin caste; these subdivisions of caste cause as great a disunion as the major divisions. A Vaidikee Brahmin will neither eat nor drink in the presence of a Neeyogee Brahmin, nor intermarry with him. He is a worshipper of Vishnoo peculiarly, and consequently wears the one yellow and two white perpendicular streaks on his forehead: his theory of divinity, so far as I understand him, is new to me: he says there is one God who has put on a thousand forms, among which forms are Vishnoo, and Siva, and Brahma, (as son of Vishnoo,) and all the train of inferior deities, besides all Avatarams, or incarnations of Vishnoo; and that God lives in the heaven without a body. On coming to the passages in Genesis i., where it is said, "God made the *whales*," I asked him the meaning of the Teloogoo word, and found that it referred to some large fabulous fish (which he did not believe to be fabulous) not less than 1200 coss (a coss is two and a half miles) in length and 800 in width, which he says lives in the depths of the sea.

June 9.—A few days ago my elder moonshee Markamdeyooloo, when he came to me, showed me the interpretation of a Sanscrit word used to express a "Brahmin," which was "one who keeps sin off from himself and from others." On my expressing my astonishment, and asking who the persons are who do so, he added, "Oh! priest could do it." I told him I could not, for that I sinned every day; on which he drew a comparison between the drunken habits of some Europeans and my soberness, to the effect that I thus kept myself from sin. He asked me what sin I did; I told him, among others, I forgot God, and neglected to worship him. "Oh," he said, "if we pray a little time to God in the morning, that is quite enough; we need not do any thing more;" and then asked me, if I knew what things were sins, why I continued to do them? I said, it was because of my sinful nature. He then made a general assent, and added, it is for this reason the world is increasing so much. I did not understand what he meant, and asked him to explain himself;—he said he would do so, by telling me what he had learned from his priest. (N.B. He is a most garrulous old man, full of curious nonsensical mythological stories.) When God had created the world, he peopled it with men without sin; and, consequently, these, after living about a 100 years or so, had accomplished so much goodness, that they all ascended to heaven, and the earth was left without inhabitants; on this God exclaimed, that "This will not do, we must not make men so good." And so he created another set of men, but put some sin into them, and therefore they had not, so many of them, left the earth for heaven, but have multiplied.

My new moonshee has a most scrupulous dread of contamination; he has not been so much in communication with Europeans, as most others with whom I have spoken; but even among them I have observed a shrinking from being touched by a Pariah like myself. This man however will not sit within a yard of me, and if my hand accidently draws near him, he draws back in haste and fear. One day a pocket-handkerchief was lying on the table before us, and the wind accidentally blew it toward us, and it seemed as if it would touch him, but he gave such a start of horror and a jump as to escape its unholy touch. I asked him to-day, when I found him at one corner of a small room, where I had put him for a few minutes, at the same time that Amah, (wet nurse,) a Pariah, was with baby in the same room, how near a Pariah might come to a Brahmin, he said, Not nearer than two yards. I asked him if the latter should be touched by the former, what he must do. He said, he must bathe. But what till he had bathed? "He must not eat, nor make prayers to God, nor do worship."

Monday, June 13, 1842.—Yesterday afternoon, as we went out for a walk before church, we met Vencana, a young Brahmin boy, a friend of ours, and a companion of his. I had the day before lent him "Draper's Sacred Stories," [one of the publications of the American S. S. Union,] and he had it in his hand to tell me the story of the part which he had read, which he did very nicely in Teloogoo. He then asked me rather abruptly, whether among my people, the birth of a female was considered a good thing, or a bad one? I answered of course, the former: he said, it was not so among his people. I told him I knew it was not, but that their opinion was a very bad one;—he quoted in defence of it some padyams, *i. e.* verses, which struck me so much, that this morning I got him to write them out for me; they were to the following effect:

"The tree may spring up in the jungle, but a female must not be born.
Mountains and great stones may be formed, but a female must not be born.
Birds and beasts may be produced, but a female must not be born."

After a few more words on this subject, Vencana asked me, what seemed to be another great question, "Whether riches or learning was best?" or rather, how they were considered among my people? After telling him how many preferred the former, and also their folly, I pointed him to the true learning and knowledge of God, and how the love of God could alone bestow happiness: whereon the other boy asked, in a tone of some surprise, "Can a poor man love God?" I answered, "Of course, he can; why not?" "How can he love God," he said, "when he has no rice in his belly?" * * *

My new moonshee is an intelligent man; the other day I was speaking about man's sinfulness, and inability to obtain heaven by his own works, and he persevered in the doctrine, that "good men did a certain amount of sin, it was true, but then they balanced it by a large share of righteousness," (punyam;) so to-day I brought before him in detail, the argument, that we may know a tree by its fruits, and as it is evident that a vast number of men sin largely, so their nature must be also sinful; this illustration he tried to answer by a second. "Take a mango-tree," he said, "the young fruit when very small is worthless; even after it is full grown it is sour; but if you wait till it is ripe, it is delicious; thus you have a variety of fruit from one tree." I think he was satisfied by my answer, that these were not different fruits, but different stages of the same fruit. His first difficulty was, his disbelief in man's nature being one only, and not varying according to individuals: we had some discussion on this point, in which he gave in to what I advanced; but whether he was convinced, I am by no means certain:—his second was, he would not believe man's nature to be *only* evil, but evil and good mixed: this point too he seemed to yield at last; but then after all, he said, "God was very merciful, and would take away our sin;" when I pressed on him that God is very just, and the case of a prisoner and judge, he at last seemed to have come to a stand-still, and exclaimed, "Well then, how can our sins be taken away?" Then I was gladly enabled to lay before him Jesus as our Redeemer and our sacrifice, as bearing our own sins, and suffering our punishment. To all which he listened patiently, but objected, how could one man suffer another's punishment, such would not be allowed in a court, &c. To which I answered, by the common, but imperfect illustration, of a man having his debts paid by another; and also that he who bore our punishment, was not man only, but God, the judge himself. He said no more about it; presently he began some sentence with the common saying, "God has made all religions, and therefore," &c. Here too I think I succeeded in showing him that these religions were contradictory, and consequently could not all be true, and how could God create a lie? "Who made them then?" "Man's evil nature." Thus our conversation ended, and we went on to chant and translate the verses of Vencana.

Masulipatam, Tuesday, June 14, 1842.—Last week I began instruction among my servants. My Maitee, who is my head-servant, is a Mohammedan, and an intelligent fellow, though he is very ignorant of his own religion, and has been cast off by his own people for marrying a Hindoo woman; he speaks a little English. Besides him I have at present the cook, two horse-keepers, the gardener, occasionally the waterman, an old man rather dull of understanding, baby's Taniketch or nurserymaid, and sometimes a little idle inattentive son of hers, Latchmi, *i. e.* the sweeping woman, who is very dull, and lastly, the two little girls of Maitee, whom Elizabeth has taken into the house to instruct, the one eight, the other ten years of age. They sit down on the ground in a semicircle before me. I began with the first two chapters of Genesis, explaining as I went on, and pointing out some of the attributes of God, the creation, fall, and punishment of man:—the last few days I have been insisting on our sinful nature, and God's wrath upon sinners, and going through a list of the most prominent sins, most of which they assent to, but they seem astonished at being told of the sin of idolatry. I am also trying to make them learn the Lord's prayer, but find them slow, both at comprehending and remembering it. Three or four of them seem to understand me pretty fairly; how far my words convey or give rise to correct ideas in their minds, I cannot well tell; for if they answer me in any long sentence, or try to explain my words to each other, I only very imperfectly catch their meaning. I find great difficulty in expressing myself to them in Teloogoo; for very many of the words which I have been in the habit of using, when conversing with my moonshees on similar subjects, have been of Sanscrit origin, and like the big Latin words in our language, are unintelligible to the poor. I have begun it, because I did not feel it right to let them go on without any instruction, when I could say a few words to them, but I am a most incomplete, wretched instrument for conveying knowledge to them. It may be, the Lord may cause light to shine in their dark understandings through my words, for it is out of weakness that he delights to bring forth strength; but I cannot at present look for any such event, according to the ordinary course of his dealings. I continue to instruct my servants every morning at nine o'clock: after going through the two first chapters of Genesis loosely, and the subjects contained therein, especially the fall of man, I for several mornings dwelt upon sin and punishment, and detailed the ten commandments, and several other rules whereby we learn what are particular sins. The servants chimed in with all I told them, except that idolatry was sin, which was evidently novel to them. I then led them to Jesus as the Saviour for sin, and read to them his birth, as recorded by St. Luke; and am now going through some of his miracles, *e. g.* casting out devils, raising the widow's son, healing the centurion's servant and Jairus' daughter; stilling the tempest; Mary Magdalene in the house of Simon the Pharisee. Two or three of them, viz. Mohammed, one of the horsekeepers, and the gardener, evidently understand me pretty well, and take an interest in what I say, but the rest are inattentive, or do not understand me. I do not think they have any *system* of belief to be overcome, but will be willing to believe what master tells them to be true, the Mussulmans no less than the Hindoos. They can now repeat about half the Lord's prayer, and understand its meaning pretty well;—as soon as they know it all, I shall commence our instruction in the morning with that prayer.

CHAPTER V.

FAILURE OF HEALTH—RESIDENCE ON THE NEILGHERRY HILLS —ACCOUNT OF MARY PATERSON—RETURNS TO MASULIPATAM, RESTORED TO HEALTH.

THOUGH apparently possessed of more robust health than his coadjutor, my brother found the Indian climate much less congenial, and it was not long before the intense heat produced a nervous debility and prostration of strength, which quite disqualified him for work. It was neccessary for him to seek for relief in a change of air; a short voyage along the coast, and a residence of a few weeks at Vizigapatam were tried without success, and it became needful to have recourse to Madras for medical advice. From thence he was ordered to the Neilgherry hills, which are the nearest sanatory station for Southern India; rising from the plain to a height of several thousand feet, two hundred miles inland from the coast, they afford a most delightful and refreshing temperature, and abound in scenery of the wildest and most romantic character. Ootacamund forms the principal residence for invalids on those hills, and thither in January, 1843, my brother proceeded with his wife and little boy, who had been born previous to their departure from Masulipatam.

It so happened that there were two children who had come down from Masulipatam to Madras, whose father, a European physician, had died when they were young, leaving them property; but the mother, a Teloogoo woman, who had been a dancing-girl, had brought them up in heathenism:—after much legal delay, Mr. Tucker was appointed guardian to these children, a girl fourteen years old and a boy thirteen, and he intrusted the former to the care of my brother and his wife, when they were proceeding to the hills. The girl was perfectly wild and ignorant, and it was with difficulty she could be taught to use a spoon instead of her fingers, to sit on a chair instead of the ground, or to wear a European dress. Her notions of religion were of the most debasing character, and her mind was thoroughly imbued with the heathen superstitions which she had learned from her mother. There was therefore a great work to be done, and that at a somewhat advanced period of childhood, which threatened to render the task more hopeless; for there was not only an entire education to be imparted, a character to be formed, and a mind developed, but there were counteracting habits and prejudices to be removed, and all the destructive influence of her previous associations to be overcome. My brother and his wife realized the difficulty of the task, but were encouraged by a hope which God was pleased most abundantly and graciously to fulfil. "We gladly accept her," he wrote, "although the responsibility will be great; the formation of her character will be a great work; assist us in it with your prayers—she may be a chosen one of God, who shall heareafter be for his praise."

After having passed through a preliminary process of breaking in, the character of this girl began rapidly to develop, and greatly to improve. During a residence of two years on the Neilgherries, so great was the change, that she returned to Madras, where she was sent to a boarding-school, quite a transformed character. This transformation consisted in her having laid aside her heathen ideas, and conformed in all outward customs to those with whom she lived; it was a great struggle for her for some time to dine at table, lest "every one should see her eat."

The improvement of her character continued after her removal from school, and there was every reason to believe that she had become a truly converted follower of our Lord, when, in the year 1848, she was removed by an early and sudden death—at the age of 19.

My brother took a lively interest in her to the last, looking upon her as one who should be the crown of his wife's rejoicing in the presence of our Lord Jesus Christ at his coming. When on his death-bed, he sent her an affectionate message, little supposing that Mary Paterson, whose spiritual welfare he so tenderly watched over, had already gone before him to the mansions of glory.

The following passage, relating to Mary Paterson, occurs in a letter dated Nellore, January 5, 1847: "Mary Paterson is now more than ever precious to me, as the crown of rejoicing of my dear wife. I saw her several times while in Madras, and it was an exceeding pleasure to have intercourse with so very transparent and beautiful a mind, which with so great simplicity is resting and living on Christ. Her's is indeed a wonderful case; the season of the year reminded us that only four years have elapsed since she was, in the same month of December, brought to us at Mr. Tucker's a heathen wild-cat, and now she is such a beautiful Christian character! yearning and striving after the conversion of her mother and her heathen relatives, and desirous of being engaged in making Christ known to the Teloogoo women."

Ootacamund, May 8, 1844.

MY DEAR MOTHER,

I had intended to have begun a letter to you yesterday, to let you know that I did not forget your birth-day; but various occupations obliged me to postpone writing till to-day. I did not, however, allow the day to pass by without especially asking blessings for you from our gracious Lord. It is one of the comforts which we have, in spite of the distance which we are from each other, that, though our correspondence takes nearly two months on the road, our prayers take not so many minutes; what we ask of God this minute for each other, may be fulfilled by him the very next. He is our most rapid, as well as most effectual medium of intercourse. My dear mother, may he richly pour out upon you and my dear father all his best gifts; so much of health and temporal prosperity as may be best for your souls' health, and to enable you best to glorify his name. There are no bounds to the spiritual blessings I desire for you. May you grow daily in him riper and riper till the day when he shall put in the sickle! May you know him more and more in his great love, in his mighty power, in his wisdom, and goodness, and glory! May he daily become more precious to you! May you continually have an increasing communion with him, and have your hope of his kingdom grow lighter and lighter as you draw nearer to it! Though we do not hear from you every mail, we still have a sort of intercourse in dwelling upon your affection toward us and in returning it; and I am often able to fancy you at your various employments. I was very glad to hear by Isabella's letters, a few months ago, that the dining-room was occasionally changed into an evening school-room. How much might be done in the mass, if every family would undertake to be teachers of righteousness, not of the alphabet only, to a few children or young people! We shall never see the church composed exclusively of godly people, but we may see a larger number of such in it than at present; and at least much happiness is gained, if not an eternal yet a temporal happiness, by increase of religious instruction. One sees that in this country, religious education, however slight and however little improved, humanizes the pupils far beyond the common alphabetical teaching. It was Mrs. Bailey's (of Cottayam) remark, that the children of her old pupils were much more manageable at first, than those who came from new families.

From your affectionate son,

HENRY W. FOX.

He returned with his family to Masulipatam, *via* Madras, in October, 1844, so completely restored in health as to give him the most sanguine hope of being able to labour for Christ in India with fresh vigour; but further trials were in store, more severe than he had yet experienced.

There was, however, a brief season of intermission; and for more than twelve months, he was steadily and actively employed in his missionary duties: studying the language, and as he got more freedom of speech, going out among the people, and preaching to them Jesus.

Masulipatam, Nov. 10, 1844.

My dear George,

* * * It is on the good sword of the word of God that I have to rely here. I go out among the people, and get a little talk with them, so lamely and poorly on my part as to appear wholly inefficient; and the people either dispute and oppose, or listen with indifference, and were it my own word I had to tell them, I should soon get out of heart; but I know the sword of God, clumsily handled though it be, must reach the hearts of some of them; so I come away quite joyfully from the midst of the opposition or the sluggishness. It is like the Woucali poisoned arrows which Waterton speaks of; the Indian blows the arrow, strikes the prey with a trifling wound, and the arrow falls out again, while the beast runs away as though unscathed; the hunter, however, follows, sure of finding the effect of his poison in the dying animal before it has gone far: so we now sow seed which we know is good and full of life; some of it must spring up, and some one or other will reap the harvest. Blessed be God for the assurance he gives us, and for the certain promises he has bestowed upon us in connection with his work. Many thanks to you for Arnold's Life, which is on its way out; it will doubtless arrive in due time. I long very much to see it, and expect to find my esteem for the subject of it much advanced, as I learn more and more of his character. How much I owe to him under

the blessing of God, I have not yet fully found out. * * *

Masulipatam, Jan. 15, 1845.

MY DEAR GEORGE,

I begin my letter with a desire to urge upon you to be very diligent in trying to get some one to come out and join us here; not that I suppose you are deficient in zeal for us, or in trying to forward God's work here; but while I feel myself so very strongly the want of more missionaries, I can do nothing else than cry out to you and others to make known our wants with glowing tongues. I daily feel increasingly my insufficiency here, single-handed among so many thousands. Our dear brother, Mr. Noble, is tied up with the management of the English school, in which he has the head class to himself, and it is a most interesting and important sphere, to which if he did not give his time, it would be my part to give mine; and this because no one will come out from England to take this work off our hands. Mr. Sharkie and Mr. Taylor, two valuable East Indian young men, are for the present occupied in the same sphere. I am alone in the work of preaching and general evangelizing in the town and villages: and what can I do? I am lost and bewildered in the multitude of work. I am yet very imperfect in my knowledge of Teloogoo, and a considerable portion of my time has to be devoted to the study of it; and when I go among the people, it is with a stammering tongue and a misunderstanding ear. There lies before me the crowded population of this large town of sixty to ninety thousand inhabitants: these are to be preached to, to have an impression made on them. If I go to one part one day, and to another part another day, my time and labour are dissipated. If I keep myself to one portion, my labour is swallowed up in the great flood of heathenism: it is like trying to clear a spot of ground in the centre of a luxuriant jungle—the roots of the surrounding trees fill up the spot I am at work on faster than I can clear. Again, there are the villages in the suburbs: fine populous villages. Again, there are the numerous villages and still more numerous hamlets studding the country all round about. Where I am to begin, I know not. Then there ought to be schools to be looked after, to be established, to be watched and taught: I cannot so much as begin them. And so, though I may be preaching continually to the adults, there is the rising generation growing up in their heathenism; the most hopeful portion untouched. Besides this, I have my servants to talk to daily—many cares and calls upon my time—and above all, it is only a very limited portion of the day that I can be engaged in out-of-door work. It is not as in England, where you might go from village to village, or spend two or three hours conversing in one village. Here we are restricted to the short periods before and after sunrise and sunset: exposure to the mid-day sun is a mere fool-hardy shortening of the time of work, at least to most constitutions. Besides all this, there comes the work of translations, (only a portion of the Scriptures have been translated,) and so far as I can judge, a great part of what has been done needs to be done over again, to render it generally intelligible. Tracts there are in some numbers; books are only yet by ones or twos. Who is sufficient to unite in his own person these multifarious duties—preacher, teacher, superintendent of schools, translator, not for hundreds, but for tens and hundreds of thousands? Pray put this to as many as you can, young as well as old, that there is a great work to be done here, and an insufficient number of persons to do it. God has, however, commenced operations; surely he is even now calling for fresh labourers: put it to them whether they are not the labourers that he is calling.

The examination began with the fourth and lowest class, and went upward. I cannot recount to you all the lessons of the different classes: suffice it to say that the first class, consisting of the young men from eighteen to twenty-nine years of age, have prepared, during the half-year, eight or nine chapters of St. Luke's Gospel in English, about half of an English grammar, a few chapters of a geography of India, most of the first book of Euclid, and have written short English themes every week. What they know, they know thoroughly, and their minds are rapidly rising above the ordinary style of that of the natives. In the first class are two very nice young men, members of wealthy and most respectable families, whose hearts seem much touched with the gospel. The eldest of the two is much troubled about his sins, and says he has often risen at night and walked about for hours, troubled with the sense of them. He prays, I believe. He is a peculiarly amiable, loving, and lovable young man, and I feel for him much of the affection of a brother. Should it please God to convert him, he would have much to give up in his family and connections. On the last Sunday of the year I baptized our little Johnny by the name of John Arnold. The same morning I baptized our ayah (*i.e.* nursery-maid) in the little native congregation meeting at Mr. Noble's house: she walks consistently, and seems to drink in with eagerness all spiritual truth we teach her. My servants, ten or twelve in number, are an interesting congregation every morning; two of them are now baptized; about two others I feel much interest, hoping the Spirit is working in them, though it is only stirring up the mind. One of them, Harry's bearer, has been hearing me now for eighteen months or more: the other is mother of one of Mr. N.'s servants, who was baptized lately.

Your affectionate brother,

H. W. Fox.

Narsapore, April 21, 1845.

My dear George,

* * * The month before I left Bunder I had a great door opened to me, only that my own defects made me but little able to enter it; it was this, that I was able to establish in the house of a poor, pious East Indian, a weekly meeting of heathens; I have to go into the bazaars, and call or drive them in, but at last I get about twenty or thirty hearers, Romanists and heathens, and have a quiet talk with them for an hour. After I have got a free utterance, and they have got over their suspiciousness, I hope they will come of themselves, or what will be better, that I shall get the same hearers to come regularly:—when I think of it, I am astonished at the wideness of the door which God has so opened; it promises so much more than mere street-talking, or rather, it is the next step above that; for while conversing in the open streets, it is necessary to raise and keep up an interest. A regular in-door meeting is much more suitable for instruction. I shall now be as it were in the school of one Tyran-

nus, alias disputing weekly in the house of one Lewis. I begin to understand St. Paul better, in his requests, that his friends would pray for him:—1st. That a door might be opened for him;—2d. That utterance might be given him;—and 3d. That he might be enabled to speak boldly the mysteries of the gospel. Ephes. vi. 19, 20, contains what I should much desire my friends to ask of God for me; an utterance and a boldness: I am often quite tongue-tied. I am at all times a wretched stammerer. I am often a coward, knowing how I stand before glibly speaking, noisy, unbelieving, scoffing fellows, much of whose language I cannot understand, and with whom my drawling tongue gives me no chance in discussion. I assure you I am often quite afraid of a noisy Brahmin. I trust that my increasing knowledge of Teloogoo will gradually set me free from this cause of fear. * * *

Your affectionate brother,

HENRY W. FOX.

Masulipatam.

MY DEAR ROBERT,

I hear you are now very soon going to be ordained; remember how that before Christ appointed his apostles he spent the night in prayer: an example to us how that we should preface so great a work as that of entering on the ministry of God's church by privacy and prayer. You may find a profitable lesson in the first chapter of Jeremiah, and in those chapters which record the call of Moses. In both, their exceeding humility is discovered, but it is mingled with a want of faith which God reproves, at the same time that he gives us the blessed instruction, that it is his work his ministers go about, his word they speak, and that it is he who guards them from evil and enemies in their work. May you have such a knowledge of the love of Christ to you in your own heart, and such a burning love for him, that you may long and yearn after the souls committed to you. It is not men's bodies which are committed to us, it is their souls, which, while it restricts us in some respects, makes our charge heavier and more difficult; but then if it was not difficult we could do it of ourselves: because it is difficult, and when we know it to be so, then we are forced to seek help from God. May Christ be with you in your ordination and in your ministry, blessing it to your own soul as well as that of others. Our united love to all at home.

Your affectionate brother,

HENRY W. FOX.

CHAPTER VI.

DEATH OF HIS WIFE AND YOUNGEST CHILD—EMBARKS FOR ENGLAND—ARRIVAL THERE.

TOWARD the latter part of the year 1845 the health of his wife began to give way; and so rapidly did it decline, that there seemed no other remedy than an immediate removal to a better clime. In this state of anxiety he embarked coastwise for Madras, purposing to send his wife and children to England, and return to his own duties at Masulipatam; but on reaching Madras, the advice of his friends and the medical attendants induced him to accompany her, for indeed her illness had become so alarming, as to render her recovery, even in a better climate, a very uncertain event. She was conveyed on board the barque "Diana," on the evening of the 30th October, 1845, and the vessel was to have sailed the next morning, but during the night, her complaint, hastened probably by the fatigue of removal, came to a crisis, and she died the following morning, owing to the bursting of an abscess in the liver, which produced suffocation.

Though the period of her labours had been brief, that labour had not been in vain in the Lord. Others besides Mary Paterson may at the day of our Lord's appearing arise up and call her blessed, who otherwise had never heard the name of Christ, nor been admitted to partake of his glory.

She was removed on shore and buried at Madras; every alleviation which the kind sympathy of Christian friends could afford was enjoyed by my brother, and it certainly was a providential mercy, that the painful event took place before the vessel had proceeded to sea; by which he had the satisfaction of having her committed to the ground by one of his dearest friends, Mr. Tucker of Madras; but all the sympathy which friends can offer at such times, falls far short of stanching so deep a wound, and unless consolation be poured in from above, and the soul is capable of staying itself upon God, of finding consolation in the sympathy of Jesus, there must remain an aching void which nothing can fill, a pain which defies the cure of human remedies.

Shortly after his wife's funeral he was obliged to embark with his three children, and proceed on his voyage to England. He had not been many days at sea, before the youngest sickened and died; the vessel put into Cuddalore, where the child was buried: there now lay before him a long and dreary voyage, during which time he was deprived of all the consolations of Christian communion; there was no one on board to whom he could open his heart, or who could enter into his sorrows; although this proved a very painful passage of his life, yet he found the promise hold good, "Whom the Lord loveth he chasteneth," and at no period did he experience the presence and power of God's love so fully as during this desolate and sorrowful voyage. During it he appears to have made a rapid progress in Christain experience: the result of his sorrows was to draw him more nearly to his God and Saviour, to wean him more thoroughly from the world, and to confirm him more than ever in his determination to spend and be spent for Christ; so that he set his foot ashore on his native land with the firm resolve, that by the help of the Lord, he would return to his work in India as speedily as possible. But his own letters will best describe his feelings during this trying period of his life.

Madras, Oct. 11, 1845.

MY DEAR ISABELLA,

I wrote a few lines by Marseilles to my father and mother, telling them of my dear wife's illness, and our purposed return home; this will reach you a day or two later, though it goes as far as Malta by the same post. I do not know what to say concerning this most sudden and great change of prospect. Three weeks ago we had not the most distant idea of revisiting England, now we are on our way there, and in the midst of preparations: it is no use trying to tell you my feelings about it. I have felt but little.

Since the plan was first decided on, I have been labouring day and night packing up, preparing,—leading Elizabeth, who is as helpless as a child,—and have scarcely a thought in my head, or a feeling in my heart. They will come in the quiet of ship-board, just as they did after leaving England: this one thing, however, you will feel very glad of our return, we feel it a bitter pain; it is bitter indeed to have plans broken up, to be stopped in the middle of beloved work, and hurried away from the spot; it will be also bitter as soon as we reach England, to be anticipating our speedy separation; and the children, how shall I leave them for so many years? It is the Lord, and we can say no more. I look forward with strong hope, that he will give us strength to bear the trial, which now seems, when we catch glimpses of it, almost unsupportable. The Lord's will be done—we are now experiencing what we have long known. Since we have got down here, the doctors have made out Lizzy's complaint to be enlargement of the liver; if it is no more, there is but little more reason for apprehension than in a healthy person, for a sea-voyage and return to a cool climate are almost certain specifics for it; we trust it is no more. But diseases of the liver are always mysterious, and no one can say but that an abscess may be forming, in which case we must expect the worst, for though not necessarily fatal, it too often is so. * * *

It was but on Saturday morning that we decided on leaving Bunder;—on the following Thursday afternoon we embarked for Madras; meanwhile I was able to leave the house only twice, and scarcely able to say good-bye to any friends, English or native; we seem to be flying the country. We left

R. Noble well, and busy in his school; we could not but envy him, but the Lord wills it otherwise for us, and unworthy we are indeed to work for him there. I left, however, in the hope of being back again within a year; it would be a piece of little wisdom to return here in June to meet the scorching wind, but I hope that August may see me again in India. Mr. Tucker says, I ought not even to talk of plans so far distant, and certainly our life in India has given us experience to this effect. I am desirous of occupying myself while in England, in trying to stir up the hearts of young men to come out here: I say *trying*, for I am sure that the getting them to come, is as much a work of God's, and as little a work of man's, as conversion or any other great work. I have a certain stock of Indian information, which I hope to be able to make good use of, but I should have been glad to have had at least two years more of information, to enlarge, clear, and consolidate what I have got. One of my pleasant thoughts in regard to returning is, that we shall all meet, dear father and mother, and all, in the bond of Christian love, and speak of Christ together. I think I shall enjoy this more than I did, and yet my deceitful heart has often deceived me on this head; and when I have looked for a full heart to have Christian communion with brother Christians, I have often found myself as cold and lifeless as can be. * * *

Your affectionate Brother,

HENRY W. FOX.

Jan. 5, 1846. Near the Cape of Good Hope.

MY DEAREST ISABELLA,

The probability of having an opportunity of sending you a letter from St. Helena, which will reach you a week or so before we arrive in England, induces me to begin to write to you at so early a time; and I am glad I have begun, for often and often have I wanted to express my thoughts and feelings to you, and have shrunk from beginning to do so—used, as I have been so long, always to have her to communicate my every thought and wish to, and to receive from her the kindest and warmest sympathy, I feel very desolate now that I have no one to tell it to. I cannot write to you at present in a sorrowful tone. I hope that the bitterest times are over, although as they have hitherto come at intervals, I do not know but that all my sorrows may be oftentimes yet renewed before I am able so fully to rejoice in Christ, as that this loss should not pain me. I look indeed to a time when my faith shall be so increased, and my affections so weaned, that *all* my thoughts of my dear Lizzy may be those of gladness and thankfulness. Now I have many such thoughts of her, and am able at times heartily to bless our dear Lord for his mercy to her, and can see her as it were filled with the fulness of his joy, free from all sin and imperfection, and so happy, and dear little Johnny with her. However, at times all thoughts of her are very full of pain: I dare not look back, for every pleasant scene is the more agonizing, because of its former brightness, and I shrink from looking forward to think of my desolateness, and how I still have to go through the rough way and weary land, without her affectionate comfort and presence. It is better to depart and be with Christ, but if he sees fit to keep me here to accomplish his work in me more fully, or to use me as an instrument, I am well content.

"If life be long, I will be glad,
That I may long obey;
If short, yet why should I be sad?
That shall have the same pay"—

says Richard Baxter; and I often repeat the words with much meaning. Again, I have also to use Miss Elliott's hymn:

"Oh teach me from my heart to say,
Thy will be done."

So you see there are many fluctuations in my state, but I think I may say that Christ has triumphed in me and glorified himself; his promises have not one of them failed, and they have shone out with particular clearness in his word.

January 8.—I have been deriving much comfort from the thought that all the pleasure and happiness which God gave me in my dear wife, was intended to foreshadow and typify, by very inferior and distant resemblance, the joys I shall have with him in heaven. I wish I had thought of this while I was in enjoyment, the thought would have led me to sanctify the pleasure; however, now it allows me to look back without the bitter pain which all recollection brought me a short while ago; for as the pain arose from the knowledge that those pleasant days were passed never to return, so now I am able to look at them cheerfully and thankfully, as pointing out what I am going to meet with in the prepared mansions. I have also, at times, great consolation in regarding the work as God's work, and bowing in submission to his Almighty will, assured not only of his right to do as he likes with me, but of his tender love in all he has done. He has made me to over-abound in numerous minor comforts and mercies, both before and since my dear Lizzy went, as though he would not let me have room for a doubt of his tenderness. This life on shipboard has been, and is a trying one for me, for I have to bear all my sorrow alone; but in this God has doubtless had in view the object of making me feel more my dependence on him. We are a small party on board, and all on very good terms, and I receive nothing but kindness from every one; but there is no one to whom I can open my heart, nor any congenial person. I hope that our captain, who is a most worthy, pleasing character, is a child of God. I have got the doctor to spend half an hour in the forenoon, in reading the Bible with me, and he likes it, and I think is thoughtful about it. I have had a good demand for reading religious books, especially among the sailors, among whom are some very decent, respectable characters, who listen kindly and thankfully to all my entreaties to give themselves to Christ.

Jan. 15.—There is one young man among them who has, I hope, been brought to God since we sailed; the commencement of the change seems to have been occasioned by his reading Baxter's Call, which I lent him the first Sunday I was on board: his progress in Christian knowledge and experience has been such as to make me very hopeful that the change (for a change there is) is the work of the Holy Ghost. He quite devours the books I lend him, and perseveres in reading the Bible. In one or two others I would hope an impression has been made; but when I think of the wicked heart within, and the devil and world without, I desire to see tokens that the impression is made, not by me, but by the Holy Ghost. I preach twice on every Sunday: if the weather is suitable, the service is on the quarter-deck in the morning, and about thirty of us are present; at other times in the cuddy, when we can only muster about fifteen. On week-days I usually go forward for half an hour in the evenings among the sailors, after the day's work is over, and get some very interesting opportunities of speaking to them in private; but if you could see my heart, I think you would wonder and be ashamed at my want of love to the souls about me, and how I have to stir myself to seek their good instead of running to do it: it is the same at Bunder, it was the same at Oxford: when I would do good, evil is present with me. I trust this lonely time of sorrow on shipboard may be for my soul's growth; but the time is slipping away, and I do not find myself so chastened or weaned from the world as I hoped I should by the grace of God have been: I have learned some lessons, if I do not forget them, of the evil within me. I wish that you all would join your prayers with mine, that my visit at home may be a blessing and grace to us all, and that our life and conversation may be such, as to stir up every one of us to more devoted and hearty service of Christ. If you can devise or plan any means to aid me, I shall be most thankful. I come home confident that all of you who so heartily bid me God speed at first going out, will not attempt to delay my return to my work. As for my own present wishes, I have not a desire except to be at Bunder again; but I know so far regarding the law of sin within me, as to be aware that my desires may change and try to lead me from my duty. I shall look therefore to you, my dear sister, to uphold me should I give way; the parting with my dear children, probably for life, will be a sore trial, and now all the more bitter since God has taken my dear

Lizzy from me. I cannot tell, nor are you likely to know, what she was to me, and how entirely we were one; there was not a plan, a thought, I believe scarcely a wish, but we had it in common: no sort of reserve existed between us. You know how much we were permitted to be together, and this enabled us to live in the closer unity; to love her was almost like loving myself, and I knew and was persuaded that I had her entire affection. You know that her affections were warm, even as your own are; and now there is this great separation of communion. I doubt not but that she loves me now even more than she could while with me, and her love is more hallowed in Christ, and I know that I do not love her one whit the less, though the yearning after and longing for her at times makes my very heart sore: at such times I have no resource but to lay up my sorrows with Christ, the man of sorrows, and he gives me comfort and even joy; "the oil of gladness for ashes." The world and life seem as if they never could be bright to me again; but if so, I may have the same brightness in the knowledge and love of Christ, and nothing shall prevent our joy when we sleep in Jesus, and when we rise in our renewed bodies to meet him as he comes down to earth. What a precious treasure is accumulating for us in the presence of God! How many are awaiting to rejoice with us! And yet I desire to look forward, not so much to the rejoicing in meeting them again, as to the joy of beholding the King in his beauty. What an all-absorbing splendour and glory must that of God be! The poor heathen have not even these prospects among those of their heaven: to meet again in the life to come, is a thought which has not entered into their heads, and when they lose their dear ones, they part with them for ever and ever. Blessed be God for his gospel, and blessed also be his name that he has made us to know it: and I add, Blessed be God for those years of happiness which he allowed me to spend with my dear, dear wife, and for the dear children he has given me, one of whom, as a sort of first-fruits, he has already taken home: I have a strong assurance that he will hear our prayers for the conversion of the other two.

From your affectionate brother,
HENRY W. FOX.

TO THE REV. R. T. NOBLE, MASULIPATAM.

Bath, April 2, 1846.

MY DEAREST ROBERT,

We reached London on March 25th. I saw Mr. Venn immediately, and met most of the committee a few days afterward; both from him and from several of them I received the greatest kindness and expression of sympathy. Mr. Venn is very sanguine regarding the increase of missionaries this year, and mentioned two or three young clergymen now about to prepare for going out. They are going to give me plenty of work at missionary meetings in different parts of the country, which I am willing to accept, as it seems to be my work while in England. I have many doubts about my efficiency; but if it is God who gives me the work, he will also give me the ability. I have no plans yet so much as talked of; the most distinct one is, that I should reach Madras, if God will, by November of this year. I am desirous, if it may be, to have the cold season to work in, and am very anxious to rejoin you, to help you in bearing the burden of the mission. You and our dear companions in labour, and the school, and the mission generally, are often in my prayers. I cannot at this distance assist you in any other way. * * * I am myself in excellent health, and only desirous to return again, if God will permit me to be employed for him at Bunder. I was very thankful to find my dear father and mother, as well as the others, more than willing that I should return to Bunder again. Believe me,

Your affectionate brother and fellow-worker,

HENRY W. FOX.

CHAPTER VII.

EFFORTS WHILE IN ENGLAND TO DIFFUSE MISSIONARY INTELLIGENCE AND OBTAIN FRESH LABOURERS—RETURN TO INDIA—ACCIDENT ON BOARD THE RIPON STEAMER—JOURNAL OF OVERLAND JOURNEY.

MY brother remained in England about six months, and embarked in the steamer "Ripon," on his return to India, in October. During his residence in England, his time was principally taken up in attending missionary meetings in various parts of the country, and in the month of May he was present at the anniversary meeting of the Church Missionary Society in London, where he seconded a resolution which the Bishop of Oxford had moved, "in a speech," to use the words of Mr. Venn, "which is remembered by many who heard it, as singularly effective in the simplicity and ability with which he described his missionary labours."

The following letters and journal illustrate this portion of his life.

TO THE REV. R. T. NOBLE, MASULIPATAM.

Durham, June 15, 1846.

MY DEAR ROBERT,

I scarcely know where to begin my letter to you: ever since I wrote in April, I have been moving about in scenes full of interest to you, as well as to myself; but I fear I shall but ill succeed in conveying to you a description of them all. My visits have been chiefly of a missionary character, and I have often wished that you could be with me, to have been cheered and encouraged by what I witnessed. It has seemed to me, that a more decided and warmer interest, and a higher tone is taken in reference to missions than used to be formerly. Men speak now of the duty and call that God is making upon us, and do not dwell so much in a self-congratulatory spirit upon successes; at every meeting which I have attended, our Society has seemed the nucleus for assembling the really pious and evangelical clergy of the neighbourhood. I may take a somewhat exaggerated view, because I now see things in a different position, as a deputation and missionary, from what I used to do before we went out; nevertheless, I think that there is much for which to thank God in the truer missionary spirit that is abroad among those who are really his children. Still the interest has not come up to the point of men giving *themselves* up to be missionaries. * * *

TO THE REV. J. TUCKER, MADRAS.

Durham, June 17, 1846.

MY DEAR FRIEND,

I could fill many sheets in writing to you, if I had time to write, or you to read them. Regarding my own unworthy self, I have arranged with Mr. Venn to return by the 20th of October overland steamer, so that I hope, if God keeps us and prospers our voyage, to be at Madras early in December. God is still dealing with me as before: keeping me in much sorrow, which time hitherto has not softened or lessened, but I feel that I need his chastening hand still. I have for six or seven weeks been running about as a "deputation;" you know the harassing work which this is, and I have found it to be very trying to my soul, by interrupting my regular seasons of retirement; I now want to be brought back again, and so God works in me painfully, but I hope it may prove profitably; though all that I loved life for is gone, and life seems very dull, still I find the cares and business of the world as much a snare as ever. I still need and shall ever be needing God's chastening and weaning from the world. How blessed a day will that be when the glories of Christ burst on our sight, and we shall be able to serve him without sin! My chief visits have been to London, Cambridge, Oxford, and Birmingham. You would hear from Mr. Venn the very favourable meeting which we had in Exeter Hall; there seems to be but one opinion regarding it, that the tone was high and yet humbled; the report was particularly good. I was myself much struck with the difference between this meeting and the one which I attended in 1840: there was no levity, no self-congratulation, and but very little lauding one another. The sermon on the preceding evening was in itself and its accompanying circumstances the most remarkable and admirable one that I ever heard. The good bishop* goes on working very hard, preaching, speaking, and travelling, but I am told he takes care of himself: he is to preach the Commemoration Sermon at Oxford this year. Cambridge is in a very hopeful state in reference to missions, as Ragland will be able to tell you. There are seven undergraduates who have made known their wish to Mr. Carus to be missionaries; but how many of them may eventually be allowed to go out, is of course doubtful. I found others, who look at the matter seriously: the subject seems really before the minds of religious men there. You know Mr. Venn's plan of paying them a visit every term, and of addressing four several parties of gownsmen. I hope things are in a train for his beginning a similar plan at Oxford. I spent a week there with Mr. Hill of Edmund Hall. I had two meetings of gownsmen, one at Wyatt's rooms, which they got ready for me, where there were about eighty present, and one in Wadham Hall, where there were about a hundred, including Dr. Jeune, Master of Pembroke, Dr. Cotton, of Worcester, our Warden, who is Vice Chancellor, Golightly, and several others. I found every thing asleep in regard to missions, but I found a large number of religious, evangelical undergraduates, among whom my visit roused a considerable interest in the subject, and among whom much may be done by a movement from without. * * *

* Of Calcutta.

TO THE REV. R. T. NOBLE, MASULIPATAM.

Harrow, Aug. 27, 1846.

MY DEAR ROBERT,

* * * About the time of your receiving this, I shall be parting with my children, and all: will you remember me before God? It will be a struggle to flesh and blood. I scarcely dare to look forward to it now. Will you ask of our Father, that he will be with me in that hour, and that I may glorify him by entire submission to his will? This life is not for enjoyment but for work, and discipline, and humiliation; hereafter, how greatly shall we rejoice in the full presence of our blessed Lord, which those dear ones who have gone before are even now enjoying: blessed be his name, both for their sake, and for our's. All you have said in your letter about more missionaries, more and more fills me with an anxious and a painful yearning to see them move; perhaps I too much strain after an object of my own heart, and yet it is God's will that they should go out, and I am quite convinced that the lack does not arise from want of God's command, but from man's disobedience. I do try earnestly in my intercourse with men, but I confess that I am not so earnest in my appeals before God. There is still a chilly deadness on the subject of our clergy going out; unless by some unlooked-for change, years must elapse before the missionary temperature rises to "go out yourself" degree. I have pressed the subject *individually* on at least 100 young men, but every one has got some one good excuse. * * *

EXTRACTS FROM A JOURNAL OF A JOURNEY TO INDIA BY THE OVERLAND ROUTE.

On Tuesday afternoon, Oct. 20, 1846, the mails were brought alongside the Ripon steamer, which was lying out in the middle of Southampton water. This was the last visit which the steam-tug was to pay us, and therefore all the friends of passengers who had lingered to see the last of them, had now to return: they quite crowded the deck of the smaller vessel, while the side of our huge steamer was also studded with those bidding their friends their last farewell. Each party exchanged huzzas as we separated, and, sore hearts as there must have been in each vessel, I did not notice many sad countenances: in my own case the bitterest scenes had occurred at a distance, and now I had to part with my faithful and dear friend E., who had continued by me to the last. At length the hawser, which held us tight to the buoy—our last link to dear old England—was loosened, our head swung heavily round, the order of "Go ahead, full speed," was given, and we rushed down Southampton water ten miles an hour. It was now about four o'clock, and the approach of dinner took us all down to the saloon to prepare for it. We were a crowded party, of above a hundred passengers, occupying every available seat at the two tables, which ran the whole length of the saloon. There were old Indian officers and civilians returning to the tropics, after a year or two of renovation of health in England: there were young cadets and writers about to launch into life, and enter a new world at a very early age, full of spirits and bright prospects; there were planters and merchants, young and old, bound for Bengal, or Ceylon, or China. There were two other missionaries, Scotchmen, besides myself, and a young clergyman, who, with a party of merry young men, was going to spend the winter, touring through Egypt and Syria. There were two or three married ladies, with daughters, returning to join their husbands in India, and one with two or three little children. There were middle-aged Indians, who had been home to recruit and to marry, and were returning with their young and newly married wives; and there was a troop of young ladies, (some almost girls,) accompanying relatives, or going out to join them. I could not help thinking how soon their fresh English faces would be blanched, and their lively health and spirits become dull, beneath a tropical sun. Long before dinner was over it was quite dark, and we had passed the Needles, and were steaming away in the open channel, with a slight motion in the vessel, scarcely enough to injure the most delicate of our party. I had the privilege of a nice, light, airy cabin all to myself, situated on the upper deck, so that I had the prospect of much comfort during the first half of our voyage. The captain of the ship, a find old sailor, had installed me in the position of chaplain, and expressed his desire for regular religious services,—a desire which, as it afterward proved, proceeded from a sincere and religious heart. Next morning, Wednesday, we found ourselves labouring against a heavy, short, but not high sea, and a blustering foul wind. On coming into the saloon I heard all sorts of complaints, how that in the middle of the night the engines had been stopped for an hour, to allow time for cooling one of the cranks, which had become almost red-hot; how, that the engine would make only six revolutions in a minute instead of sixteen, and how that the lower-deck cabins were all full of water, which had dashed in through the ports: almost every one had their beds wetted, together with their carpet-bags and portmanteaus. The steamer, a very fine vessel, was on her first trip, and had been hurried prematurely out of dock, so that every thing went wrong about her. We continued in this way, steaming slowly down the channel, with the head sea rising, and the wind increasing to a gale: she rode it out well, however, but in consequence of the state of her engines, at twelve o'clock the officer in charge of the mails ordered that her helm should be put up, and that she should be run into some port on the nearest coast. We now lay broadside to the sea, which occasionally gave us some heavy blows and made us roll, and also washed over the fore-part of the vessel, and poured down into the hold through the open hatchways, which, in the hurry of departure, had no covering whatever over them. About an hour after, the head of the rudder broke off, so that the wheel was useless, and the ship unmanageable. We were now for several hours in the most imminent danger of going to the bottom, and it was only the goodness of God which preserved us. The water which poured down her hatchways was gradually rising up to the level of the fires, and there being no command over the vessel, the sea washed over her more and more. The captain, as he afterward told me, gave us all up for lost, and retired several times to his cabin, and there kneeling down prayed to God to deliver us from the danger. The only hope consisted in our being able to make the land and get into smooth water before the water gained on us.

About four o'clock the boatswain very gallantly volunteered to be let down over the stern and hook on two chains to the rings on each side of the rudder itself: this he did, plunged under water every other second as the waves dashed up; by this means we again had power of steering, by bringing the chains round the capstan, and steering by men at the capstan bars. By half-past four we saw land right ahead, and also on the weather-bow. It was five or six miles distant, high, and dimly seen through the haze. Up to this time I had been lying quietly in my cabin, reading and dozing, and utterly ignorant that there was any thing the matter, for we did not roll or pitch much, and there was not nearly so much noise on deck, as there would have been in bad weather in a sailing vessel. When I came to dinner I was much startled by one of our party saying, with a gloomy face, "It will be well if we get ashore at all; the rudder is gone, and we are in the greatest danger." I was glad to go to my own cabin to commend us all to God, and to seek for his presence and strength in the hour of fear, and he mercifully granted it: for though some natural shrinking from death remained, I felt happy and confident in reunion with Christ, after all should be over, and meeting those dear ones who have passed through the river of death before me. It was growing dusk as we neared the shore, but some one on board recognised the coast, and we found ourselves running into Torbay, a secure and sheltered anchorage. By half-past seven we had anchored in smooth water, and all our danger was over: had we been out at sea, in the Bay of Biscay for instance, or had the ship's head not been put up toward the land before the rudder broke, it would have been barely possible that we should have escaped. As it is, our deliverance has been one conspicuously from God. When all was over, and about forty of the passengers were waiting in the saloon for tea, our captain sent for me, and asked me to return thanks to Almighty God for our great deliverance, which I did; all knelt, and I hope many joined sincerely. There has been since then a return to usual thoughts and feelings on the part of most of us, at least so far as is observable, although there is a general expression of thankfulness and acknowledgment of God's hand in the escape, from most of us. Seldom perhaps has there been so much danger with so little suffering or inconvenience. We have in no ways suffered any thing, except the wetting of some of the luggage in the cabins and in the hold.

Thursday morning, Oct. 22.—At sunrise we found ourselves lying in Torbay, a fine semicircular bay, with bluff cliffs, and green hills surrounding it: on the right was Torquay, with its white houses perched up on the hill, about four miles off; in the centre was another pretty town, and toward the left, lying snugly under the shelter of the western horn of the bay, was the small fishing town of Brixham. Four or five small ships lay in-shore of us, and a fishing-smack soon paid us a visit. By eight o'clock the purser of the ship started for the shore to convey the news of our disaster to London. He reached town by four the same afternoon, and a telegraphic express was immediately sent down to Southampton to order the Oriental steamer round to our assistance: he returned himself on board about one o'clock on Friday, to announce the result of his expedition. Meanwhile we lay perfectly quiet, as steady as if we were on shore, all Thursday and Friday, with a fine bright sea and clear sky the greater part of the time, and with fine views of the beautiful coast around us: numerous fishing and other boats perpetually in motion enlivened the scene. A few of the passengers landed at Brixham or Torquay for some hours, and some even ran up to London and back. Late on Friday night the light of the Oriental steamer and another smaller vessel were seen, and they soon ran alongside and anchored near us. The whole of Saturday was a day of bustle and confusion, baggage and cargo were being transhipped into the smaller steamer or into boats, and thence into the Oriental. By four o'clock they carried the passengers over in the smaller vessel, the weather being all the while very favourable, and while we were dining on board our new home, they finished all the carrying process, and we expected to start the same night. We did not do so, however, till daylight the next morning.

Sunday, Oct. 25.—On coming on deck I found that we were running along the Devonshire coast, about a mile off the shore: the coast was fine, precipitous, and hilly: the cliffs often tinged with a ruddy colour, mingled with the greenness of the grass which clung to their face. Many little combs and valleys appeared, in which lay hid a clump of trees and a cottage; we passed on beyond the Start point, sighted Dartmouth, lying in its little rocky cleft in the hills, and gradually edging away to the southward, lost sight of land in a few hours. Although the wind blew fresh, the sky was bright, and the sea was smooth. Eleven o'clock was the hour for morning prayers; but as the time drew on, those ladies who were able to leave their cabins, together with most of the gentlemen, were assembled on deck, lying along the seats which were fixed there: most of them declared their inability to descend into the saloon, through fear of sea-sickness, and so it was arranged that we should have service on deck. I was glad to find that many were really anxious to have the service, and did not really make their sickness an excuse. Accordingly I read prayers on deck; the ladies lying at full length, the gentlemen sitting or standing as they could, with their hats on, my hair blowing in the wind, and my voice going everywhere. I had to strain my voice, and found afterward that I was heard, but at the time thought otherwise. I however preached, or rather made a short address on Rom. xii. 1, drawing attention to the call which God had made on us by his late deliverance, and then to his great *mercy* in Christ. The party, about forty in number, were attentive, but cold. All the afternoon I was qualmish and sleepy; I had several walks and conversations with fellow-passengers on deck, and in the evening we had service again in the saloon, with about twenty present, and I preached from Luke x. 25–27, the obligation of the law. The day was to my own soul very lifeless and cold, and my preaching was similar. Toward evening the wind became light and the sea fell.

Monday, Oct. 26.—A beautiful bright morning with a calm sea, saluted us on going on deck; we are now well in the Bay of Biscay, and still quiet, although the wind and sea are rising during the afternoon.

Tuesday, Oct. 27.—When I went on deck this morning there was a very perceptible change in the temperature; which showed we were approaching southern and warmer climes: it was a beautiful, bright, and cloudless morning; we were nearly across the Bay of Biscay, and had met with neither storm, nor sea, nor swell: it was more like sailing down the channel in mild weather. About noon the high land above Cape Finisterre became indistinctly visible from deck, and all the afternoon was enlivened by the brighter and ever-changing views of the coast, as we neared it and ran along it. As we drew closer to it we saw a long line of rocky and mountainous coast, running from north-east to south-west, the most westerly point being Cape Finisterre, which literally *finished the land* of Europe to the west, and the most easterly, dimly seen in the distance, indicated the neighbourhood of Corunna. It has a curious effect, this seeing from the ocean, coasts and countries familiar to the ideas, and represented to the mind chiefly by a red or yellow mark on a map. One fancies Spain to be something peculiar; and so no doubt it is, when the traveller is winding among its hills, and can notice the costume, the style of building, the altered vegetation, and other objects which present themselves to him. But seen at a distance which precludes minute observation, while it allows of distinguishing the outline, and even the colouring of the scenery, one country looks so like another, as almost to disappoint the spectator.

I have got nice opportunities of getting at the sailors in their quarters forward, and am able to enter into profitable conversation with some of the passengers as we walk about the deck. It is, however, a time of great distraction. My cabin is so dark that I can scarcely see to read in it, and in the saloon I read or write in the midst of talk or card-playing. My cabin-companion has the merit of never being in the cabin, except at night, so that I have as many opportunities of privacy as I wish.

Thursday, Oct. 29.—By sunrise this morning we came in sight of Cape St. Vincent, and about eight o'clock were abreast of it. As we passed within half a mile, the cliffs and all upon them were distinctly visible. The Cape consists of two headlands, separated by a slight bay a mile wide; the cliffs are 200 feet high, either sandstone or magnesian limestone, or rather they presented the appearance of both these kinds of stone. They were precipitous, cut into numerous clefts, and many caves; and only in one or two small coves offered a narrow beach at which a boat might land its crew. The first headland was crested by a monastery converted into a light-house: its chapel was marked by a black cross painted on its end; the whole was whitewashed, and dazzling in the morning sun. Above twenty men and women were looking at us over the walls. On the next point was a small fort, also white, in which the most conspicuous building was its chapel, with a tiny plastered dome over the altar; it seemed scarcely to possess a window, and reminded me very much of the Romish churches in India. After passing three headlands, the coast receded a little, but still presented a pleasing view with its variously coloured cliffs, its low hills covered with bents, and dotted with a few white specks of houses, and one or two mountains in the distance.

Friday, October 30, 1846.—And now we have been at Gibraltar; and how shall I describe it? We were but three or four hours on shore, and in continual excitement for some hours before and afterward.

All Thursday afternoon and evening we were steaming along out of sight of shore; during the evening we were talking over our intended trip ashore, and making inquiries of those who had been there before, regarding the objects of interest and the method of seeing them. We expected to reach our anchorage shortly before daylight, and proved to be correct in our calculations. About half-past two in the morning I was called up with the announcement that we were passing through the Straits, and on going on deck found the land visible on both sides; the night was a starlight one, and the outline distinctly visible of hilly promontories on each side of us, apparently not two or three miles distant. In reality they were more, for the Strait is twelve miles from shore to shore. Here were the pillars of Hercules, and the boundaries of the ordinary navigation of our true ancestors of classical days. On we steamed, with several light-houses on the European shore guiding us into port, and soon we drew near enough to distinguish the rock of Gibraltar itself, and some of the lights in the town at the foot of it. Gibraltar is not strictly the narrowest part of the Strait—it is rather beyond it.

By four o'clock in the morning we were deep in the bay, lying about a mile off the western face of the rock, fired two guns, showed a blue light, and cast anchor. By six o'clock there was enough daylight to distinguish objects, and presently the view became, not only interesting, but beautiful. We were lying in a glassy bay about three miles deep and as many across; immediately to the eastward rose up the rock of Gibraltar, forming the greater part of that side of the bay.

By seven o'clock we embarked in one of the numerous boats which were clustered about the ship, whose owners were clamorously in broken English seeking for a freight: they called themselves Englishmen, but their complexion and countenances told their Spanish origin at least on one side. They soon rowed us ashore, and we set foot on English ground once more, with some feeling of pride at the sight of the red-coated soldiers here in the land of Spain. We were no sooner landed than we were bewildered by the variety of novel sights which beset us on every side: nor were these diminished as we proceeded through the double gateway into the main street of the town. I had previously heard that at Gibraltar every costume might be seen, and the fact was speedily verified, to our great delight. There was the tall Highlander in full costume mounting guard at the gate, and the English soldier, in his red or blue artillery uniform; then there appeared the stately Arab, with his handsome features, and curled beard, his long blue coat with hanging sleeves, and large white turban;—next came the Barbary Jew or Mussulman, distinguished from each other only by the black colour of the cap of the first, or the red of the latter: their shorter tunic of blue with a red band round the waist, or their long loose *capote* of heavy cotton striped blue or white, formed their summer and winter dresses. Then came the Gibraltar Spaniard, in trousers and jacket, or shirt sleeves, like the untidy English of the lower orders, and most of them with jaunty-looking round beaver hats, low crowned and adorned with a couple of tufts or favours of the same material and colour as the hat. Presently there came a Spanish muleteer, the very original of the pictures of a brigand so familiar to us in England. A short, tidily-cut blue jacket, dark breeches, open from the knee to the calf of the leg, with buttons for show rather than use, white stockings, and a knowing hat or cap, formed their costume. The women, of the upper ranks, were in black, with shawls or vails over their heads, instead of bonnets; the poorer women with scarlet cloaks, adorned at the cape and armholes with black cloth. All had a dark hue, a sort of black pallor, an inky blood peering through a white face. The appearance of the town is not English, yet it is difficult to say in what particular point it differs from an English town. The streets and alleys are regularly built, though rather narrow: the houses are substantial, and, in the main street, three stories high; in some quarters, only two stories. They are all plastered and washed with either white or yellow; the absence of all smoke and the light colour of the dust renders every thing clean. The most remarkable features are the flat roofs, with occasionally a row of flower-pots adorning the parapet, and the green Venetian shutters at every window. There are abundance of shops, for articles of English or French manufacture, but they make no show, as they have but in few cases regular shop-windows; the goods are exposed in windows like those of an ordinary house. However, the motley appearance of the crowds in the streets, and that of the mules dragging the carts, instead of horses, sufficiently show the foreign character of the place.

The Journal is continued, giving a lively description of first impressions at Malta, Alexandria, Cairo, and the Desert; but this is a journey so frequently performed in the present day, and possesses so little novelty, that the remainder is omitted. He reached Ceylon on the 6th, and Madras on the 10th of December, 1846.

Madras, Dec. 12, 1846.

MY DEAREST SISTER,

Here I am at last, by God's mercy, surrounded by much kindness, and attended by gracious marks of God's love on all sides. I looked forward with many painful anticipations to my arrival here, and I have found them fully realized. Every sound and sight recalls my dear Lizzy to mind; there is not a spot in Madras which is not associated with her; many houses and rooms remind me of her presence, and I cannot go about the streets without remembering the last time I did so, when I had left her for an hour or two only. The children also continually come to my mind, and I feel that I am very desolate. Last evening I went as usual to the Friday evening meetings at the Brownes, and how empty did the house seem, for when last there, she was lying in one of the rooms below, and the dear little children's voices were scarcely hushed before the hour of the meeting: every one there looked just as they did a year ago—husbands and wives still preserved to each other—but to me how great the change! Do not think I am complaining. I can call God to witness, I do heartily bless him for the change, both for her sake and for my own. I would not have it otherwise, but yet it is full of sorrow for the present. I do not want you to grieve with me, for I cannot think of giving you sorrow; but I want you to pray for me, that I may glorify God in this land, and time of trial, by looking beyond this life, and rejoicing in his promises. I have had many sorrows of late, and I feel I am going to have more, but I think I have learned to look on sorrows with a welcome eye, as God's best gifts. I have been thinking of God's tenderness in his dealings with me ever since my dearest wife died. If I had had to go back to Bunder, and let the children go away at once, how almost insupportable would have been the trial! But he allowed me to come home to you all, and be comforted by your affection and love; and in England I visited but few places which were closely associated with her: and now, after I have had thirteen months of teaching, he has brought me back to Madras, first to break, as it were, the greatness of the pain of revisiting the scenes of our happy days at Bunder. The sea-voyage home was indeed a time of great trial; but then to make up for that, he made it a time of much converse with him, and of many consolations. * * *

Your affectionate brother,

HENRY W. FOX.

JOURNAL.

Cullapilly, February 13, 1847.—I am now out on my first excursion to the villages, since my return to India. I have commenced by coming here to the great annual bathing festival, which occurs on "Sivarátri," or the Siva-night. It is a considerable village about twelve miles due south of Masulipatam, situated on the most northerly branch of the river Kistna, and containing a considerable pagoda, devoted to the god Siva, under his common name of Nagaswara-swámry, or the Lord of Snakes. It is curious that the bathing in the river Kistna, a personification of Vishnu, should be held in connection with, and in honour of the rival god. It is a festival of three days' continuance, the main features of which are the religious bathing by thousands in the river, and their repairing to the temple of Siva to make their obeisance and offerings to the idol. I left my house at four o'clock in the morning, and proceeded through the entire length of the native town on to the open country beyond it. In consequence of the many showers which had fallen rather heavily a few days previously, I found the wet portions of the plain filled with water; in crossing the first the water reached my horse's girths, and in the second he began to sink so deep in the treacherous mire, that I was obliged to leap off and lead him through the mud and water for two hundred yards, knee deep. A great part of the rest of the country (for there was no road) was of a miry and treacherous character; so that when the sun rose I had still three or four miles of my journey before me. By this time I had no longer any difficulty in discerning my way, for I found crowds of people streaming in from all directions along the main path; and for the last two miles I was continually passing a string of people trudging to the festival, the majority on foot, and a few in common bullock-carts. There were old and young, the tottering and bent figure of the old woman, and little children toddling alongside their parents, or carried on their sides. There was about an equal number of men and women, but nearly all were of a poor and shabby appearance. On reaching Cullapilly, I found the pagoda very prettily situated, on the side of a tank full of water-lilies, both red and white, and the whole place alive with the visitors to the festival. After giving directions about the pitching of my tent on the bund of the tank, about a quarter of a mile from the pagoda, I rode down toward the river, which lies at about half a mile distant from the village. There was a solid stream of people the whole distance—a few return ing from the water-side—but the majority on their way thither; and already I could hear the roar of the voices of the multitude engaged in their ablutions, and the occasional screechings and drummings of music, proceeding from them. As we drew near to the river we passed several small raree shows, consisting each of a box gayly painted with mythological figures, and opening with folding-doors so as to display inside the tawdry image of either Vishnu or Siva; these were placed in the road by their owners, who stood by begging for money, and reaping a rich harvest from the piety of the people! When I asked some of them why they provided mere toys for worship, instead of serving God, they made the common answer of patting their stomach, to show that it was their livelihood. There was also a large number of clamorous beggars, lining one side of the road for the distance of about a quarter of a mile: each beggar spread out a long cloth or mat by the roadside, and as the people came back from the river they threw a few grains of rice, or now and then a single chili, or less frequently a cowrie shell (in value about one-fiftieth of a farthing) on each cloth; so that there was a prospect of two or three handfuls of rice being gathered from each cloth. I found the crowd of bathers lining the river-side for a distance of 600 yards or half a mile: the river here, though the smallest of the main branches of the Kistna, varies from a quarter to half a mile wide, and at present is about seven or eight feet below its banks: on the higher bank were collected the crowds of visitors; some sitting, some standing idle, some engaged in preparing their food, but the majority were changing their wet clothes, or rubbing their coloured powders on their foreheads, or preparing their diminutive amount of alms: in the river itself stood hundreds in the act of bathing. The process appeared to be generally of this kind: the party after scrambling down the steep and slippery bank, proceeded into the water till a little beyond the knees, of course without removing any part of their dress. Some friend commenced by pouring a number of pots full of the water over their head and back; then there was the raising of a little of the water to the mouth in the two hands and drinking it, then the throwing two or three handfuls of the water upward, by way of libation, then some over the head backward, and then plunging the whole body several times in the water. Men and women were mingled together promiscuously. I stood watching them for a considerable time; the noise of so many voices was sufficiently great to render conversation of scarcely any use, so I was a silent observer of many hundreds going through a ceremony which they all believe to acquire for them a great amount of religious merit, and which many believe removes their sin. I saw two or three men with little baskets, which they took into the water with them and dipped in the water. On inquiry, I found that the basket contained the little household god of the party, an image a few inches long.

On my return I found a boy going about chanting and begging, with a long piece of wire run through both his cheeks. Siva is the bloody deity, and it is in honour of him or his wife that cuttings or mutilations are made: this is the only one I have seen today, but I am told this evening, that near the temple there are some men cutting themselves, and piercing their flesh.

As I returned, I found the same close streams of

people still moving down to the river: there could not have been less than four or five thousand in all, either on the river banks or on the way thither, during the three quarters of an hour that I was there. There were about twenty bullock-carts covered with mats, in which women of the wealthier class changed their dress, and about a dozen palanquins, in which those who could afford the expense had come to the festival; but the mass were on foot. Before I left Masulipatam I was told that not many people of wealth come out to this festival, on account of the sums they are expected to expend in case they do so. I found this to be the case; the majority of the visitors seem to be of the lower classes. On coming back I found a considerable part of the road leading to the temple lined with temporary booths for the sale of toys, bangles, ornaments, or simple articles of food. The booths reminded me much, as indeed did much of the scene besides, of the outskirts of an English race-course: of course the booths had no table or any thing to raise them from the ground; they consisted of a few sticks so arranged as to allow a cloth or mat to be stretched on them, which sheltered the seller and his goods from the sun. I was glad to take rest and get my breakfast in my tent; it was not long before all the neighbourhood was covered with groups of people cooking their food, eating it, or lying down to sleep after it: for out of the six or seven thousand strangers, who have come for this occasion, none seem to have any place to lodge in,—the open field is their parlour and their bed-room. The continual noise of their talking, and the unceasing hummings of the large drums at the pagoda, have been far from agreeable all day. In the afternoon, finding that no one came to my tent for conversation, I went out into the crowd and wended my way to the temple, after two or three conversations by the way. The people were loitering about, with no other occupation than that of a few jugglers and mountebanks to amuse them. While waiting about the temple gateway, watching the continual passing of the crowds in and out, there came forth a bridal palanquin, in which was placed a small brazen trident, eight or nine inches high, half wrapped up in cloth. This is the "Trishúlam," and is, I believe, a representative of the god: by the side walked a man with a horse-hair flapper, to drive away the flies from the god. Before the palanquin went a Brahmin, who laid down on the ground, every here and there, a large leaf, and on it placed a handful of boiled rice: he was followed by a boy who gathered leaves and rice into his basket. I found that nearly every one that went into the pagoda, purchased, as he went, a little earthenware saucer, such as is used for a lamp, with a wick and a few drops of oil to offer to the idol inside. There was no uproar, or riot, or excitement, only a large crowd; I obtained a good many opportunities of speaking to groups of people, and two or three times went over the history of Christ as the only Saviour from sin. I had no opposition, for which I was thankful. On returning, after about a couple of hours' ramble, I brought with me to my tent a crowd of people, and sitting there I continued for two hours more to talk to successive groups who sat on the ground, until I was quite tired. A good many asked for tracts, which I supplied: I was glad that there was not any of that eagerness for tracts which I read of, as sometimes occurring; for on such occasions I feel the consumption is not repaid by the number who read

Tent of Rev. H. W. Fox, pitched near Cullapilly. p. 149.

them; the desire being, not that of reading, but of possession. I have had many good listeners, no positive opposition; my only annoyance has been that of two or three people, who were so fond of hearing their own tongues speak, as not to allow me to finish a sentence.

It is a serious reflection that I am here alone in the midst of Satan's kingdom: here he is rampant and triumphant: not a soul out of the thousands here but is a sworn servant of his: he has all his own way with them, and would do his worst toward me; it is a consideration to make me run to Christ more lovingly and earnestly, as my only defence against the powerful and evil one.

Cullapilly, Monday, February 15.—The noise on Saturday night of the crowds of people who were bivouacking in the open air all round about, and of the beating of the drums at the pagoda, continued till a late hour: and I was wakened about four in the morning by the same drumming, and by the voices of the crowds who were beginning to wake up. During the night there had been a minor procession of the idol in a little car: the great procession in the great car was to take place this afternoon, Sunday. When I went out for a morning walk soon after daybreak, I found the people streaming away to their villages just as they had been crowding from them the previous morning; though the festival is one of three days' duration, yet the greater number are content with the first day, and before mid-day about two-thirds had left the village for their homes. There was some bathing again in the morning, I was told, but the number of bathers could not be great. I had all the forenoon to myself in quiet, but from the middle of the day I had a quick succession of visitors, some boys, some grown-up men, who came to hold a conversation, but most of them to ask for tracts. I had again many favourable opportunities of telling them of Christ as the only way of salvation. Their continual struggle is for works of their own; I as continually press upon them the impossibility of bringing out of the unclean man any thing which can cleanse him. I had a long and very interesting conversation with a well-behaved and intelligent Mussulman, who, with every appearance of lively interest, honestly confessed, when it was pressed upon him, that a forgiveness of sins from without was necessary, and that he could not find any such in his religion. In the afternoon I went to the pagoda, where the crowd was great, as well as the noise. I could not hold much conversation in consequence, but I was remarkably enabled, as to-day also, in giving such ready answers to those who put foolish, captious questions, as quite to silence them. About half an hour after dusk they began to prepare for the car procession; the car, a lofty frame-work of wood of a pyramidical form, strongly tied together with a net-work of ropes, was covered over with dingy red cloth, and adorned with long strings of leaves, on which were suspended pumpkins and gourds. No fewer than three "zemindars," or wealthy land-holders, (they call them "princes,") attended the festival, and added to its splendour, such as it was, by their own bejewelled persons, their matchlock and spearmen, and three or four elephants and camels. I stood near the car, to see the idol brought from the pagoda in order to be placed in the car: the crowd was great, but a number of lighted torches made every object distinctly visible. Just now several Brahmins came forward in a rude manner and told me to move out of the way, for the god was coming: at least their gestures told me so, for the sound of the drums prevented me from hearing more than a word or two. I took it to be merely a piece of impudence on their part to require me to do that which they had not the slightest right to do in the public street, and so I stood my ground. Several with vehement gestures told me again, and one of the zemindars talked at me with words inaudible from the great noise. As I thought it better not to oppose their wishes, I moved on a few yards: but that would not content them, and presently I found that the spearmen and others who were pushing the people about, began to push them against me, and others began to hustle me. I fancy that had it been right to do so, I might easily enough have stood my ground against them; but as I had no reason to irritate them, but the contrary, I moved down the street, and as I went, I found three or four people throw dust upon me. I was more astonished than annoyed at this rudeness, which is so unusual toward a European. I presume that the excitement of the festival, the concealment which the darkness afforded, and the presence of the zemindars, emboldened them to forsake their usual submissive conduct. I stood in a side street and saw the cumbrous car dragged slowly on, and when it was passed I looked down the street filled with a dense crowd, upon whom the light of the torches streamed. I returned home to the quiet of my tent, to reflect on the contrast of a quiet English Sunday, with the singular, profane, and idolatrous scenes I had witnessed.

To-day I have had numerous visitors in my tent. One man much interested me: he stayed more than an hour, spelling out, for he could not read well, first the ten commandments, and afterward a little tract of eight pages. It was a laborious task for him as well as tiresome to me, but he persevered through it, asking me questions as he went on about what he did not understand. I told him all the way of salvation; he seemed cordially to approve of all, and to be pleased with the good news he heard; he was not one of those dull men who chime in with any new thing which they hear, but an intelligent, lively person. I have had no great opposition or discussion, or any new subjects started. Several have harped on the trite topics, that all things are God, and that he is materially the substance of all: others again, that our bodies are created by him, but he is the soul of all men, that there is but one spirit, ours and his being the same; others, that God is the author of sin, "for if he is not," they say, "who is?" Others, that the way to purify the soul is, to restrain and get under the senses: others, that believing in or serving God is necessarily connected with the ascetic life of a hermit. It is quite remarkable how readily they fly off from the subject; pretending to answer some questions I have asked, they will go on with a long rigmarole about what has no more to do with it than the man in the moon.

All these three days God has very mercifully kept me from the adversary, by keeping from me those noisy and difficult discussions which, from my imperfect knowledge of the language, I so much dread. He has also kept me in great peace, and made me feel much enjoyment in this sort of life.

I have given away about 150 tracts; rather withholding them than offering them to the people: most of my visitors have been from Masulipatam; of the rest, not above half a dozen are inhabitants of this village.

Sallapilly, February 16, 1847.—This forenoon was spent like several others; in the early morning I took a walk, and on my return through the village I wanted to find out the school. It is curious what falsehoods they unblushingly tell: from not less than eight or nine people I have had an answer to my question of where the school was, to the effect that there was no school at all in the village; while some of them, on my charging them with the falsehood, have pointed out to me where it was. In my tent I had visitors for two or three hours: among others a man came and sat down outside (he would not come in) and conversed for about an hour: he had the usual appearance of a "Sanyàssee," a mendicant friar, but was not one of the filthiest and worst class: the marks by which I discovered his character, were his greater quantity of hair on his face, the larger amount of ashes on his forehead, and particularly his strings of beads on his neck and arms, his cloth of the sacred yellow, and the tiger's skin carried on his back. He was not strictly a Sanyàssee, but was employing himself in going about to beg money to build a pagoda in his native village: he had collected, he said, 400 rupees, (£40,) but 200 rupees more were needed: for some weeks past he had not got a farthing. He was a cheerful, good-natured fellow; had no objections to make to what I urged upon him, both in regard to his sins and to Christ's redemption, and appeared an ordinary sort of man, unable to read. Though I had dwelt for some time on their sin of taking God's name in vain, at last he went off in a jovial mood, chaunting, "Bhagavan! Bhagavan! Naràyana! Naràyana!" names of God.

This they think purges the sins away. He, like other religious characters I have seen among them, seemed to be totally devoid of any thing like seriousness or devotion. As I sent off my tent about two o'clock, I walked into the village to get into the shade of the houses, and went to a street full of Brahmins, where I had been treated somewhat rudely in the morning. In a few minutes I had the whole horde upon me, and there ensued a discussion most utterly profitless, except to myself, to whom it served as a grindstone to sharpen me for further contests. About two o'clock, Brahmins, old and young, with pride and impudence strongly marked in their faces, surrounded me, and sometimes one, but more commonly three or four at once, assailed me with childish and ludicrous questions, many of them of a quite unanswerable character: "Why were some men born rich and others poor?" "How was it that my caste (which they confound with religion) had denied the divisions of caste?" On my telling them of the evidence we had to the truth of Christ's life from enemies as well as friends, one of them answered me in a thoroughly Hindoo fashion: "Probably," he said, "these were only sham enemies pretended for the occasion; for instance, (pointing to two men,) if I want to get possession of this man's house, I persuade the other, who is a friend of mine, to pretend to be my enemy, and then I bring him into court to swear that the house is mine, and the circumstance of his being my enemy adds much to the weight of his evidence." Sometimes they were so eager to beset me with what they thought flooring questions, that one would pull the other by the arm to stop him, in order that he might get his word in, and then they would ask me a series of questions one after another, giving me no time to answer. "Is there any difference between God and your body?" "Who knows the difference between right and wrong?" "Is your God, the God of the whole world, or only of your country?" I turned the tables on them by laughing at their hot eagerness to assail me, and at their unfair dealing. I could only feel, at the end, that God had graciously delivered me out of the hand of the enemy, and also I felt sorry at these poor men wilfully refusing the light and the treasure. But I rejoiced to find Satan alive to the fact of his kingdom being disturbed; any thing is better than the deadness of some places; I had not expected such decided opposition as I have found here: they are quite alive to the fact that Christianity will not allow idolatry, and fight shy of this subject. On leaving Cullapilly I took a Brahmin village in my way here, intending to leave a few tracts in it. I found a boy to whom I had given a book at Cullapilly: he first told me that he had read and understood it all, but immediately after he said he had not looked into it, but had placed it upon one of the rafters of his house: when he went in to look for it, he came out again and said it was gone, some one had thrown it away; but when he was urged to produce it, he presently pulled it out; and that without any marks of shame at his falsehood.—When I had offered the tracts I had brought, the Brahmins would not have them: they said, "We believe our religion, and don't want to hear any thing against it." I had a ten minutes fruitless discussion on horseback with five or six of them; they were so silly and captious that I could tell them nothing valuable. If I asked them, "Have you not committed many sins?" They answered me, "What difference is there between sin and righteousness? Who can tell?" Here however I made them look foolish by obliging them to answer their own questions, by further asking them whether lying, stealing, &c. were not sins? Nevertheless they shuffled, as well as they could, by mentioning cases in which, according to their views, it was necessary, if not right, to lie and steal. If I incidentally spoke of God, immediately they interposed, "Who is God? What God do you mean? What form has he got?" When I illustrated the sure punishment of sin by the case of an English judge punishing a convicted felon, they tried to be off at a tangent, by appending the statement: "Yes, one of your judges will punish the felon, but if he was open to bribes he would perhaps let him off," although this was nothing to the point, for I had distinctly stated the presumption that the judge would act justly. I was glad during the discussion that a couple of women were standing listening in the doorway of the house where we were talking; to have a female listener, is to me, as yet, a very rare occurrence.

I have changed my quarters by coming to this village, about five miles north of Cullapilly: it is a considerable village, the capital of the country, and the residence of a zemindar, or land-holder, who has quite a grand palace, far superior to any thing I have seen elsewhere.

Thursday, February 18, 1847.—The last two days have been occupied with visits from many of the residents of the place: a great many Brahmins have come to see me, but none of them disputatious, or noisy, or learned. A young Mussulman has struck up quite a friendship with me; and I have had many interesting conversations with him. He consents, he says, to our religion, and he listens quietly while I speak to *others* of Christ, as the Son of God, and the only sacrifice for sin; but as soon as I begin to press it on *him*, with much bitterness he repudiates the idea of Jesus (whom he acknowledges as a great *prophet*) being divine; nothing he, says, shall convince him of it: in this respect, he says, "Christians resemble the heathen—the latter worship a stone, the former a man." I have been pressing him, however, with—1. The absence of any remission of sin, in the Koran, or by his religion; 2. The total want of evidence of the divine authority of that book; 3. Strong evidence to the facts of Christ's life and death; and 4. That if Christ is not God, there is no forgiveness of sin for mortal man. I think he feels the force of these points; and as he lives in Masulipatam, I hope to have many more conversations with him.

A man yesterday fancied that we Christians were Buddhists, and disbelieved the existence of God. One of the village school-masters came to me to-day: his object was to beg a present of me. He was a man of about forty years of age: his wife was dead about four years ago, and he wanted to marry again, and had made proposals for a girl in a neighbouring village, but the sum required for her was 150 rupees, (£15,) a sum equivalent probably to a year and a half or two years' income. Part of this sum was to go to the parents, part to buy jewels for the girl, and part for the expense of the wedding. When I told him this was buying a wife, he did not deny it; and when I advised him, as he was a poor man, to look out for a cheap bargain, he told me that this one was very cheap; he could not get one for a less sum, and this was confirmed by the bystanders. When I told him that the next best plan was to wait till he had saved money enough for the purchase, he was not at all satisfied. The girl is eight or nine years old; and on my asking him by whose wish the engagement had taken place—the girl's or her parents'? he answered, "Of course the parents; she is only a child; how can she know any thing?"

The young Mussulman told me, as we were walking through the burial-ground of his people, that the graves for men were dug about three feet deep, but those for the women about four feet: the reason of this is, that the women, being shy and modest, like to lie deep, well out of sight!

Weyoor, Wednesday, Feb. 24.—I remained at Cullapilly till Saturday morning, when, striking my tent at daylight, I started across the country ten miles, till I came to the high-road at a village called Neddamole, where there is a travellers' bungalow. On my way I passed through two large and several small villages, which I hope to visit in due time. The impression left on my mind by riding about the country is that of a thick population; the ground is at least three-fourths under cultivation, though in a slovenly style. At Neddamole I stayed till Monday afternoon; being in the bungalow instead of in my tent, the people did not come to me, but I went to them morning and evening; and Sunday being cloudy, I went also in the middle of the day: it is a small, poor village, inhabited by Brahmins, Sudras, and Mohammedans; of the former many are unable to read at all; I had paid two similar visits to the place before, two years ago, but I found nothing but languid indifference: it was difficult to get a small audience, and when got, it was difficult to retain it. On Sunday afternoon I walked over to a village about a mile off, and coming to a house where a blacksmith was making a cart-wheel, and the owner of the cart, a good honest Sudra farmer, and one or two others looking on, I sat down beside them and had an interesting and friendly conversation with them for more than an hour. The former, speaking of the famous idol of Juggernaut, in Cuttack, affirmed, that at the time of the car festival, the idol miraculously ascends into the car itself; similarly regarding the *lingam* (φαλλος) idol at Cullapilly, the story is current, that it sprang out of the ground itself, and they say that the zemindar of Cullapilly possesses an ancient description, bearing witness to the fact. The Hindoos abound in miracles in defence of their idolatries, which, however, like ghost-stories, always occur at some distance, or else took place in their father's time, "a long while ago."

On Monday evening I moved on along the northern high-road to a village called Pràmarra, about seven miles distant from Neddamole. It is a large village of about 300 houses, and at least 1500 inhabitants; here I met a very different reception from that at Neddamole. Before my tent was pitched, I had four or five of the chief men of the village, of both the Brahmins and Sudras, waiting upon me, and addressing me in most humble terms, "Your worship, my lord," &c. They showed me all over the village the same evening. With this commencement all was in keeping during my stay: my tent was crowded for two and three hours at a time with attentive, obsequious visitors: the Curmuns (the chief Brahmins) were in frequent attendance. One of them much interested me; he was a rough, sturdy man, apparently of an independent character; from the first conversation I had with him he seized with apparent heartiness upon the truth of Christ, and continued to reprobate idolatry: he paid me no less than six visits in two days, and in the presence of many people continued to denounce the idols and to tell them that "the only way of remission of sins was steadily to contemplate Jesus Christ, the only true God." He and another of the same family told me, that though worshippers of Siva, yet they did not worship any image, nor go to the temples: the man's manner marked his sincerity, at least I hope so. He confidently said, that on my return to the village on my way home, he would accompany me to be baptized, and "as for his caste-people rejecting him, what did he care for that?" It may be that the Holy Spirit will work in him as a chosen vessel: it may be on the other hand a mere trick of his to obtain some end at present concealed. I fell in one morning with the astrologer, or walking almanac of the village. His business is to tell the people about the day, its luckiness, or otherwise; for instance, he began reading to me from off his almanac, "This is Tuesday, such and such a date of such a month; there will be a conjunction of the planets at four o'clock: at that hour no work must be done," &c. He and many others are fully persuaded, that according to their mythological geography, there are seven seas surrounding the earth, severally composed of salt water and fresh, of milk, of spirits, sugar and water, butter, &c. They all cry out in astonishment when I tell them I have been in Ceylon, or *Ravana Lauka*, as they call it; they all think it is a land of hobgoblins and giants, which no man can visit. I find also a very common notion among them that we Englishmen will not let Hindoos go to England. They are delighted to hear any accounts of England, and I kept some of them interested for a long time to-day on that subject. One of their first questions is, "What sort of grain grows in your country?" Another is, "Are all the people there white?" or, "Are there any labourers there, or are they all gentlemen?" They are ludicrously personal in their inquiries, not intending them as rudeness, but knowing no better manners. Their salutation is, "Where do you come from, where are you going to; in what employment are you, how much pay do you get?" Then they go on with, "Have you a father and mother, brothers and sisters; are you married, have you any children, are they boys or girls?" More than once I have been asked by Mussulmans why I had no beard.

After staying two very interesting days at Pràmarra, I came on this evening seven miles to this place, where there is a travellers' bungalow, and a large village. I passed through three considerable villages on the road, and saw many others at no great distance; when will men come out from England to preach the gospel up and down the country-side?

Beizwárah, February 27, 1847.—I have advanced twenty miles from Weyoor, straight along the high-road, in order to be in time for the Mangalagherry festival to-morrow. This place is a town rather than a village, and has the greater number of its houses tiled, instead of thatched; though still their walls are only made of mud. I have now reached the foot of a long range of hills running north and south, which, though not above seven or eight hundred feet high, are steep and rocky; just at this spot there is a break in the range, of a mile in width; the break is entirely filled by the river Kistna, which here makes its escape into the interminable plains eastward. A steep hill on either side, whose rocky foundations dip into the water, seems to keep guard over the stream, as the Pillars of Hercules guard the Straits of Gibraltar. In consequence of its being situated on the Kistna, Beizwárah is accounted a holy place; and at the same time as the Cullapilly festival, there is a great concourse assembled here from the neighbourhood "to bathe and to visit the god." Perched up on a lower crag of the hill, is a small pagoda to Dúrga, or Káli, the bloodthirsty wife of Siva. It is the first I have ever seen, for her worship does not seem to be at present common in these parts. I went up to it last night, and though of course I could not go inside, the priests, who were Brahmins, showed me the goddess. It was an ugly image, two or three feet high, of which the head only was visible, the rest being concealed by a sort of cloth which was tied to the neck, and fell down on all sides like a pinafore; it was sprinkled with red drops—I suppose, to represent blood. The eyes were two glittering pieces of tinsel, with a black spot on each for the pupil. I had a long conversation with one of the priests, a poor half-clothed young man, who wanted to be very civil, by bringing me an orange from among the offerings before the idol. I, of course, would not take it; he pretended to believe that the idol was divine, but it was painful and piteous to observe the poor man thinking only of his livelihood, and sticking to that first and last. Truly there is no life in these people, no sense of any thing greater than themselves, or any belief in any thing more important than this life: this is visible enough among worldly-minded people in England, but even they acknowledge such existence by shrinking from and disliking allusions to them; but these poor people play with such subjects, as a child would with a snake, not knowing that there was more in the reptile than what it saw. I passed from him to visit the hermit of the hill: not one of those dirty, obscene beggars who call themselves Fakeers or Sanyássees, and hang about towns and villages, but a real hermit, who has lived there in his cave, as he told me, for thirty-five years. I had heard of him from others, and found him just as I had expected. I believe that formerly he really practised asceticism, but he has long given that up, and seems to be enjoying the results of his asceticism in the respect and presents of the people. His cave is made into a very comfortable abode, and its site is particularly well chosen, inasmuch as it escapes all the heat and glare of the sun after an early hour in the morning. I found him sitting on his stool with three old Brahmins from the town chatting with him; he had chairs, a cot, a table, and many more little conveniences than most natives have. On an old rug on the cot sat cowering and mumbling like a monkey, a young man, who apparently aspires to be the future possessor of the cave. The hermit, himself, was a comfortable, fat, elderly gentleman, with a clean cloth round his waist, and a clean skin on his body, which, by its comfortable folds, showed the good living he enjoyed. He saluted me in a very friendly manner, and gave me a chair, and then began to enumerate the number of European gentlemen who had paid him a visit, and exhibited their kindness by leaving him a present. I treated him with great respect, and after some general conversation, I told him I had a question to ask him, for which I should be much obliged if he could give an answer. "I had committed many sins," I said, "and I knew that it was only just that God should punish sin; how could I escape this punishment?" He answered me very readily by the old tale, "You must meditate upon God, you must pray, you must give alms," &c.; and he was quite satisfied with his answer, as were also the Brahmins who sat listening. I told him in an humble way, that even I was able to discover that this would never do to remove my sins; for all these prayers, devotions, alms, &c. proceeded from out of my evil heart, and how could they, being evil, cure its corruptions? I added, by way of illustration, (what I find to be unanswerable, and a most useful simile,) that in Masulipatam there are salt wells, and consequently the water in them is useless, and I knew that if a man was to draw a few buckets full of the salt water out of one of them, and then pour it back again into the well, he would never by this means make the salt water sweet. He acknowledged my illustration, and passed on to general conversation: but I brought him back again, reminding him that he had not satisfied my question; he merely repeated his former recipe, and I told him again that I knew it would not do, for that for years past I had been praying to God, &c. as he told me, and yet all this so-called righteousness had not removed my sins, nor given me that peace of mind which ought to accompany forgiveness. He still had no other remedy to give me, but said if we poured good water into the salt well, would not that cure it? I acknowledged it might, but "where is the good water to come from? my heart produces only salt water." At last I told him and his friends that I would go home and try their experiment with a salt well near my house; this made them laugh, for they saw my intended application. On finding that the conversation was going to turn in other directions, I told them plainly that I knew a way of remission of sins: and then unfolded Christ to them, dying on the cross to suffer our punishment and to pay our debt. After talking on this subject some time, I left three or four tracts with them, and came away.

This morning I spent an hour or more in the street, in a warm conversation with about twenty people, chiefly Brahmins: they maintaining the efficacy of self-righteousness and the very divinity of the stone idol, I preaching to them "God is a Spirit," and the alone efficacy of the blood of Christ to remit sin and to give righteousness.

Mangalagherry, March 3, 1847.—I had a pleasant ride here on Saturday afternoon, being in the shade either of a range of hills, which skirted the road for some distance, or of that of an avenue of trees under which the road ran the whole way. I arrived at the close of the first day of the great annual festival. Mangalagherry is a small, but for India, a well-built town: that is, its houses are all made of mud, but the largest number of them are tiled; and there is a regular street dividing the town into two equal parts; it probably contains 3000 or 4000 people: there is a large temple with a handsome goparam (*i. e.* tower over the gateway) about 120 or 150 feet high: just beyond it rises the hill to the height of 600 or 700 feet; half-way up the hill is a small pagoda, where the most sacred idol is kept.

It is a stone one, about two feet high, called Narasimha, and represents an uncouth incarnation of Vishnu, half man, half lion. There are several miracles connected with it: the first is, that when the people come to make their offerings of sugar and water, the priest pours them into the mouth of the idol, which as soon as it has received half of them begins to reject the rest, as a sign it has had enough: the next is, that whatever quantity, even a hundred gallons, is poured into the idol's mouth, small as the idol is, it holds it all: the manifest refutation of this is, that from out of all the crevices of the rock round the temple the sugared water trickles down in large quantities; but the stupid people are persuaded that this arises only from the spilling at the time of pouring it into its mouth. Another is, that if a number of vessels full of this liquid be left in the temple during the night, next morning they will be found half-emptied; the idol never taking more than half. I told those who reported this miracle to me, the story of Bel in the Apocrypha, and it greatly amused them, being so closely to the point. The fourth miracle is, that if this sugar and water be left on the hill any time, neither ants nor flies are atracted to it. The festival consisted in nothing more than certain nightly processions. On Sunday night an indecent representation of one of the scenes of Krishna's life (another incarnation of Vishnu) took place in the public street by means of figures about two feet high. The next night was the marriage: this consisted of a procession of an image of the god, so wrapped up in swaddling-clothes, that I could make out nothing of its shape, seated upon the folds of an enormous *cobra da capello*, and overshadowed by its outspread hood: along with this image, and, like it, borne aloft on men's shoulders, was a small shrine containing two brass idols, which represented the two wives of the god. The procession moved slowly about the town, pausing every now and then, while music was played before the idols, rockets were let off, guns fired, and a fire-work or two burned. The great night was Tuesday, but nothing else took place beyond the dragging about a great car, in which was seated a little idol. The crowd was enormous; on Sunday the town was crammed, but on Monday all the ground round about was also covered with people, and on Tuesday it was still closer and more widely crowded. The poor people came from all directions; many of them twenty or forty miles, and some even more. Of course there was no room in the town for them, so they just lived day and night on the open plain. Each night, about seven or eight o'clock, I saw numerous groups of women and children, worn out with the heat and excitement of the day, lying down all round the temple asleep; the men were still moving about. All the main street and neighbourhood were crowded with booths, where ornaments, toys, food, or sweetmeats were to be sold; indeed, in many respects, allowing for difference of customs, it was like a great English fair, without its riot or drunkenness, but instead of that defiled with idolatry. In the place of mountebanks or wild-beast shows, were a number of people whom I might call fire-dancers: a man, three parts naked, would take two thick torches made of cotton rags with oil on them, and having lighted them, he would dash them one against another until he was enveloped in the cloud of sparks which flew from them. All this while dancing about violently, he would vary the spectacle by beating his naked breast and back with the burning end of the torches, or hold them both before him in such a position that the flames pass close by his breast and face. Sometimes he would sit down on the ground, and take a roll of rags about an inch thick, light one end of it and put it into his open mouth, holding it on his tongue without extinguishing it; meanwhile another man fantastically dressed was beating a small gong: I saw four or five sets of these characters in the space of one hundred yards. Another man varied the amusement by mounting on stilts and running through the skin of his back and arms four skewers of wood, the farther ends of which terminated in small flaming torches. On inquiring many times the cause of all this outrageous and unmeaning self-torture, I was assured it was not from religion or devotion, but simply to collect a few pence from the by-standers.

On Sunday I was alone, and spent the greater part of the day quietly in the travellers' bungalow just outside the town; in the morning and evening I spent more than an hour on each occasion in disputing with and preaching to large numbers of listeners. Unlike the people of Cullapilly, they everywhere, and at all times, treated me with great respect and civility: the immediate cause of which is probably the well-known good-will of the excellent collector of the district to the missionaries. On Monday morning I was joined by Mr. Gunn from Guntoor, the American Lutheran missionary; for in India we are able to put the Evangelical alliance into practice: and morning and evening we sallied forth into the crowd: however, the better to get at the people, I pitched my tent in a grove of tamarind-trees, in sight of the great temple, and just outside of the crowd. Here I had crowds of listeners: as many as could find room sat down in my tent; they crammed all the space round about the doors on each side of the tent, and looked in through the windows. I must have had from fifty to sixty people at a time, most of them attentive and continuing for a length of time: among them were a good many women. I continued for an hour and a half or more, at a time, to preach to them, about idols, sin, and Jesus Christ the one sacrifice for sin. When tired, I read to them the ten commandments, explaining and applying them, or else a tract, commenting on it as I read. The crowd being great, and the noise from the distant crowd reaching to the tent, and as I had my audience not so much before me as at my right hand and left, I had to exert myself much, and to shout loudly: this, with a temperature of about 94°, was exhausting, and when the two days were over I was greatly fatigued, and my throat very sore. But it was a subject of great rejoicing that I had been permitted to preach Christ to such great numbers, who had never heard of him before, without obstruction or opposition. Though I sat preaching in Satan's own seat, yet he seemed restrained, and the power of God to be withholding him that he should not work out his malice against the gospel on its ministers. I was not a little amused at the looks of wonder which I saw continually in the crowds who looked at Mr. Gunn and myself, and at the crowds which usually followed us to the bungalow; for their looks confirmed what they told us, that they had never seen a white face before. I believe this is the case with a large proportion of the villagers.

Wulloor, March 5.—I have returned again into the Masulipatam district, which I had left on going to visit Mangalagherry: in doing so I had to recross the river Kistna; the branch in which I found water was about half a mile wide, and in parts fifteen feet deep. I crossed three other branches of about a quarter to half a mile wide, but at this season they are only dry beds of sand: during the floods they tell me that not only are all these branches filled with deep streams, but the intervening islands are also covered, so that the stream flows along a mighty river five miles wide. I pitched my tent in a clump of tamarind-trees just outside the village, and for these two days I have had conversations with the people much as usual. I had a variety however in the case of one man, a Sudra, who has learned Sanscrit, and read some of the Purànas, and is a Pedànti, one of a sect similar to the new Platonists. He professes to reject not only idols and their worship, but also all distinction of gods, affirming there is only one; yet like the Greek philosophers he conforms to custom, by a large mark of Vishnu on his forehead. I first met him in a crowd in the village when I was talking to a number of Brahmins about their idols; and then he was violent and almost unmannerly in discussion. When however he came to my tent he spoke more quietly, and was very much interested in the answers I gave to a variety of questions he asked; many of my answers, regarding the spiritual nature and the unity of God, quite agreed, he said, with his own views: there were others which no less pleased him, although novel, for they approved themselves to his judgment. Although he made no objections to the great scheme of redemption, yet he did not grasp it with any readiness; the reason was plain, as I afterward told him; he did not *know* or *feel* that he was a sinner, and therefore cared little for the good news of forgiveness of sins.

The village is a large one, and is the residence of the richest zemindar, a large land-holder of this district. He lives in a good-sized house, inside a fort with lofty mud walls: this is erected, not for defence, but only for show; for the grandfather of the present possessor was the first of this race of zemindars, and made his fortune since the commencement of this century; since which time all these districts have been as secure from an enemy as the inland counties of England. On the same principle of display, he keeps in his service 400 men, about sixty of whom are dressed and armed as Sepoys, and about a dozen as cavalry. He has seven fine elephants, and a large number of camels. He is a man of Sudra caste, but like the rest of his tribe, he is fed on and led about by a number of Brahmins: he is fond of hog hunting, and keeps about fifty dogs for this purpose. The only useful thing that I heard of his doing was, the establishment of a native school inside the fort. Though he was for several years the ward of the East India Company, being a minor, no pains were taken to give him any instruction: he does not know English, and is as little fitted to perform the duties of his station as any other zemindar; and it would be difficult to say less of his qualifications than this. I understood that his wife could read Telugu, and even a little English. I learned this by a little boy who is a scholar in the school, coming to me for some tracts and books for her ladyship. The mother-in-law of the zemindar also sent for several tracts, which he specified, and afterward sent one of his chief people to see if I had got "any curious books:" by which he meant, any copies of their religious books, concerning the possession of which I had been speaking in the morning.

Neddamole, Bungalow, March 9.—Leaving Wulloor on Saturday morning early, I rode over to

Weyoor, distant only four or five miles. I remained there in the bungalow all that day and Sun day, visiting the village in the evening and morning. I had long conversations on either occasion; on the latter the only noticeable points were a testy old Brahmin who would be satisfied with nothing I could say, and a younger man who maintained with vehemence that the idols were not idols, but gods: when I used the term idol, or image, he shut his ears and cried, "Alooh! I cannot listen to such a word." I think he was only half serious; the rest of the people laughed at him. He reminded me of a Roman Catholic priest at Secundrabad, who was very indignant at his opponent in a controversy charging the Romanists with worshipping a wafer. "How unfair it is of you," he wrote, "to say we worship a wafer; you know that if we thought it was so we would not worship it: we believe it to be the body of Christ: it is *that* which we worship, and not bread, when we adore the host."

At daybreak on Monday morning I left Weyoor for Pràmarra, where I had been so well received ten days before, and whither I had promised to return. I met on going into the village several of my previous acquaintances, who seemed glad to see me; they had many questions to ask me about Mangalagherry, so that two or three times I had to go over the stories of the trickery of the priests, and the story of Bel. It was excessively hot all day in my tent, and I had not so many visitors as before: but of those that came I had the opportunity of repeating the gospel to several, and of pressing upon them the danger of delaying to come to Christ. I found the Brahmin in whom I had been much interested before, still professing the same belief in Christ, and distrust in Vishnu, Siva, and all other idols. He did not conceal however from me that he received four rupees a month for singing Siva hymns in a neighbouring village. He had a long conversation about how he was to get his livelihood in case he was to turn Christian, and wanted me to promise I would support him; I told him I could not promise to do that, but that God's promise was true, and consistent with reason, that those that come to him he will provide for. "Oh," said the man, "that won't do for me." So I said to him: "If you cannot trust God's promise for support in this life, how can you trust his promise for what is so much greater and more difficult, eternal life in the world to come?" I afterward could not help thinking how inconsistent we Christians are on this point, trusting to God for forgiveness of sins, for a kingdom and a throne, and yet mistrusting him daily in matters which concern our temporal support or comfort.

On both occasions I have pressed him to take a copy of a tract or a gospel: but he has with unusual pertinacity declined. I was pressing him to take and read a copy of St. Luke, and asking him how he could expect to know the way which leads to life, if he did not read regarding it. "How can I understand it?" said he, pointing to the book; "perhaps it has sixteen different meanings, and how am I, even though I sit all day over it, to find out the right one?" His notion is an authorized Hindoo one, viz. that the sacred books are purposely so written, that every sentence may be capable, not of one meaning only, but of many: and a teacher or a commentary is thus required to understand the text In ingenuity this exceeds the pope's reasons for keeping the Bible from the people. In regard to the variety of meanings capable of being drawn from one set of sentences, it shows that "there is nothing new under the sun." Yet who would have expected the principle of tract No. 90 to have been forestalled in an obscure Hindoo village.

I still have hopes of there being something at work in the man's mind. I had intended to have remained there two days, but I found the heat to be so great that I judged it better not to remain in my tent any longer.

Masulipatam, March 27.—I have been here rather more than a fortnight since my return from the villages. My employment is to go out before sunrise into the town, which is close to my house, and there spend an hour or so in conversing, preaching, and disputing with a crowd of people in some corner of a street. I get ready listeners, though not so favourable ones as in the villages. Nevertheless, I make the name of Christ known to many, and give away a few tracts. Nearly the whole day I am engaged with visitors in my house: many boys from the English school come and spend hours with me: many grown-up natives pay me visits, with whom I have long and interesting conversations. I have adorned the walls of my principal rooms with pictures, some portraits and views, others of birds and animals, and on my tables I have placed a variety of nicknacks and curiosities—little mummy figures from Egypt, chimney-ornaments from England; a small globe; and these form grand attractions to my visitors, who are as delighted to see these things as a child is to see a raree-show. Besides this, fame has carried abroad that I possess some magnetic fish and ducks, and a camera obscura, and other wonderful things from Europe; and I often find, after a long conversation on other matters of a higher kind, that I have been honoured with the visit in consequence of my visitor's curiosity to see the wonderful things I possess. I, of course, gladly exhibit them, and so I hope I prepare the way for more confidence and kindly acquaintance with my native neighbours, besides conveying to them as full statements as I can of the way of salvation through Christ. With the younger part of my visitors I find that so simple a thing as a magnetic toy goes to shake their confidence in their heathen miracles, as exhibiting to them the existence of natural wonders greater than those which their people tell them regarding the gods. The fish and the duck that will come when they are called, and have the semblance of life, although they are manifestly only tin toys, afford a ready comparison with the idols, which can neither stand nor walk, nor hear nor see, and yet are said to be alive.

A few days ago, while conversing with a crowd of people in the street, and when some of them were asking me the common question, "Suppose we join your religion, how shall we get our livelihood?" and while I was endeavouring to show them that those who committed their souls to God would be found far from losers in regard to their bodies, I used the illustration of the Prodigal Son: "Suppose," I said, "a little boy was to leave his father's house, and go to a far country, surely he would soon find himself in want: then half starved as he was, if he was to return home, and humbly ask for food, would not his father most joyfully receive him, feed him and clothe him, as a recovered lost one?" "No," said the man I spoke to, "the father would have nothing to do with the lad; how could he tell what he had *eaten*, while he had been absent from home?" meaning, that as the father could not tell whether the boy had not eaten food prepared by people of inferior caste, and consequently lost his caste, he would count him as unclean and drive him away. I was scarcely prepared to hear so unblushing a statement of the hard-heartedness to which the system of caste reduced people. The speaker was not a Brahmin, nor apparently any thing more than an ordinary Sudra working-man.

On several occasions of late I have had the low morality of the Hindu religious books brought out in common conversation. Pressing on the people the fact of their having sinned, which some deny, but which they commonly evade by asking, "Who knows the difference between right and wrong? what is sin?" I asked them, "What is lying; what is theft? Are they right or wrong? are they sins or not?" I have been answered several times, "Why that depends on the occasion; if a man lies or steals to satisfy hunger, of course there is no harm in it." Sometimes they say, "Of course everybody tells lies; how could the world go on without lying?"

I was much shocked one morning by that old wicked statement made to me by a farmer just come out of the country. I was asking him as above mentioned, whether he had not sinned; whether, for instance, he had not told many lies. "And if I have," said he, "who is it that made me to tell them; who else but God? It is not my fault." I told him that thus he was charging God with being a liar, for if I was to send my servant into the bazaar and make him steal, I should be just as much a thief as he was. "Well, what then," said the man, "God *is* a thief and a liar; if not, how does it happen that some men are born rich and others poor." I turned away from him, saying, I dared to speak no longer with such a blasphemer, and began to express to the by-standers my horror and grief at these expressions: they only laughed, but the man seemed a little ashamed, for he came back presently to justify himself, saying that in his religion, his god (Krishna) was related to have both committed thefts and told lies, and as he believed all this, he was surely right in saying what he did. The worst of it is, that it was not the man's own idea, but the systematic doctrine maintained by a large proportion of the Hindus, that men are mere puppets, and God is the immediate instigator of all their actions, both good and bad!

Sallapilly, Feb. 17, 1847.

MY DEAR GEORGE,

I have no one to disturb me here, but the natives who come to my tent, and this is in the way of business; the intervals between their going and coming, and my evenings, are all my own for reading and writing. I thus combine more active employment in real evangelization, with improvement in Telugu, and leisure for my own use. I am more and more inclined to carry out Mr. Venn's proposed plans, so far as the seasons allow me; about six months I must be under cover of a roof, but the rest of my time I hope to spend in my snug tent. I wish some of the Cantabs knew what a happy life it is; to have it actually one's business to be preaching Christ to those who have never before heard of him, is very joyful:—when I have been to a village and told the people there of him, and left tracts with them, I come away joyfully, recollecting that there is one more obstacle to Christ's coming removed: whether they will hear, or whether they will forbear, he has been preached among them, and so the end is coming all more quickly: besides this, the seed is sown, and some will spring up to bear fruit, and Christ shall see of the travail of his soul in that village. * * * I look back to my visit to England with much thankfulness and pleasure: perhaps with more than if it had been made under more outwardly happy circumstances. I feel so thankful for all the happy intercourse we had together, and the interchange of affection between all the members of the family, and especially for the love you have all shown to my dear little children. But I cannot say I look with satisfaction on my missionary work there. I look indeed with exceeding pleasure upon all the meetings in the North, which I went to with Blenkinsopp: I enjoyed them thoroughly—but what I considered my more important season in the South, I regard with less satisfaction. It is perhaps because I expected to see results in the shape of men, and saw none, nor any prospects of any. This is want of faith, but it also arises from feeling that I might have said and done more.

Your affectionate brother,

HENRY W. FOX.

REV. J. Y. NICHOLSON, EMMANUEL COLLEGE, CAMBRIDGE.

Masulipatam, Feb. 25, 1847.

MY DEAR FRIEND,

I have been purposing some time to fulfil my promise of writing a long letter to you: I promised Ragland that I would try and do so on my journey up here from Madras, but that journey is over; and I have got myself settled in my new house, and I am out in my tent in the villages, and yet my promise is unfulfilled; so I take advantage of a forenoon in which I am staying in a travellers' bungalow, and therefore have no native visitors as I have when I am in my tent. I wish that you and all your missionary circle could be with me, either in my house at Masulipatam, or in my tent in some of the villages, that you might yourselves see how free from personal hardship a missionary's life is in India. I have a large new house, one end of which lies empty for want of some brother missionary to come and occupy it: in it I have every comfort and convenience I could wish. I have my drawing-room and dining-room, my bed-room and bathing-room adjoining, and my study besides: so that I live like a prince. Then I have the society of my dear brother Noble, and of two Christian families, and sometimes of one or two others like-minded, among our European residents: so that I am really without any outward want. When I come out in my tent, my servants pitch it for me in an eligible situation, in or near a village; it is just twelve feet square inside; it has double walls and top, separated the one from the other by a space two feet wide—and here I have my tables, my chair, my bed, my books, and a great part of the day long I have an audience of black faces and turbaned or shaven heads inside and outside the door. I say, that I wish you could see how free from outward hardships we are; for I fear that it is the dread of them which keeps so many men from coming out to us; and yet, supposing a missionary's life was one of hardship, surely we have no right to shrink from it on that account. Our dear Lord's life was one of hardship, and we are not to be above walking in his steps: as Christians, we are born to hardships, and blessed is the man who receives them from the Lord! Through much tribulation must we enter into the kingdom of heaven; why then should we shrink from our allotted tribulation? All the way as I came along the road from Madras, I was thinking how I could tell you of my journey; it is scarcely worth while to describe to you the journey itself in detail; it is enough to say I was on horseback, and travelled a stage of from ten to fifteen miles every morning and evening, halting at comfortable bungalows, or houses built by the government for the use of travellers; there is no inn-keeper in them, but the people attached to them are always ready to procure me milk, and boil my kettle, and for dinner kill me a chicken and curry it. I enjoyed my journey greatly, as the season (the beginning of January) was cool and bright, and the crops on the ground made the boundless plain through which I rode greener and prettier than I had ever seen it before. In the loneliness of my journey,—for I had no one to speak English to, except in two or three towns where I stopped for a few days,—I had much enjoyment. But the subject about which I was continually thinking I would speak to you, was that of the desolation of the country in a spiritual point of view. I rode 250 miles in a straight line, through a populous country, passing through villages every three or four miles, and seeing many others in all directions, and occasionally coming to considerable towns; but in all that district there was not a single Christian missionary; not one person from whom a heathen might hear the word of life;—my road lay parallel to the sea-coast, at no great distance from it, but I might have gone inland for 100, or 200, or 300 miles, and except in one place have found the whole land equally wanting in Christian teachers. On Sunday evening I went into a village and had a long conversation with some Brahmins; the discussion coming to no satisfactory conclusion, the chief speaker said, "Well, come to-morrow, and we will have a full talk on the subject: you shall bring your books, and I will bring mine, and we will see which is true." I could only tell him that by the next morning I must be on my journey again; and I thought of the almost impossibility of a Christian preacher ever reaching him; the village lay 200 miles from Madras, and 150 from Guntoor, the next missionary station. And now that I am moving about in my own district, I often think of you and the missionary collectors who assemble in your rooms: I pass from one large village to another, I see the intermediate distances broken by smaller villages;—the country as distinguished from the town is, I think, more closely peopled than that in England, and yet I am alone in visiting the people; I find generally the very name of Christ unknown, and perfect ignorance as to either the sin or folly of idolatry. The whole district, without another missionary in it, is nearly 100 miles each way; it is impossible that I can visit even the chief villages for two or three days each, during the six months in the year in which the weather allows me to be out.

How gladly should I welcome some one or two of you, who might come out overland by July or August, when the worst of the hot season is over: a couple of months spent in Masulipatam would give the bare rudiments of the language, and then we could go out together into the villages for six months, and hear nothing but Teloogoo all day long. I would suggest in answer to any one who might say, "I have not qualifications for a missionary life;" that so various are the spheres of missionary labour, requiring such very different kinds and degrees of talents, that if a man is not fit for any of them, he is certainly not fit for any ministerial sphere in England. Some have great difficulties in regard to opposition on the part of their parents; I would suggest in such cases that they should get some friend, whose age, character, and position has weight with their parents, to open the subject to them. The subject which, coming from a young man, a father might at once treat as visionary and absurd, may, when quietly brought forward by one of riper years and judgment, at least claim a calm consideration. My paper obliges me to conclude by assuring you of my being

Your very sincere friend,

HENRY W. FOX.

Mangalagherry, Sunday evening, Feb. 28, 1847.

MY DEAREST ISABELLA,

I have been thinking about you often to-day, and so I think I will spend half an hour this evening in writing to you. The cause of my thoughts recurring to you so often I believe is, that I have been reading Newton's Cardiphonia, which I used to read at Rugby, and have scarcely ever looked into since. Newton is much mixed up with my recollections of Rugby, and that brings to my mind the time when I used to receive from you a long letter regularly every Sunday morning, which served as my food during the following week. I believe those letters of your's were, under God, among the chief means of fanning into a flame the smoking flax, and bringing the full light of Christ's sun to break through my twilight. I was then, as I am now, lonely: I had friends and companions, but none in Christ, for it was before —— was touched by the Spirit of God; and I used to look to you as my chief, and indeed only Christian companion, though so far off: and now it is the same, my heart flies to you as the dearest companion on earth, and distant as we are, I seem to have more and closer communion with you than with any one alive. While I am writing, (nine o'clock at night,) the roar of the devil's festival is going on, about a quarter of a mile off: the cracks of the fireworks, the braying of harsh trumpets, the screeching of clarionets, and the hammering of tom-toms, rise above the confused sound of a thousand or two of people, and tell me that the procession of the god has set out from his temple. I have only just come back from the town to the bungalow; crowds of poor beings, worn out with the excitement of the day, were lying asleep in all directions on the ground; vast crowds fill the street and neighbourhood of the temple, in the midst of whom are several men like madmen, dancing about with two lighted torches (made of cotton rags) in their hands, which they dash together till the sparks fly out, and almost cover their naked bodies; or they beat themselves with the lighted ends, or they hold them, so that the flame scorches their chests or their faces; and one man was walking about on stilts, with four long wooden skewers run through the skin of his arms and back, and the farther ends of them on fire: and all this is not for devotion or religion's sake, but to get two or three pence by it. This, for the time being, is Satan's seat, where he sits triumphant; but I trust the time has come, when the Lord Jesus is going to turn him out of it. After a long talk in the morning, for an hour and a half, till I was quite hoarse, about idols and the true way of salvation, I have been spending a quiet Sunday in the travellers' bungalow, reading the first nine or ten chapters of the Acts, which I thought was a good preparation for going to the people again, when the heat of the day was over. However, I shrank a good deal from going into the noisy crowd of devil's servants, all alone,—not that I had any thing personally to fear, but the contest seemed great. I was able to remember, and take courage from the remembrance, that the one Lord of heaven and earth was on my side, and would be with me in the midst of them; and when I went, I had about an hour of remarkably quiet, satisfactory preaching, to attentive and assenting listeners, many of whom were Brahmins, and one or two learned ones; so that Christ has prevailed, and would not let Satan have his way. Leaving the noise and crowd of the town, I walked up the silent and lonely steps on the side of the hill which led to the pagoda of the idol which is so fond of sugar and water, and there looked down on the town, half hid among the trees, and the tall goparam, a tower rising above all, and the milk-white buildings inside the pagoda, gleaming in the bright moonlight, and the many lights down the street, reaching far away; and as the roar and drumming came up to me, I remembered how, at that hour, (eight o'clock,) our friends at Guntoor, only thirteen miles off, were met together for evening worship, and how at the same time the thousands of congregations in quiet, happy England, were just assembling for afternoon service: while here, the thousands assembled to worship a dirty stone were indulging in dissipation and devilry. Blessed day when Jesus shall come to set all things to rights; "The times of refreshing from the presence of the Lord," poor souls, now taking it all easy, but then shrinking with horror from the sight of him coming on the clouds of heaven. Oh, dear sister, what a joyful day for us! to rise with dear Lizzy and little Johnny, and our dear brother and sister, and the other loved ones in Hove Churchyard, to meet him in the air, and so we shall ever be with the Lord. We may well work on with patience, so long as he has work for us to do, with such a joy set before us. May it please God early to make my darling Harry and Mary rejoice in this prospect through their love to Christ! I do greatly long and pray, that they may be spared the uneasy pantings after the world, and from the dishonour done to Christ by most in their youth; and that they may early, even from now, know what is the settled joy and peace of real believers.

Your very affectionate brother,

HENRY W. FOX.

Masulipatam, March 22, 1847.

MY DEAR FATHER AND MOTHER,

I cannot sufficiently thank you for the letters which I have received from you so regularly every mail since my arrival. I received my mother's letter of January 29, yesterday. The receipt of them is a great break on my solitude: at times I feel downcast by my loneliness, and at such times it is an inexpressible relief to look across the water and feel your affection and your sympathy. Your love toward, and care of, my dear children, is a fresh source of love to you, and most thankfully do I feel to you for your kindness to them. You may say that they are your grand-children, but it is not all grand-children that receive such parental love. I have returned from my village tour, as the weather was becoming too hot to live in my tent: the last day it was up to 98° for some hours. On my return, the weather feels cool enough, but it is beginning to warm up; the season however is favourable as yet, and we have had several cloudy days, very unusual at this season, and I am in excellent health and strength. I am too busy at present. I cannot get my work done: as my house is near the town, I have visitors half the day long, occupying all my leisure time and a good deal more. I also go into the town itself morning and evening, and have long and animated discussions. You remember that till now I had kept to the outskirts and villages in the suburbs; now I am able by Christ's help to go into the streets and bazaars and meet all comers. So that I am able to attack the stronghold of Satan. The English school is also beginning to receive its visible blessing; there are two dear little boys in it, —one fourteen, and the other almost sixteen, very desirous of being baptized, and showing marks, as we think, of the work of the Holy Spirit in them. One is a very respectable Brahmin, and the other a respectable Sudra. We must wait a little time before we take the step; they come to Mr. Noble or to me every day. I see also a good deal of other boys in private: the magnetic fishes, ducks, &c., and other toys and pictures, are a great attraction, and make my house quite a show-room; and as I generally get an opportunity of telling my visitors of Christ before they ask to see the curiosities, it all works for good. * * *

Your very affectionate son,

H. W. Fox.

TO THE REV. JOHN EMERIS.

Masulipatam, March 27, 1847.

My dear John,

I feel that I must at last begin a letter to you this Saturday evening, though it is late, and I can do no more than begin it. For on looking over my old journals, (teeming with the sins of my youth,) I found lately, that the 27th of March was the day on which, in 1840, I came to the final decision to be a missionary. Do you remember the occasion when you came to my lodgings,—those nice little rooms of Sims' in Holywell Street,—and after spending the evening together and praying, I made the decision? It is a memorable day for me, and it might be well to keep it as a day of commemoration; but I am no longer master of my own time, and I can keep no days except Sundays, and they are busy ones. It was a day ushering in great mercies and much toil, for both of which God's name be praised. Instead of seven years, it sometimes appears to me like seven centuries, and I am tempted at times to complain, "When will my weary time be over and I shall be at rest?" Nevertheless, it has been more a time of work in me, than of work which I have done all this while. I seem to have been only learning: now I hope I am at work, but it is only since the last two months. If God gives me work to do, and life to do it in, I hope I may be able to thank him for it. At times I am able to feel very thankful for my work, and to wonder how I could wish to be anywhere else; at others, I am ready to faint and complain of weakness, want of refreshment, and of the sorrows laid on me. I arrived here on January 20th. Very soon after the bishop paid a visit of a fortnight here. * * * When he was gone, at once I called for my tent and baggage, and went off into the villages, where I spent a happy, and I trust, profitable month, daily preaching to numbers the free remission of sins, through our precious Lord. To my astonishment (and it was all *his* doing) my loneliness, for I scarcely spoke a word of English all the while or saw a white face, was so far from being a burden, that I actually enjoyed it. I look forward with great pleasure to going out again as soon as the fire has gone down sufficiently, in August or September: for while I have more continual and favourable opportunities for preaching the gospel, I have also abundant time for reading and writing. * * * Many of the boys in Mr. Noble's English school come and spend hours with me during the heat of the day, and with some I am almost as affectionate as a father and his sons. There is one of them, a dear boy of fourteen, who wants very much to be baptized, but whom we delay, as he is still in the legal power of his father: he is, I am sure, a true child of Christ, and a few days ago had a great struggle to go through, on occasion of an idolatrous ceremony in his father's house. After a long debate with himself, whether he would worship the Brahmin priest, if required to do so, and many inward struggles, at last his eyes brightened, and he said, "He (meaning his father) can only hurt my body; he cannot hurt my soul; I will not worship the man." And afterward, when he had been spared the trial he dreaded, the first words which he spoke, on coming to tell me of it, were, "Sir, Christ has heard our prayers." * * * Believe me,

Your own affectionate,

HENRY W. FOX.

JOURNAL.

Masulipatam, July 8, 1847.—In my usual morning visit to the streets of the town, I fell in with a boy who had lately left Mr. Noble's English school. After an interesting conversation, in which it appeared what a consent of the understanding there might be to the truth without any inclination of the heart toward God, he began to speak about my going regularly to the streets to preach and converse about religion. He said, "The people crowd around you, not because they care to hear what you have to say, but they think you are mad, and so they come for mere curiosity's sake." I was struck with the remark, which was made in great simplicity, and I believe that there is a great deal of truth in it. Indeed this regular street-preaching quite puzzles them; they do not know what to make of it; and from the remarks I hear about it, many of them do not like it, for it seems like a systematic attack upon their religion in their homes. They are on the whole, however, very civil and attentive, though very often silly.

A few days ago a Brahmin, with whom I have been long and intimately acquainted, lost his only child, a little boy about two and a half years old. Added to the natural feeling of a parent, a Brahmin has an additional source of grief in the thought that it is only by the ceremonies and prayers of his son after the father's death, that he can be delivered out of the pains of purgatory; and so he who dies without leaving a son behind him is especially cursed. How far this feeling affected the individual in question, I cannot say, for he is a believer in nothing save money; but it is probable that superstitious feelings may have remained where belief has ceased.

However, his natural feelings were roused, and when he came to see me next day, he told me that it was no use staying in his house: if he sat down to do any thing, he could not do it, and that he got up and wandered restlessly about; and besides, there was the baby's poor mother crying without stopping. I felt much for him, knowing that in all the range of his thoughts, and in all heathenism, there was not one word that could afford him any comfort. I pointed this out to him, telling him how much I felt for him, and begging him, as I knew he placed no belief in heathenism, to look and see if the comfort during sorrow which we Christians receive, and of which I gave him assurance from my own experience, was not a most forcible evidence of its divine authority. "You *are now* in sorrow," I said, "and feel what it is; and you find that neither in yourself nor in that which is around you, have you the slightest alleviation of it; surely that religion which does what man cannot do, must be from God." He acknowledged with much heartiness that it was so, and said that it was an undoubted proof, much stronger than external proofs. I asked him then where he believed his child was; he said he believed it was with Jesus Christ, but he should never go there, nor see it any more. I asked him if he had a word of comfort to give to his poor weeping wife; he acknowledged that he had none; nor indeed could he have, for if he did believe in his fathers' religion, he must suppose that he would never meet his child again—for already it was probably wandering about in some other transmigration; nor could he look to the sorrow as being from a Father's hand, but only that it was a curse incurred by sins during some former state of being. However, having learned from me before, he now said, "God has given me two blows,—the death of my relation a week ago, and now the death of my child; my sin must be very great." These were ideas he had gained from me, and were not indigenous ones. He promised to consider the Christian religion closer than he had ever done, and took away a Gospel of St. Luke, with the promise of reading it carefully.

Masulipatam, July 15, 1847.—Yesterday morning I went to a collection of huts, inhabited by Chuklus, and lying on the outskirts of the town, half a mile distant from my house. These people are shoemakers and workers in leather, and are consequently considered the most unclean of all the most despised of the pariah class: their habits have not indeed much to recommend them. As soon as I entered the thick cluster of huts, I was surrounded by twenty-five or thirty of them; half were men, half women and boys. After a while I asked where their god was; they pointed out a square hut in the middle of the cluster, with mud walls four feet high, and a sloping roof of palmyra-leaf thatch. There, they said, was their Ammavâru or village goddess. On asking what was inside, they said, "A stone." Reproaching them for worshipping a stone, I said, "Go and fetch it to me." They made excuse first, "It is too heavy to carry;" and when I said, "Let two or three carry it," they next said

"It is planted in the ground." After ten minutes conversation with them, telling them of Christ and his love and death, I went up to the hut and crept in at the low door-way, and at once noticed the lies they had told me. On a little raised daïs of dry clay reclined, first, a slip of wood two feet long, on which was cut very imperfectly a rude figure of a man, four or five inches long, and in the style a school-boy might carve with his knife; next to it was an old worm-eaten piece of wood, ten inches long, resembling nothing so much as an old tent-peg, or a withered root of mangel-wurzel: these two, they said, were the husband or husbands of the goddess; next was a misshapen rough stone, about a foot square,—this was the Ammavåru herself: farther on lay three stones, about the size and shape of small paving-stones, these were her children. It is difficult to conceive that state of mind which should believe such coarse and common materials to possess a divine nature; yet many, if not all the people about me, seemed quite serious in believing these stones to be their deity. They did not regard them as the creator or creators of the world, but simply as their gods; whom if they were to forsake, they would pay their lives in forfeit.

After leaving the hut again, I returned to the subject of Christ, and called on them to forsake these miserable stones, and come to him as their dying but living Saviour. One man said, quite seriously, "But if we all turn Christians, what will become of the dead cattle?" For the Chuklus are the privileged consumers of all bullocks, cows, and buffaloes which die of disease or old age. "Suppose," he added, "some of us join your religion, and we will leave some behind to eat the cattle."

I suppose that, so long as the human heart can escape humbling itself before God as worthless and unprofitable, and to accept the righteousness of another and not its own, there is nothing too vile or degrading to which it will not descend. For, indeed, what difference is there between these worm-eaten stumps of wood and shapeless stones of the chuklus, and the silver and marble be-jewelled figures of the Virgin and saints which I saw the people adoring at Malta, except a few degrees of civilization and elegance? Religiously and morally viewed, the one worship is just as degrading and humiliating as the other.

Masulipatam, July 31, 1847.—Ten days ago, Mr. Sharkey and I went out to the public bungalow at the village of Neddamole, ten miles from here; our object was partly to preach to the people in the neighbouring villages, but chiefly to obtain, in the quiet of the bungalow, that seclusion which we cannot obtain in our houses here, where native visitors are coming and going all day long: for we wanted to make progress in revising and preparing some Telugu manuscripts for the press. We stayed three days visiting the villages, morning and evening, and having some interesting opportunities of making Christ known.

Last Sunday, July 25th, we baptized in our little congregation Sitapàti, a young man of a respectable Sudra caste, and about twenty-one years of age. The way in which he was brought to us encourages us in the hope that God has many other hidden ones, whom he will in due time bring out from among the heathen. About six months ago, he became acquainted with David, a young man of about his own age, who was baptized last autumn, and who had once been of the same caste as Sitapàti. I do not know that the acquaintance led to any thing about that time, but two or three months ago, Sitapàti speaks of himself as beginning to think about his sins, and to feel anxious concerning them. In this state of feeling, he asked his acquaintance, David, what was the cure for his sins? David told him of Christ: and it seems that almost immediately the young man was led to desire to be a Christian. When in this state, David one day informed me of him, and at my request brought him to me. I found him very ignorant, yet desirous of being taught, and professing a desire to be baptized. He came to me several times for instruction, and read a little of St. Matthew's gospel. However, his relatives seem to have found out the turn his mind was taking, and he told me he was afraid of their locking him up in the house and not letting him go out. This led him to spend a great part of his time at the school-house, where David lives, as it was then the holidays; and during the time, of his own accord, he broke his caste by eating of David's supper, prepared by a Pariah cook. His father and elder brother—the former an old man who had once been a gardener; the latter a strong, stout, and violent young man—at last, finding that Sitapàti absented himself much from home, came one Sunday afternoon to the school-house to seek for him. This led to two or three interviews between him and these relatives, in the presence of Mr. Noble or myself; in which they endeavoured by threats and enticements to induce him to come home with them; but he steadily resisted, and said he wished to become a Christian, and told them their efforts were useless, for he had already broken caste.

On Monday morning, when they came to my house, the brother used all sorts of entreaties, urging how he had fed him, and taken care of him from a child, and taught him to read, &c., and would he now leave them? All the while his face quivered with passion, and had not the interview been in my presence, I am sure he would have endeavoured to drag his brother off by force. Next day, when Sitapàti was in Mr. Noble's compound, his brother and another person, who apparently had been lying hid on purpose, sprang out and seized him, and taking him head and feet, dragged him out of the compound, and some little distance toward the place where they lived. However, the alarm was given, and Mr. N. and two or three servants ran out and overtook them, and insisted on the young man being released; which, after a short while, was done. Mr. N. then asked him where he wished to go, with him, or with his brothers: it did not require much for the poor young man, whose face was bleeding from a blow received from his brother, to decide to return with Mr. Noble. Next day, with the too ordinary barefaced falsehood of a Hindoo, the brother laid a complaint before the magistrate, that Mr. N. was detaining his brother by force. The collector sent for the young man, and in public court examined him for a long time, concerning the correctness of his brother's complaint: Sitapàti publicly declared that it was of his own good-will that he had gone to, and was living with Mr. N., and as publicly declared his purpose of becoming a Christian. This was truly making a good confession; for all round about were crowds of Brahmins and others, whose enmity against the gospel is not small: some of them said among themselves, as I was afterward told by one who said he heard the words, "I wish I could get hold of that young man—I would murder him." The magistrate, of course, dismissed the complaint, with a warning to the brother. Since then Sitapàti has been going on steadily, and daily receiving instruction in the knowledge of the leading truths of the gospel, till last Sunday, when having assurance of his sincerity, and being satisfied that he knew what it was into which he was to be baptized, he was received into Christ's visible church. His coming over to us, and the publicity which was given to it by his examination before the collector, made a much greater sensation in the town than I could have expected: it was added however to a recent baptism of a young Brahmin at Vizagapatam, which caused great sensation there, and was well known here; the effect was, that nearly half the boys in Mr. Noble's English school were withdrawn. After a while many of them came back, but in all he lost fifteen, among whom were some of the most hopeful and interesting youths. The school, however, was not left empty, for the vacancies were rapidly filled up by new applicants who crowded to gain admission, among whom were the sons of the principal Sudra Ameen, and the Sheristadar of his court. The story which was current here, as it has been elsewhere on similar occasions, was that we had given the young man a potion, the effect of which was to attach him to us: the way in which they supposed it was done, was to sprinkle a powder on his head. The parents of some boys feared, or pretended to fear, that we should do so to their boys, if they remained in school: not considering that it would have been easy for us to have done so any time these last three years past, or when the boys come to our houses, which they freely do. But the fact is, like the Jews of old, they cannot but acknowledge that a wonderful thing has happened, an influence has been produced on a man's mind to induce him to deny himself, and give up his family and his caste; and not knowing whence it proceeds, they attribute it to magic or medicine. I do not think the Hindoo system knows any thing of an influence of Divine power on the heart or feelings of man: it is more conversant with mere outward ceremonies, or at least with a mere intellectual theorizing on deity.

Neddamole, Aug. 11, 1847.—Mr. Sharkey and I have started for a month's tour through the villages, being desirous of taking advantage of the continuance of cloudy weather, which enables us to be out much during the day-time. There is so much rain, however, that we are not able to take out tents with us, but keep ourselves to the line of road on which there are public bungalows, and from them visit the numerous villages which lie within two or three miles of our resting-place.

Yesterday morning, at sunrise, we rode out to a large village named Tarakatoor, about two miles off: the land is about two-thirds under the plough, and at this time the crops of black paddy are a few inches above the ground, and resemble young wheat. The village is inhabited almost entirely by Sudras who live by cultivation; there are only four Brahmin houses in the place; one of them contains a school, in which a small portion of the boys of the village learn to read and write. The village is under a zemindar, or landholder, and seems to be in a more prosperous condition than many others; for the bullocks seemed to be numerous; no less than five ponies, not very much starved, were grazing outside the village; the houses were not ruinous, and several were of a slightly superior style to the mud cabins of the villages; and lastly, the pagodas to Vishnu and Siva, besides being rather larger, were in much better repair than usual. Both of us had several very long and interesting conversations with separate groups of people. At first, they were very suspicious of us, and would not so much as touch a tract, and fancied we came out as spies of some kind: when we told them we were preachers, as usual, they concluded that the East India Company had sent us.

In the evening we went to two distinct villages: Mr. S. to the main village of Kurumalapád, about a mile from this village, and I to the Pariah hamlet near it. Every village has such a hamlet situated about a quarter of a mile distant from it: in it live the poor abject Pariahs, who are not allowed to live in the main village where the Brahmins and Sudras dwell, and who are the farm-labourers, or almost serfs, attached to the soil which belongs to the village. Some Sudras and Brahmins, who are very poor, drive the plough themselves, but the majority employ these Pariahs instead. I found most of the men out in the fields weeding the corn, and for some time could only get desultory conversations with two or three women at a time. As it was growing later, one of the farmers of the main village was passing through, and I had a long talk with him in the hearing of a dozen or more of the Pariah men and women—he sitting on the ground, a few yards off, with his back against the mud wall, and I on a heap of lumps of dry mud, which had lately formed a wall. When I had told him at length about Christ, his birth, labours, sufferings, and his death, and had dwelt on these as the only expiation for sin, and then on the duty of all to turn to him, and call on him, he at last said, "Sir, I will ask you one thing. It is somewhere about a hundred years since your Company people (*i. e.* the East India Company) came to these parts; now, how is it, if all this that you have been telling me is so good, that they have never sent to tell us about it before?" I could only acknowledge that it was a grievous sin and offence of the government, for which I had no excuse, and over which I often mourned. The extraordinary and unfounded dread which some people entertain lest the Hindus should be ready to rise in arms against the English government, in case it was to begin to teach them and to send preachers of the gospel among them, is daily refuted, not by theories, but by facts. For the natives, one and all, believe the missionaries to be emissaries of the Company, until we undeceive them. Yet neither on the establishment of the English school in Masulipatam, the declared and published object of which was the conversion of its scholars, and which was generally believed by the natives to be established by the government; nor on our going out to the streets or villages preaching against idolatry and proclaiming Christ, and supposed to be the Company's missionaries, has a word reached our ears hostile to the Company on this account. In regard to the civil and military administration, complaints (often unfounded) are not unfrequent: with respect to its supposed proselytizing, or rather preaching department, not one word. So much for the fears lest God's work should impede the progress of man's dominion.

Weyoor, Aug. 13, 1847.—After visiting two or

three more villages from Neddamole, we started at an early hour yesterday morning for this bungalow, which is fifteen miles farther on. I did not, however, like to pass by the large village of Prámarru, where I had been so well received at my two visits in February and March. It lies nearly half-way, and so on our arriving there about eight o'clock in the morning, left our horses with our horse-keepers, and entered the village. We soon met the Naich, or head Sudra of the place, with whom I had formed an acquaintance before, and he led us to the chief school,—the friendship of the master of which I had purchased by putting the Naich's little boy to his school, and paying for him for four months. The school-master was not there, but was away getting shaved, as it was a lucky day for that rare operation, and an old blind superannuated master was keeping in order about twenty boys. Here we spent more than an hour sheltered from the sun,—Mr. S. in one part and I in another of the spacious room where the school was held: he was speaking to and reading with some adults and a few boys. I had a small congregation, varying from six to a dozen of the elder boys, to whom I acted as school-master, sitting down and making them sit, and then making them read the Ten Commandments, and explaining them to them. Afterward, when I began to speak of the forgiveness of sin, and asked who can take away sins, one quiet little lad gave me a nice answer: "Only God," he said, "can take away sin." When I praised him for his answer, the other lads, who were several of them Brahmins, looked rather contemptuously at him, and said, "Oh! he is only a barber!" for the barber caste is an inferior one. When we had tired the patience of the school-master, who had meanwhile arrived with his new-shaven head shining like an egg, and who ought to have dismissed the school nearly an hour before, we went out, and crossing the narrow street, entered the house, or shop, of the village carpenter. He is not paid as such an one would be in England, by the job, or for the article he makes or mends, but is a regular village servant. Every villager who possesses a plough pays him (in grain) about half a rupee annually for each plough, that is about four or five days' pay, and for this the carpenter has to make, if need be, or keep in repair, the farmer's ploughs and sledges on which the straw is carried from the field. Carts are a separate charge; perhaps because they probably scarcely existed in the days of old when this village custom was established. Sitting down on some logs of wood, we had more than a dozen men and four or five women as listeners. Mr. S. had a long discussion with a Brahmin, who was a Vedantist, and maintained first that "all is God, and God is all," then, that he himself was God, and lastly, that God was the author and agent of all sin. He was no stray infidel; the same doctrines meet us on all sides, and it is difficult to say whether such men are better or worse than atheists.

It is one of the painful parts of our dealings with the people, and particularly with the Brahmins, that their mouths are so full of lies; it is scarcely possible to speak five minutes with one of them, but he utters two or three palpable falsehoods. When rebuked for them, all they have to say is, "It is the custom of the country;" or, "How could the world go on without lying?"

On leaving Prámarru, about eleven A. M., we had

a sunny ride for nearly two hours, rather warmer than we had hoped for, but a cool breeze in our faces prevented our feeling it oppressive. Each time I pass through this part of the country, I am struck with its numerous population: the villages lie round in all directions in clusters: from one spot I counted no less than fifteen in sight within a circle the radius of which was about three miles, and probably I overlooked some, for the low thatched huts which compose them are not very conspicuous in this flat country.

Yesterday evening in this village, and this afternoon in the large village of Wulloor, about four miles distant, we had crowded audiences, from twenty to thirty persons standing round one or both of us, and generally listening very quietly. The burden of one man's argument yesterday was, "All our gods are one and the same; whomsoever we shall worship, we shall go to heaven." Not only is this absolutely false, and contradicted by almost every popular book, but I have little doubt but that the speaker knew it to be so, just as well as I did; and it was not difficult to point out his mistake. This afternoon one clever old man would consent to every thing that was said: "It is all right, this is just what our books say," &c.—except the way of deliverance from sin; and, as usual, he was slow in discerning the fact of Christ's atonement, however clearly stated. "You expect to be saved by believing in your Gooroo, (teacher, meaning Christ,) and we expect to be saved by believing in our's; the only difference is that of language: you in English give him one name, we give him another." When, however, pressed to state his way of forgiveness of sin, it was the old story, "You must live purely, and pray to God, and this will be your deliverance." It was easy to point out to him by the usual illustrations the folly of trying to purge away the sin of an unclean heart, by that which comes forth from that heart, and is consequently itself unclean.

Weyoor, Aug. 15.—Yesterday, in the middle of the day, I went into the village, to the parts of it inhabited by the toddy-drawers and the cow-herds: for the different castes, especially such as these, generally cluster together in a distinct spot. After addressing a few Pariahs and toddy-drawers, in the locality of the latter, I went in quest of the cow-herd's house, where Pèrentálew, the village goddess, is kept. Her little temple lies about a quarter of a mile from the village, and she is famous all the country round for the swinging festival which takes place here in February annually; but from some reason or other, she, (that is, the image,) is kept in a house in the village belonging to one of the cow-herds, who are her patrons and priests. On mentioning my wish to see the image, the man I spoke to offered at once to show me the way, and to my astonishment led me to the house, and took me inside the little court of the house, and pointed out the door of the room where the goddess and her husband Chintanna are kept. I sat down, and had half an hour's opportunity of addressing about a dozen common people on the subject of idolatry, and of Christ's death and sacrifice for sin. When I rose up, I found that while my back was turned, a lock had been put on the door where the idols are kept, which had been unlocked when I first entered. On my noticing this, they all said, "Oh, the old man who has got the key is not here;" and when I pointed out to them, that the lock had been put on during the last few minutes, they pretended not to know of it, though every one in the place but myself, who had my back turned, must have seen it done. Oh, lying, lying! it seems to be the very meat and drink of the people. While talking of this goddess, I said I had witnessed a swinging at Peddana, (near Masulipatam,) and that then the victim had shown considerable symptoms of pain when the hooks entered his flesh, contrary to the usual story that the goddess preserves him from pain, and I asked if the same ever occurred here. "Oh no," said the man; "this goddess has great power." "But has not the goddess at Peddana also great power?" "No, *she* was only made by men; *this one* is not so, but was a gift from Siva." I was here amused with a nice little girl about five years old, who came feeling my clothes, and with much curiosity asked her father what I was: she had never seen a white man or English clothes before, and seemed scarcely to know what sort of animal I was. In most of the villages off the road which we visit, the people, particularly the women, look at us with wonder, being probably the first of the species whom they have ever seen.

Both yesterday and this morning, I visited a small Pariah hamlet, half a mile distant, and containing seven or eight huts: the people do not engage in agriculture, but are weavers of the coarse cotton cloths worn by the lowest classes. I had good audiences each time, of ten or twelve men and women, who were much interested in all I said. I spoke of sin, read the ten commandments, and enlarged on them; I dwelt much on heaven and hell, and the deliverance from fear of death, and the joyful prospect of the day of release which Christians enjoy, and then went through the history of Christ, and showed how his atonement removed our sin, and set us free to serve God with thankfulness. They had no opposition to offer, and seemed to like all I told them, and to accept it: they asked several questions, and wished to know if I would come and see them again. This work among the Pariahs is so entirely different from our conversations with Brahmins, as to remind me much of missionary labours in lands where caste, civilization, and a *system* of heathenism are all unknown. To the natural eye it looks more hopeful and pleasant, but we have never room to forget that the whole work of converting and fixing the truth in the heart is the work of the Holy Ghost.

In this village, where the Pariahs are very few in number, and not all are farm-servants, most of the land is ploughed by Brahmins and men of other castes. A large plot of land is a mànyam, or freehold, of certain Brahmins who cultivate it with their own hands; but as I was told by a Sudra I met on the spot, it is the worst cultivated in the village; "for," said he, "the Brahmin ploughs one day, and next day he is off to some festival or other, anywhere in the country-side, and when he comes back, the time for ploughing is over." We see many marks, and hear many expressions of the hatred of the Sudras toward the Brahmins, because of their local oppression and insolence.

Beizwarah, Aug. 17, 1847.—We made a short ride from Weyoor yesterday morning, to the next bungalow at Kankepad: on the way we entered a village of middling size, in order to speak with the people; but though we stayed more than a quarter of an hour there, and walked about the little lanes in it, we could not find a single man: they were all Brahmins and Sudras, out ploughing, for the village has only a tiny Pariah hamlet of three huts under it, and so the inhabitants have to labour in the fields themselves.

On the way we again stopped at a considerable village named Parunky, and walked into it; near a pagoda, (in better order than usual,) we found two or three people, and others joined us as soon as we stopped to speak to them. They of course received us with profound respect: there was one, an old Brahmin, who had a musical instrument a good deal like a guitar, with three metal strings of similar size and tone; he was a "singer of songs," they said; so we asked him for a song, and sitting down on the mud ledge against a mud wall, he began to sing a song in praise of Ràma. Unlike Hindu instrumental music, their songs are by no means tuneless, and on the whole, the song, accompanied by a little twanging of his instrument, was not unpleasing, though his voice was not musical, and his time poor and monotonous. When he was done, Mr. Sharkey began to tell them that he knew of a better person to praise than Ràma, and went on to tell them about Christ. This led us into a general talk about him which lasted more than half an hour: they were quiet people, and had no serious objections to make, or at least made none: the few they made were at once answered without difficulty, and they had no reply to make. They were such as these: "Nay, but we have always hitherto believed these images to be gods;" "Our fathers believed them;" or, "This is all related in our books." "But are your Shasters true, or false?" "Of course they are true." "How do you know them to be true?" "Are they not *books?*" "But what support have you for them, what evidence?" "They are their own support, their own evidence." In this village, as in many others, on our producing tracts, the question was put to us, "Is this your own hand-writing, or is it printed?" For in most places the majority, nay, rather, the whole of the people have never seen a printed paper. Of course, in all these villages, the very name of Christ is utterly unknown; and to be told that there is sin in idolatry is as great a novelty to the people as the names of their gods are to the most ignorant of our English villagers.

We have fallen in two or three times with a party of "Medicine people," *Rasayogulu*, as they call themselves. They live, that is, they have houses in Masulipatam, but seem to spend a large part of the year in wandering about the country. They seem to be wandering village quack doctors, and like the apothecary of old, they adorn both themselves and their families with strings of uncouth beads and nuts, to acquire a sort of mysterious character. Their little encampment was the exact counterpart of a set of gipsy huts on an English common; only, instead of cloth, the covering of the low oval tent consisted of a coarse sort of mat. Each tent was about seven feet long, five feet wide at the ground, and three and a half feet high. Inside was a low rude cot, upon which sometimes a child was lying: before the doors were plenty of ugly black sows with their young ones, all grubbing up the ground: snarling Pariah dogs were near them, and at a little distance was a crowd of forty or fifty donkeys grazing. Whenever near a town or village we see donkeys, we may be sure that there are either washermen, (who use the poor creatures to carry bundles of dirty clothes,) or basket-makers, (a wild, curious race,) or jugglers, or some similar wandering low class. There is no animal so deeply despised as the poor donkey, and to speak of riding on one excites a sort of derision and amusement.

Beizwarah, Aug. 19, 1847.—This place is a small town, if it deserves the name, of 3000 or 4000 inhabitants, and lies at the crossing of the great north road from Madras to Calcutta, with the great road from the coast at Masulipatam to Hyderabad. It is close on the edge of the sacred river Kistna, now a full mile wide, rolling its muddy, yet sweet water rapidly to the sea. From these two reasons it is both a place of travellers and the abode of many Brahmins—for all places on this river are sacred—and wherever any pickings or stealings are to be had, either from festivals or from visitors to sacred spots, there are abundance of lazy, vicious Brahmins to be found. It presents to us all the signs of a bad place; and what we have seen of the Brahmins tells us this too plainly.

On the afternoon of the day of our arrival, we went into a street inhabited by Brahmins, and fell into conversation with a man squatting on the mud ledge beside his house-door. Not many minutes had elapsed before there was a crowd of thirty or forty people, chiefly Brahmins, many of them sitting along the same ledge as the first man was on; others, who could not find room, standing in the street like ourselves. For some time Mr. Sharkey had a very interesting conversation with a very old intelligent man, who said he was eighty-four years old, and who did not speak for the sake of controversy, but, as he said, in order to acquire information. He began by saying he rejected and disbelieved all Hindu systems: "The Adwai system (or the wild pantheistic creed, which is so common, 'All is God, God is all, I am God, you are God; there is no distinction between right and wrong, truth and untruth,') is false; the Dwaitam system (or the Gnostic doctrine of the eternity of two principles, good and bad, of which *matter* is the evil one) is false; the Vasishta Adwaitam (a mixture of the other two) is also false, and nonsensical." But though the old gentleman went on in a garrulous manner to tell us what his system was, and though he greatly approved of the Christian scheme which Mr. S. set before him, yet it was not very clear that he had any distinct system at all, but rambled into loose metaphysics; and as for including the subject of the remission of sins in his system, he never seemed to think of it. All this while the other people kept very quiet and listened, but finding the old man did nothing but ramble in the fields of most unprofitable metaphysics, we began to speak to the rest of the crowd; and then we discerned their want of manners and of virtue; they showed no personal rudeness or insult toward us, but as soon as we began to talk, half a dozen at once began to talk also, either to one of us or to one another, and no peaceable opportunity of speaking to more than two or three at a time could be obtained. They stood up for the worship of idols,—they denied the existence of sin,—they mocked the idea of any thing spiritual, any thing which was not productive of vice, money, or bodily pleasure. At last I drew near to one man to speak to him; he said, "I want none of your books, not I." I answered, "I have no intention of giving you any, I force my books on no one; but listen to me for a few moments." And I then began to speak seriously of his sins and of the coming judgment; but his continual remark was in this strain, "What care

I? I don't know whether I have sinned or not: I never saw the hell you speak of." I said to him, "Now answer me one question: Which do you count of most value, your soul or your body,—things present, or things to come?" His answer was, "Of course things present; of course my body is most important to me." It was the bold bad acknowledgment of, and glorying in, the principle which is the chief feature of the "body of sin" within us, and which every unconverted man steadily acts on; but the shameless boasting about it marks a hardness and a deadness of conscience which is very painful to the hearer.

As we walked away from this painful conversation we took our course down to the river-side: it was now a little after sunset, and several of those with whom we had been speaking, followed us to perform their evening devotions. Stepping a yard into the river, or squatting down at the edge of the water, they began to mutter some Sanscrit verses or charms; presently the man would take up a little water in his hand and carry a few drops to his mouth three times in succession, then he went on with his mutterings, then he threw up three or four libations of the water with his right hand, then he turned to the west, then to the east, then he made crossings on his breast, not to be distinguished from Romish crossings, and so went on with a variety of signs and symbols, and gesticulations and mutterings. There was something ludicrous in seeing some of the men going through this unmeaning child's-play (to them it is neither more nor less) with all gravity; but it was also painful to look at these, or at others who were smiling at us from time to time, and to remember that all this was a pretence of religion on the part of evil men, who had only a few minutes before been uttering blasphemy, negations of all religion, professions of utter ungodliness, and viciousness. I could not help being much reminded by this scene of the inside of a Romish church; the same muttering and running over of charms and prayers in an unknown tongue, the same cycle of bodily gesticulations, and then the rising and going away with the same appearance of self-satisfaction, with the same deceived conscience and unforgiven soul.

The Pariahs employed in agriculture, all the district through, receive as daily pay a quart measure of dry grain: of course this is inadequate to maintain a man and his family, so they eke out a poor livelihood by digging grass for cattle, by gathering sticks for fire-wood, and by stealing from the crops in the harvest season, and from the stacks at other times. When compelled to do unpaid work, they of course lose their allowance of grain. They are a poor-looking race, not so much in figure as in their ragged dirty clothes, and in the uncombed, dishevelled state of the hair of the women. Their huts are small but compact: and not unfrequently a cow or a buffalo, or a few fowls, are to be seen in the little enclosure round a hut. A Pariah is not (at least in the villages) allowed to enter the (otherwise) public court or cutchery of the native judge or magistrate, whose authority is derived from the British government. If he wants justice, or has any business to be done in these places, he stands in the street outside, and the judge or tahsildar (too generally a Brahmin) comes out to him to inquire the business of the poor Pariah. This fear of defilement by the near approach of the unclean one to their holiness on the part of the vicious and godless Brahmins, reminds one of the similar dread of pollution by entering a Roman court of justice on the part of the Christ-crucifying Jews. The Pariah is regarded by the Brahmin as a beast of a lower creation, as we might look upon a pig.

We visited these poor people twice, and Mr. Sharkey *at length preached Christ* to them: they received the doctrine very readily, and expressed themselves willing to follow it: they had no objections to make, but only asked a few questions about their stone goddess, whether they ought to worship or not.

Beizwarah is not only situated close on the banks of the magnificent Kistna, but it is at the most picturesque spot of the lower part of the river; it is here that the low range of hills which runs irregularly the greater part of the length of the presidency, crosses the river, which is not so much narrowed as guarded by two steep rocky and pyramidical hills which dip into the water on either side; I call them the "pillars of Hercules." The town lies immediately at the foot of the hill on the north side of the river, and two or three of the lower projections of the hill are crowded by small pagodas. The town is said to have once been very extensive; it now covers a piece of ground nearly half a mile square, and about half its houses are tiled; but the empty and desolate spaces among the houses are numerous and extensive, and by the remains of mud walls in them, show that the town must have been almost as populous again, previous to the last great famine which occurred twelve or thirteen years ago. There is scarcely a village which we have visited which does not tell a similar tale: and from the testimony of English eye-witnesses, I should conclude that the famine in Ireland, even in its worst places and features, was not a half, nor a fourth so terrible or destructive as that which occurred in these districts. There are many ruins about Beizwarah, showing the sites and remains of massive and elaborate carved pagodas, and two or three of those which exist are a curious medley of old original building mingled with new building erected with old materials: they doubtless tell the tale of the ruthless destruction of the idol temples by the Mohammedans, and of the subsequent rebuilding of them on the same spot, and with the same materials, by the Hindoos. Just at the end of the town we witnessed an instance of this in a Mantapam, or isolated portico for exhibiting the idol. It consisted of a raised basement three or four feet high, and four elegant pillars at the corners, the capitals of which were richly and gracefully carved. There was no roof to it, and not far from it were lying the massive capitals of two other pillars similar to those which were erect. That it was not simply an unfinished building, was evident from some large blocks of stone carved with groups of figures, which had once formed the frieze of the Mantapam, being built irregularly and disjointedly in the basement. All the figures were human, and perfectly free from the misshapen deformities which abound in all the Hindoo pictures and sculptures of more modern date which I have seen. Several of these figures were grotesque, little fat children or satyrs, but yet in good taste. The whole was composed of a very hard dark granite, and the edges of the figures were as fresh as if newly cut. There must have been a time when taste existed among the Hindoos, and some skill in the fine arts; yet the contrast of the greater part of Hindoo buildings, new and old, which I have seen in South India, including the two famous pagodas of Conjeveram and Madura, with the Hindoo religious buildings seen by Bishop Heber on the Ganges, is very great. These sculptures at Beizwarah go some way to redeem the character of ancient Hindoos as artists, but they are too limited to enable the framers of them to be commended as great architects who could raise large and magnificent buildings.

Condapilly, Aug. 20, 1847.—At an early hour this morning we left Beizwarah, and passing by the Northern pillar of Hercules, by a road cut out of its foot, and overhanging the river, we again found ourselves in a plain, bounded by another and somewhat loftier range of hills at the distance of nine or ten miles. In striking contrast with all the country from Masulipatam to Beizwarah, this plain, ten miles wide, and reaching northward for many miles more, is very thinly inhabited, and only half cultivated. From the top of the hill above Beizwarah, which I ascended yesterday, I saw only four or five villages. The range toward which we were proceeding across the plain was about 800 or 900 feet high, rather falling off at either end: under the centre part of it lies the little town, or rather village of Condapilly: during the Mohammedan rule, and probably previously to that, this place was the capital of the district, and a place of much importance, as well as size. At present it consists of a ruined fort and palace at the very top of the hill; —the walls of a fort skirting the foot of the hills, the face wall of which is about a mile long, and must have been built by the Hindoos; within this there are no living inhabitants, but a company of Sepoys with their families, detached from the regiment at Masulipatam, the officer commanding, and the apothecary attached to the company. The ground is covered with irregular mounds of ruins, a ruined mosque or two, and abundance of jungle. Outside the wall lies the village; it is difficult to judge of its size at once, for it is absolutely hid in ruins and rubbish, and the trees which grow out of the same. We were both of us laid up all day with headache: in the afternoon, Mr. Sharkey had an interesting conversation with two young natives who came to see him, and in the evening we spent half an hour in the bazaar, speaking of Christ to a crowd of people. The hill which is immediately above our heads is very beautiful; it is composed of a fine purplish rock, of which many massive projections stand out precipitously, but it is otherwise pretty plentifully covered with bushes and small trees, which at this season are beautifully green and refreshing. A slight valley or hollow just behind the house, reminded me for a few moments of Nightingale valley at Clifton; but it has not its depths, nor its richness of wood; still more, it has not the attendant softness and moisture of air, and the gentler light of an English sky. There are a few leopards among the jungle, and one was killed quite close to this house a short while ago, but I believe they seldom or never attack men. The greenness of all around and the abundance of trees make me almost forget that I am in India.

As we were leaving the fort this evening, we found one of the Sepoys busy adorning a little stone image of Hanuman, (the monkey-god who helped

Ráma to conquer Ceylon;) he was daubing red paint over it, and lighting lamps before it. We stopped to speak to him, and tried to point out to him the absurdity and the thousand contradictions involved in supposing the dirty stone to be a god. His answers and his manner greatly struck us, for he really *seemed serious* in what he was doing; he really seemed to believe the thing to be a god, and to be hurt at the contrary being stated: this is a rare occurrence. Lightness of mind, half-belief, want of seriousness, are the almost universal characteristics of the people regarding the idols, and were exhibited in another Hindoo who stood by, and laughed at the absurdities of the idol.

Beizwarah, Aug. 23, 1847.—Saturday was a very interesting day to me. As Mr. Sharkey was poorly, I sallied out by myself at sunrise, and passed right through the village to the adjoining hamlet of Pariahs: here, as usual, I found more women than men; yet after half an hour conversing with these former, I had also an audience of about six or seven of the latter for a similar length of time: they have as it were no religion to give up, having only a loose attachment to a shapeless stone lying in the adjoining field, and no system of priesthood or books to keep up superstition. They listened therefore, and as far as the natural man goes, consented to all I told them of our dear Lord's suffering and sacrifice for them, and some promised to pray to him. These poor folk are always delighted when I tell them we are all brothers and sisters, and that the distinctions of caste are human and false: the whole burden of the evil system bears down on them who are (not out-castes, or people without caste, according to European notions, but) at the bottom of the list, and are trodden under foot by all. Leaving them and returning to the town, I fell in with two or three Brahmins settling accounts with some farmers; and had a conversation of some length with them : one of the Brahmins expressed himself dissatisfied with idolatry, and professed to be desirous of learning something better. The roguish cast of his countenance made me suspect that there was little sincerity in what he said. Walking down the street with him, we stopped beside where the school-master, and another man with great daubs of Vishnu's mark on his forehead, and who was said to be a Guru, or learned teacher, were sitting. I did not intend to stay, but soon found myself sitting down in the verandah, and having an amicable discussion with the latter of the two men, in the presence of twenty or thirty other persons.

Though said to be learned, (Hindu learning is about as much as that of a school-boy who can construe Ovid's Metamorphoses, and knows a little of Lemprière's Dictionary,) he was not a very acute man, and I found no great difficulty both in answering his objections and overthrowing his defences. After some little time spent in pointing out the inconsistencies of the existing system of religion with the original Hindu books, in which I exhibited my little acquaintance with those books—which, though little, is great in comparison with that professed by Brahmins, which is none at all—then quoted to them the ever-sacred *Gáyetri Muntram*, the very sound of which, from unhallowed lips, astounded them; and having thus acquired a character of being learned, I was led naturally to unfold the Christian system, Christ crucified, and man saved and renewed through faith in his blood. After this the discussion kept harping on this great topic, in which I had to answer a variety of objections and difficulties, chiefly of a trifling, childish character, such as, "How can a man save others, who could not save himself?"—although I had particularly dwelt on the fact that Christ's sacrifice was a voluntary one, and that he was born in order to be slain. I was also led to the subject of evidences, and this is a very difficult one. With the Hindus, as with some Oxford doctors, the harder a doctrine is to swallow, and the less evidence there is of its truth—the truer and greater is the exercise of faith in believing it: that is to say, if the doctrine is one of their own. Consequently, in regard to religious and moral questions, the Hindus generally do not seem to understand what is meant by the word *evidence.* "The book" is evidence not only for the doctrine, but for itself also. Again, the utter ignorance, not only of history, but of the very existence of such a thing as *history*, prevents a Hindu from at all appreciating the value of external evidence. The proofs I made use of on this occasion, as being at least the most handy, were two. First, if a book contains within it doctrines which are in accordance with the character of God, so far as our moral sense enables us to know it, that book has probability in its favour that it is a Divine revelation. This principle they are willing to admit, as well as the reverse one, that a book which contains statements and doctrines contrary to the Divine character, is not of Divine origin. With these two I was able utterly to overthrow their abominably vicious books, and to give some authority to the gospel. Secondly, I brought forward the case of Josephus, as an enemy living in that time and country, uniting his evidence to that of the apostles, who, although friendly, were yet eye-witnesses. Coming further to the question of the evidence of my friend's books, he asserted the Vedas to have sprung incarnate from the mouth of Brahma, far back in the depths of eternity. I asked him for the proof of this fact; "for," said I, "in your authoritative commentaries (for they also have "fathers," whose word on religious subjects is counted to be as good as their god's, and whose interpretations alone are to be received as expressing the meaning of their scriptures) on the Vedas there are mentioned the names of the very men who wrote the different hymns, and yet you say the books were never written at all, but are born from Brahma." He appealed to the Puránas, a set of books holding very much the position of the semi-fabulous monkish tales and lives of the saints. "Very good," said I, "let us, then see what weight is to be rested on the word of these same Puránas;" and so I went on to remind him of some of the monstrous fables contained in them: *e. g.* the length of India being said to be 90,000 miles; Mount Meon, in the centre of the earth, being 800,000 miles in height above the earth and 160,000 below it; the seven concentric rings of land and seas, the latter of sugar, water, butter-milk, spirits, &c., and to assert my own experience and that of eye-witnesses that these statements were false. He could not deny my statements, but said, "Never mind the Puránas, what have they to do with the subject?" He had already forgotten that he had himself mentioned them a few minutes before as his authority for the divinity of the Vedas. I now pressed him for some evidence. "What sort of evidence do you want?" he said. I answered, "Any will do, so long as it is good; please to say what you believe about your books, and give me evidence for your statements." So he began: "The Vedas are the personification of God, that is, the word of God." "Now," said I, "please to tell me what proofs you can give for that fact." He was nonplussed, and had not a word to say. So before I went away I said, "This is always the way; I have asked the most learned men in Masulipatam the same questions, and they, like you, have not a word to say: how is it possible for you to allege a proof, seeing that none exists?"

About the middle of the day, the persons who had visited Mr. S. the day before, made their appearance again, bringing with them three or four others, among whom was one particularly sensible, well-behaved Brahmin, who had received a little English education at Vizagapatam, and knew the outlines of Christian truth, and greatly approved what he knew. They stayed with us about two hours, and came the next day also, while we were at morning service, and afterward remained with us about an hour and a half, and even came for an hour more in the afternoon. The most interesting questions were put, and the difficulties started by this Brahmin were just such as we might expect to come to the mind of such a man: points of evidence, both Hindu and Christian, the nature of sin, man's corruption, the work of Christ, how it was to be applied, how it was satisfactory, the new birth, and many other subjects were discussed. I was thankful, not only that we were able to give answers, but that our hearers were satisfied, and went away apparently (especially the above-mentioned Brahmin) convinced of the truth of Christ, but exclaiming, "How can a man forsake all?"

The same afternoon I ascended the hill immediately behind our little bungalow: my path lay up the slight hollow or valley which separated the rounded purple crags of two projecting parts of the mountain: it was a good path consisting of irregular steps, made of large blocks of granite, and was probably formed 300 or 400 years ago, when the Hindoo kings dwelt in the palace on the rock. The ascent was delicious; the sun was just hid from me by the crest of the hill I was ascending, but shone brightly on the sides of the projecting rocks, and made the green trees that fringed them yet greener, and filled the plain below me, and the wooded range of hills beyond it, with a flood of bright light. The path lay through a low but luxuriant wood, and the rich scent from numerous flowering creepers, so filled the air as to remind me of the deliciousness of an English hot-house full of tropical plants; but there was not the moist closeness of such a place. Twenty minutes of delightful ascending led me to an old ruined gateway, overhung by the dilapidated remains of the palace, beetling over the rock. I pushed on through it, and had not gone many yards before a most lovely spot opened itself to me: my path lay on the edge of a small basin, in the heart of the hills: a level bottom half a mile across was covered with marshy grass, and in one corner had a rocky pool of clear water. I stood about twenty feet above it; at its edge were two or three large banyan trees scattered about, with their pendent threads hanging down to the marsh below, and full of parrots and minas: on all sides rose and fell the ridge of the hills in a most irregular broken line, sometimes presenting bare crags, but more commonly chiefly covered with irregular wood and bright-green tufts of grass. Winding my way by the edge of this beautiful nest among the hills, full of greenness and of bright light, and not altogether without marks of human work, for the crumbling wall of the fortress here and there showed itself among the trees, or crowned the peak of the hill,—I arrived at the gate at the opposite side to that by which I had entered; and here there burst on my sight a view as beautiful as it was unexpected. At once stretching away below me, and reaching to the right hand and the left, lay quite a sea of bright-green forest, closely covering the rugged spurs and supports of the main ridge of mountain, which reached away to the distance of three or four miles. Beyond this was the level plain in sober colouring; but a little to the left, glowing like silver in the rays of the evening sun, which dazzled my eyes as I looked westward, lay the great river Kistna, a couple of miles in width and studded with small islands. I had not seen so fair a scene since I left the Neilgherry hills, nor can I call to mind any one spot there which was so lovely; there were many on a larger and grander scale; I think I know of none more beautiful. I spent an hour in scrambling by rugged paths, all made in olden days, up to the top of some of the surrounding peaks and ridges, which were surmounted by long walls and bastions, except where the rock was so precipitous as not to need any defence. I then returned to look at the palace, which I had passed on my entrance through the first gate: the ruins are extensive and rambling, interesting from the tale they tell of days gone by, and of the triumph of those who bear the name of Christ over the heathens and Mohammedans. The building is, however, so much ruined, that it is impossible to judge of its former splendour. The main building is raised on a series of arched crypts, which remain in good order; the arch is the common Mohammedan one of this part of India, viz. a flat-pointed arch, somewhat similar to that of the late Tudor style in our English churches. The building above has consisted of four or five long, roomy aisles, corresponding to those of the crypts below, but both roof and arches are gone, as well as the greater part of the walls; the sole marks which remain to show that kings once dwelt here are a few square yards of plaster on the walls, cut or carved with very graceful tracely; a style in which the Mussulmans seem to excel. The utter want of beauty in the rest of the ruins, partly arises from the style of Mohammedan building in these parts; for they do not seem anywhere to carve the stone as the Hindus did, but are content with building their palace or mosque of rough stone, which they cover over with a coat of fine plaster, and adorn it with lines of tracery cut in the plaster. The effect is, when the plaster is fresh and white, and shining like marble, exceedingly pretty; but it wants grandeur, and looks as all plastered buildings do, weak and mean, and as in this case, the ruins have none of their former beauty to show.

We spent Sunday at Condapilly, and were joined in our morning service by the apothecary and his wife, and the wife of the drummer—the drummer himself being unwell, and the commanding officer absent.

The same evening, as I was returning to our bungalow, I fell in with a most interesting character: he was a Sepoy, who I found, after a few words of conversation, was there on leave of absence, and was about to join his regiment (the 16th Madras Native Infantry) in a few minutes. I discovered that though he was a stranger to me personally, yet by his gallant exploit he was well known, not to me only, but to thousands more. In the war in the Sawun Warree, in 1845, he had been taken one day as an orderly by a Lieutenant Campbell, of the Bombay European Infantry, who with a party of thirty or forty of his own men, had been ordered to dislodge a party of the enemy in the dense jungle close at hand. This Sepoy, Kótappa by name, was the only native of the party—all the rest were European soldiers: when they had advanced a little way into the forest, they were fired on by an unseen enemy with deadly aim, and nearly half the soldiers were struck down dead. He described here the wounds of several of them: among others, the officer was shot in the forehead, and fell dead. The soldiers retreated; Kótappa, who was thus left alone, threw himself flat on the body of the officer, and after a few minutes discovered that the enemy had retreated, as well as his friends; so, rising up, he took the dead body on his shoulder, and carried it some little distance to the rear, where he laid it down, to return for the cap, sword, and double-barrelled gun of Lieutenant Campbell. While he was returning with these, five of the enemy made their appearance, armed with matchlocks; one of them fired at him, and wounded him in the fleshy part of his arm. He said that he was in a great fright himself, expecting that his last hour was come, but he knelt down and took deliberate aim with the officer's gun, which was in his hand, and shot one of the five men in the knee; the others seeing him fall, took to their heels; and some of our officers hearing the firing, concluded that there must be some of the party who had advanced into the jungle yet alive, and sent forward some troops to bring them off; these brought back Kótappa, the wounded enemy, and the dead body. For this gallant action, Kótappa has been rewarded by the Madras Government with a star of merit, to be worn on the breast, and with promotion to the rank of Naick, (corporal,) but the circumstance which led to my being familiar with his story was this:—Some of the inhabitants of Perth, in Scotland, of which town Lieutenant Campbell was a native, had struck a large and beautiful gold medal, on which was recorded, both pictorially and in Hindustani and English, the event which drew forth this mark of their gratitude; and sent the medal to Kótappa. He brought us the medal to the bungalow, to show it to us, and seemed to be justly proud of the distinction conferred on him, though at the same time he was a man of quiet and humble manner. He was very grateful to the East India Company for the rewards which he had received from them. He is a native of Condapilly, and of the Golla or cow-herd caste. I was reminded of David, the shepherd, who went up against the lion and the bear and slew them, and I grieved at the difference of this poor man and the Bethlehemite; for the former knew not how to "go up in the strength of the Lord." We took the opportunity of telling him of a yet better Master than the Company, and of yet more glorious deeds done for him than he had done for his officer, and gave him a couple of tracts to read on the way.

Gannáveram, Friday, Aug. 27.—On Monday afternoon, Mr. Sharkey and I separated—he returned to Masulapitam, and I to make a two-days' detour to Guntoor, to see my dear friends there previous to continuing my tour in our own district. Having carried my horse across the deep-rolling stream of the Kistna in a horse-boat,—which is a considerable advance in civilization beyond the old plan of making the poor animal spend half an hour in the water swimming for his life,—I rode to Mungalagherry, in time to go into the village for a conversation. I had about an hour and a half of useful talk with a crowd of twenty or thirty people of the upper ranks, before returning to the bungalow. Early next morning I rode over to Guntoor (twenty miles from the river) just in time to be present at the half-yearly examination of the schools, both English and Telugu, of boys and girls, under the care of the Rev. and Mrs. W. Gunn, of the American Lutheran Church. The last, viz. the girls, some thirty in number, were particularly pleasant to see and hear; they are all day-scholars, and most of them of decent, though ordinary Sudra caste.

After greatly enjoying for two days the society of the little Christian circle at Guntoor, I left late on Wednesday evening, and reached the river Kistna soon after sunrise on Thursday morning. I had proposed to have visited the Pariah settlement and another part of Beizwarah, the same morning, but the boatmen were so slow in crossing the river, and the sun was so bright, that when I had crossed I was glad to get into the shelter of the bungalow.

In the afternoon I started off to explore a new line of country, viz. the high-road to Ellore, the only other town in the whole district besides Masulipatam. I had a long ride of fourteen miles to this place, through an imperfectly inhabited and three-fourths uncultivated district: low hills covered with bushes lying a few miles to the left. The only villages almost which I saw were four or five which lay on the road. It does not promise much as a missionary sphere. The village adjoining the bungalow here is not large: I spent two hours in it this morning, in conversing with and addressing the chief people in it, together with some of the Sudras of less note. Except with a young Brahmin with a smattering of English, who wished to show off and seem a little impudent, (and he was soon settled,) I met no opposition, nor yet much encouragement, though one or two made inquiries of interest.

Gannáveram, Friday, Sept. 3, 1847.—Since I was here a week ago, I travelled two stages to the town of Ellore, the only other town in this large district besides that of Masulipatam. I found it a larger and more prosperous town than I expected: its width I could not judge of, but I rode more than a mile through a long, crowded main street, and it has besides two or three large suburbs. I took up my quarters with some friends in the regiment stationed there, and enjoyed a few days of happy Christian intercourse with them: on Sunday we had two English services, with the Lord's Supper, at which about twenty were present. In the mornings I visited the lines of Sepoys, some of whom I had become acquainted with at Adur, or when they landed at Masulipatam, and also had two or three interesting conversations in the suburbs of the town nearest my friend's house. I had proposed leaving Ellore on Tuesday afternoon, but was induced to change my mind from a circumstance of a purely Indian character. In and near Ellore are the beds of three small streams, one of which lay just in front of the house where I was staying, and when I arrived it had not a drop of water in it, consisting only of a dry, yellow sand. On Monday afternoon, however, it rained heavily, both at Ellore and on the hills about twenty miles distant, so that on rising next morning, I found a rushing stream three or four feet deep, and twenty yards across, filling the whole bed, and preventing convenient ingress or egress except in one direction. On Wednesday afternoon it had fallen again, so as to be scarcely ankle deep, and I started on my return. I spent all yesterday at a village called Apparowpett, in which, and in a neighbouring village, I had interesting opportunities, both in the morning and evening, of telling willing audiences of Christ. This morning I came on to this village, a distance of fourteen miles, but stopped for an hour at a village which, on my way to Ellore, had appeared to me to be a large one. On dismounting, however, and walking about it, I found nothing but ruined mud-walls, with here and there a dilapidated house. I could, with difficulty, get an audience at all, and this only by going to one of the grain-shops on the high-road, and so gathering five or six villagers around me, and as many travellers. They told me the village had been ruined in the great famine thirteen or fourteen years ago, and had never recovered, in consequence of insufficient supplies of rain for the rice cultivation, on which the village depends, during the years which had elapsed since. But I could not but think that want of energy had had its share in continuing the destitution. Two-thirds of the land near and in sight of the road to this village, as well as from Ellore to Apparowpett, are uncultivated, mostly covered with low bushes and jungle.

This afternoon I was much amused at the novel case of a haunted house. The pensioned Sepoy attached to the bungalow, who had been an acquaintance of mine at Masulipatam three years ago, came about the middle of the day, and told me that since I was here last, his house had tumbled down, and he and his wife and nine children were all living under the trees! I recommended him to set to work and build another, for his pay is seven rupees a month, and he could easily build a good one for two, or at most three rupees, (four or six shillings.) However, I found that the house had not really fallen down, but, as he said, "The day after your honour went, a hand rose out of the ground in the house, and we can live in it no longer." I could not understand him, and asked, whose hand? What did he mean? He said he could not tell whose hand it was, perhaps it was God's hand, but there it was, all the village had seen it, sticking as far as the elbow out of the ground, fingers and all. I asked what he had done, he said he had taken a sword and cut it off, and blood and matter had flowed from it, and it smelt offensively. His story greatly puzzled me, for he evidently was not deceiving me, and I suggested that some man had been murdered and buried secretly in the ground of his house. This did not satisfy him, and I promised I would come in the afternoon and see it, for he said the hand he had cut off was there still. As I went with him, I found all the neighbours confirmed the story, and he told me on inquiry, that the hand was white, not a black one. On entering the court-yard of his deserted hut, he pointed to a spot in and under a hedge, as the place where the mysterious hand had arisen: it was so situated that it was impossible any thing could have been buried there since the hedge was formed, nor was there room for any thing to have risen out of the ground more than six inches in length. "There," he said, "is a piece of the hand," pointing to a little crooked thing on the ground, like the dried claws of a bird, as large as a crow. "What," said I, "is this the wonderful hand?" He assured me it was, and I took it up and found it a brittle substance, which, on closer inspection, turned out to be nothing more than a piece of the clay formed by white ants, and often formed out of the ground to the length of several inches in one night. In this case the clay had taken the form of a hand, or of claws. Hindu exaggeration had made it as large as that of a man, and a superstitious imagination had supplied both the blood and the bad smell. I found however that it was not a solitary case:—some years ago, a similar hand made its appearance in a house belonging to a neighbouring zemindar, which was in consequence deserted. My amusement at the discovery of the hobgoblin did not seem at all to shake the belief of the Sepoy, though he acknowledged it was strange that a limb should both bleed and emit an offensive smell at the same time. I afterward spent nearly two hours with some Brahmins in the public cutchery; but as the discussion chiefly turned on the viciousness of their gods, it was, I fear, to little profit. I told them of Christ, but he did not form our chief topic.

Neddamole, Sept. 8, 1847.—From Gannáveram I rode ten or twelve miles across country, by a country road, that is, a miry foot-path, about twelve miles from Weyoor. I stopped an hour by the way at the village of Mánakonda, and preached the gospel to some twenty of the farming people. I had more freedom of tongue than usual, but I long for that freedom and full command of the language to enable me to enlarge a little on the *fulness* of Christ, and to tell them of the sweets of his love. I fear my method of conveying the gospel message is a very dry one.

TO THE REV. J. TUCKER, (LATE OF MADRAS,) CHURCH MISSIONARY SOCIETY, LONDON.

Ramacherdra, Apparowpettah Bungalow, Sept. 2, 1847.

MY DEAR FRIEND,

The very name will remind you of dear India, which I know is as dear to you (or more so) as it is to me, in spite of its hot sun and dry dull plains. I am out now on another tour; but as we are in the middle of the monsoon, I cannot bring my tent, and consequently keep myself to the high-roads, and the bungalows on them. We have only two high-roads, or I may say roads of any kind, in the district, running at right angles to each other, viz. that from Bunder toward Secunderabad, 100 miles of which are in our Zillah, and the Calcutta road, of which about the same length runs through the Collectorate. I am now on the latter, one stage short of Ellore, from which I returned yesterday, after staying there four days with Major —— and Captain ——, two Christian officers in the 47th native infantry. Sharkey started with me from Bunder nearly a month ago, and we travelled together for a fortnight as far as Condapilly and back to Beizwarah: when, as he was not very well, he returned to Bunder. We visited a great many villages together, and in most of them found the gospel a new subject, and the name of Christ quite unknown: printed characters have never been seen by the majority of the village readers, though the villages we have visited have all been within two or three miles of the high-road. No less than four times has the question been put to me, twice by Sudras, and twice by Brahmins: "If all you say is true, how is it that during these eighty years that the Company have ruled this country, they have never, till now, sent to tell us of these things? since then, what millions have perished in ignorance!" This, coupled with the fact that, until undeceived, the people, both in Bunder and in the villages, supposed us to be the Company's missionaries, most practically refutes the foolish cry, that if the government were to attempt to preach the gospel, the people would rise in arms against us. The Hindoos have the perception, as we have, of the simple principle, that if a man believes a thing to be true, he is right in making it known to those who are ignorant of it. Sharkey's power of speaking greatly astonishes the people, and no one is able to answer him; for by adroitly expressing his argument in clear, forcible language, he places the truth in fair contrast with the gross falsehood of Hindooism, and they are compelled to acknowledge the truth of what he says. However, I am thankful also to say that he preaches Christ, and is anxiously desirous of making him known. He will have told you of Mrs. Sharkey's little girls' school; it has increased in numbers since we came out, and will increase yet more.

We have sent David (who was baptized last August) down to Madras for a wife out of Mrs. Peters's school, so that I hope we shall soon have a really native-christian sister in our congregation, which I cannot say we have had hitherto. Jacob has gone to Vizagapatam to fetch his two little daughters, Maria and Anna, and his heathen wife, if she will come. About five weeks ago we baptized Sitapàti, a young Sudra, who joined us at the end of May. He was quite unconverted and unknown to us before he came to seek for baptism; nevertheless, his coming being known through the town, in consequence of his having to witness a good confession in the public cutchery, was the cause of a good many scholars leaving the English school: their places were filled up immediately by crowds of applicants, and the school is now larger (about sixty) and in better order than formerly. I and Sharkey go on in the town quietly preaching and discussing in the streets: of late I have decided to go more among the Pariahs and Chuklers than I used to do, both because it is to the poor that the gospel is peculiarly to be preached, and also they are less bound by prejudice and priestcraft than the upper classes. I have been spending a very interesting afternoon to-day. In the early morning when I was talking in the village here, I had for one of my hearers an old man of respectable appearance, who took an interest in what I said, and asked for a book; he turned out to be the land-holder of a neighbouring village, and begged that I would pay him a visit at his own house. I went therefore about four o'clock to his village, which is a very small one, about a mile distant, and consisting of Sudras, most of whom are farmers of his land. He spread a little cotton carpet (you know the striped blue and white tent-carpets) before his door, and when I had squatted down on it, he sat down beside me, and about a dozen of the Sudras of the village came around us; the conversation soon turned to religion, and I had a good opportunity of telling them of Christ's history and his redemption of man, to which they listened with much interest, and consented to it all. After half an hour thus spent, the old man sent for the tract I had given him in the morning, and asked me to read it to them. It was a very clever and pointed tract, on the follies and wickedness of caste, and they all listened with delight, and often repeated expressions of admiration at the *exposé*, and particularly at the hits against the Brahmins. In the middle, a Brahmin came past, one of the learned class, so they stopped him to ask him some questions; and I had half an hour's discussion with him, exposing the wickedness of their gods, to which he could make no answer; all the other hearers chimed in with what I said. After he was gone, and I had read enough of the tract, I opened St. Luke's gospel, and read the parable of the prodigal son: they were delighted with the story, but not so much so with the explanation of it. It grew quite late before I was done, when I left them with a warning of the responsibility they had now incurred by having heard of Christ. In many places we find a strong dislike of the Brahmins among the Sudras, arising, I think, from all the power of the country being in the hands of the former, who occupy almost every magisterial and revenue post, and from the consequent tyranny they exercise. I am continually forced to feel that our present work is that of preparation: if there is to be any extensive conversion of the people in this neighbourhood, it will be in the days of our successors, but whether those days will ever come or not I cannot tell: at all events the gospel has been preached among the Teloogoo nation, and that is enough to satisfy God's prophecy. * * * Believe me,

Your very affectionate friend,

HENRY W. FOX.

CHAPTER VIII.

LOSS OF HEALTH—OBLIGED TO ABANDON INDIA—RETURN TO ENGLAND—DEATH OF HIS FATHER—IMPROVEMENT OF HEALTH—UNDERTAKES THE OFFICE OF ASSISTANT SECRETARY OF THE CHURCH MISSIONARY SOCIETY.

TOWARD the close of the year 1847 my brother's health again failed, not as before, from the nervous irritation produced by the heat upon his system, but from repeated attacks of dysentery, which so weakened him as to render a voyage to sea essential for his restoration. After a short voyage along the coast, he was obliged to resort to Madras for medical aid, and it was there that, after mature deliberation, the professional men in that place declared that his constitution was not suited for India, and that he must proceed home immediately, for ever renouncing the hope of being able to return.

This decision was too plainly in accordance with his own experience to allow of its being disputed, and it was with a heavy heart that he bade adieu to India's shores. After his return home he frequently expressed his lively sorrow on this account, and said he found it more difficult to submit to the will of God in this trial, than in any other he had ever experienced. He returned home by the overland route, and arrived in England in the month of March, just in time to have the painful satisfaction of closing his beloved father's eyes, and ministering to him in his last hours. He reached Durham on the 15th of April; on the 18th his father died.

Masulipatam, Oct. 2, 1847.

MY DEAR FATHER AND MOTHER,

I very much wished to write to you yesterday, but was quite unable to do so, not as usual, because I was too busy, for I have had time enough on my hands for some days past; but I was not strong enough, as I am only recovering from a sharp, though not severe, attack of illness, which has laid me up for a fortnight. I trust that now, by God's continued mercy, I shall go on improving, and be about my work in another week. My ailment was a slight dysentery, arising from and accompanied by biliousness. The depressing and weakening nature of the disease itself, added to the remedies used, brought me low enough. * * * I am thankful, however, that the attack was checked at once, and I do not suppose I shall be any the worse for it when it is over. Among the other mercies I received was that of the unremitting and kind attention of the doctor of the station, who visited me every morning and night. My servants also were very kind, and my butler waited on me with the attention which one might expect from an old attached servant, rather than what I should look for from a man not ten months in my service: so that my illness has been full of marks of my Father's tenderness, just as the stars shine brightest in the darkest night. In this, the sharpest attack of illness I remember to have had, as well as in other slighter illnesses, I have found my mind and spirit greatly to fail me: for two or three days, when suffering from weakness, I was unable to collect my thoughts to pray, or my desires to have any longing after God. I was however kept resting on him peacefully, without doubts or anxieties, or those temptations which Satan likes to bring against an enfeebled child of God. Though I knew I was in no danger, yet my mind often ran on my death, as this was just such a shadowy valley as leads to it, and I desired rather to go to the end of it than to turn back. I could desire to have more lively sights of Christ during illness; I know not whether the absence of such does not mark a too dull looking at him while in health, or it may be greatly the physical depression of the soul which hides him from me. I can see, however, that my various little illnesses are all given me by way of training and preparing me for the last struggle: from my late experience of the *pain of weakness* I could almost shrink from the dark valley, but *that* were to mistrust my Saviour: David says, I *will fear no evil.* And he can, if it is good for me and for his glory, make the valley shorter even than the few days of weakness I this time suffered, as indeed is common in India; or what is best, he can make his presence to shine in the darkest part of the valley, and in "His presence is the fulness of joy," whether in sickness or in health, on earth or in heaven. I am thankful now to be raised up again, to be allowed to go on in my poor way with the glorious work which he permits me to be engaged in. Yesterday, thirty years ago, I was born to you: the round number of thirty seems to make this birth-day one of the stages of life, and I feel all the older for having passed out of my twenties, though I suppose to you the age seems a little one after all. What an unspeakable mercy to be quite freed from all those uneasinesses of growing older, and so nearer the end of life, with which the men of the world are troubled at every memorial of the passing away of their years? The poor heathen are terribly afraid of death: to mention the subject to them is almost a piece of bad manners, and to speak however incidentally of any man's death with whom we may be conversing, is an evil omen, and causes a shudder of pain in the poor listener. What a bondage is this to be freed from! They are astonished to hear me speak of death as a thing greatly to be longed for. I knew that you would all be thinking of me yesterday, and especially I knew my dear children would pray for me.

October 6.—I have had a letter from each of you since I wrote last: very many thanks for them. I am very thankful to hear by the last, that you are both so well again after having been both tried by illness: it is like the bright clear shining after rain: nevertheless, we must look for the return of the rain again and again as long as we are in this stormy, sinful world. Your account of Seaton meeting interested me much. I have heard very little of the meetings of the Church Missionary Society this year; I should like to have heard more, as I feel strongly interested in the places I visited as "deputation" last year. I wrote a long letter to Mr. Dixon, to be in time for the September meeting at Shields, which I think was the meeting I liked best of all I was at. * * *

Your very affectionate son,

HENRY W. FOX.

Masulipatam, Oct. 18, 1847.

MY DEAREST ISABELLA,

You will be anxious to hear how I am, after my last fortnight's bulletin of bad health, and I am thankful to be able to give a better report of myself: indeed the doctor pronounces me to be rid of my complaint, and all that remains is the danger of a relapse through incautiousness of diet or exposure, and considerable weakness. I have not made the progress in recovery which I anticipated when I wrote to father and mother, but after all it is only a month and three days that I have been laid up. The exceedingly damp weather, tremendous falls of rain, and a saturated soil, with pools of water in all directions, seem to have been the secondary cause of the delay; but it is well to look higher to the first cause, and to see God prostrating me and keeping me low for purposes of his own: some of which I now see. During the first week of my illness I was much reduced by my disease and by the remedies; and I was astonished and amused at one of the effects of my languor and weakness, which was the springing up in my heart of strong desires for the scenes of natural beauty which I used once to enjoy; and not only a desire for them, but a strong assurance, that if I was in them, I could enjoy them, as I did of old. It was indeed a partial lifting up of the curtain which has fallen over boyhood and its bright feelings; and I could not help thinking of Wordsworth's Ode on Immortality. It seemed also to be a hint how easily God can restore, in the *right time and place*, those powers of enjoyment. Now I beg of you not to be anxious about my having been ill: the anxiety which you all show about my ailments causes me more uneasiness than my sicknesses themselves do. I have never yet been seriously ill, nor have I had any complaint likely to injure me for the future. In this climate I must expect periodical attacks of some kind; and if they weaken my body, I hope they do good to my soul. But above all, I am in God's hands, and not one day's illness shall I have beyond what is good for me, and for his glory. It would not be strange if he was to make some illness the instrument for carrying me home, where my dear Lizzy and baby are, in his bosom; or he might drive me to England; but again, it is not improbable (and I continually pray for it) that he may permit me to remain a little longer to preach his gospel here. My utter unworthiness to be so employed makes this last seem less hopeful; yet even here there is hope, for he may purpose to show his power to perform his work with the most inefficient of all instruments. * * *

I trust I shall find profit from this dealing of God, and glorify him by patiently suffering his will; but I see not much of this yet. My thoughts have been led much to dwell on the insufficiency of lively piety among us missionaries: the same is the general fault of the church of God at large, in present, and perhaps in all times. But for missionaries to be half-hearted, cold of prayer, sluggish of faith, it is grievous! and what can Satan want more to check their inroads on his kingdom. I greatly desire that in your own prayers for me and for missionaries, you would entreat God for more graces of the Spirit in our own souls—more faith, more untired zeal, self-denial, deadness to the world and flesh, more love for souls, showing itself in continued and earnest cryings and prayers for them; and do you speak of this matter to others who pray for the extension of God's kingdom, who wait for his redemption in Israel. People think missionaries such good folk as scarcely to need prayer, except perhaps that they may be consoled in sorrows, &c.; we much more need to be prayed for, that we may not settle on our lees.

Your very affectionate brother,

HENRY W. FOX.

Madras, January 13th, 1848.

MY DEAREST SISTER,

I am writing to you from the same house in which I wrote my first letter in India. I have been here nearly a fortnight, after a three weeks' voyage from Vizigapatam, which, though unusually protracted, did me some good. As soon as I got here I sought the advice of Dr. Sanderson. He has always inspired me with confidence in him, from the very careful and minute examination of a case which he makes at first, and his clear insight into the real ailment. After examining me, and watching me for a week, he spoke decidedly to me a few days ago, referring to his former experience of my constitution. He considers my liver organically affected, though slightly, and gives no hopes of my recovering from this state on shore: thinks I may more or less completely recover from it by a voyage to sea for a few months, but believes I shall never be able to continue in India, and that my return to Masulipatam will be attended with great probability of a return of disease, and consequent risk of life. He says my constitution is unfit for the tropics, wanting *nervous energy*, so that when a complaint lays hold on me, I sink under it at once. This I know to be true by experience; and indeed much of what he said to me is confirmed by what I have heard from doctors about my health in time past, though unconnectedly and not so decidedly. I tell you all the worst, because I know you would wish me to reserve nothing from you, and at present there is no risk, so far as man can see, of life. I have pretty well decided to take a sea-voyage, perhaps to the Straits of Malacca, perhaps to the Cape of Good Hope, for a few months: not that Dr. S. thinks I shall return set up again for work, though he anticipates much good from such a step; but I do it for my own satisfaction and that of others, that I may not forsake my missionary work too lightly: my own thoughts at present are that I ought to make every endeavour to stay by my work as long as I possibly can, even at some risk. I have asked the advice of —— and ——, whose judgment I value highly; the former thinks I ought not to remain in India, to run the risk predicted by the doctor: the latter advises a good sea-voyage, and after that another experiment at Masulipatam, taking every and even peculiar precaution to avoid exposure. I shall be better able to decide when the time for decision comes: for God does not always make our distant plans clear to us; only if we have sought his guidance, he will make the next step to be taken clear to us. I wish you therefore, dear sister, to help me in this matter both with your advice and your prayers. In case I return from a sea-voyage, recovered from my present state of health, and Dr. S. continues to affirm the same risk to attach to my attempting to renew my work at Bunder, ought I to run the risk or not? I wish to have an impartial judgment, as little influenced as you can by your feelings of affection, and with such reasons as appear to you on the subject. Secondly, pray for me, that I may with a single purpose seek God's glory in my decision, that I may have no wishes or will of my own in the matter, and that he will guide me aright. Your letter directed to Madras, in reply to this, will probably arrive before I have to decide. * * *

Your very affectionate brother,

Henry W. Fox.

TO THE REV. R. T. NOBLE, MASULIPATAM.

Madras, Jan. 18, 1848.

MY DEAR ROBERT:

This day last year I was on the point of setting out from Guntoor to rejoin you at Bunder, and to re-enter on my work in full health and spirits; to-day, what a change! broken down and enfeebled, and with prospects far from raising my spirits; I am beginning to write to you in preparation for retiring from my work: I can only say, God's will be done: he has shown me endless mercies in India: his goodness in bringing me and employing me here for a little while has been great, and now if it is his will to send me away to a less honourable position in his vineyard, who am I, that I should gainsay it? Only I would desire to be humbled at his rejection of me: and I do pray, and will continue to pray and to labour that he may send out to you others more and more fitted for his work than I am. * * *

Your affectionate brother in Christ,
HENRY W. FOX.

Madras, Jan. 22, 1848.

MY DEAR ISABELLA:

I write to you by Marseilles with the view of preventing you from writing by return of mail in reply to my last letter: for I have come to the decision, earlier than I anticipated, of at once leaving India and proceeding to England. On consideration I saw, as I might have seen from the first, that considering Dr. S—— said, his view of my case would remain unaltered, however much I might be benefited by a voyage to the Cape, England, or elsewhere; it was my business previous to starting on such a voyage, to make up my mind regarding my future course, or rather that the making such an experimental voyage and returning to India was in itself an opinion in opposition to the doctor's opinion. I waited however for a few days, till Dr. Sanderson called in another and senior doctor, and they unitedly condemned my residence in the country: upon this, I came to the conclusion above-mentioned, considering it to be my duty not to run the risk predicted by competent medical judges, while an important though inferior sphere of work lay open for me in England. I trust I have judged according to God's will. I have sought his guidance, and prayed that I might be unbiassed, and I have used the means of asking a few friends most competent to give advice. The giving up my Indian work is very painful, as you will well know; but my weak state of body, and callous, enfeebled feelings, do not let me feel at present so much pain as I might. Indeed, I seem able to feel nothing, neither love nor hatred, joy nor sorrow, but I believe this is chiefly physical. I am not, however, worse, though feeling poorly. In all probability I shall embark in the steamer of the 13th of February, and proceeding from Alexandria by the Trieste and Germany line, which is now open, reach London about the end of March. I suppose I shall be just in time for the Clifton Church Missionary Society meetings: I hope to be stronger by that time, if it pleases God to bless the cool climate to my recovery. Believe me,

Your ever affectionate brother,

HENRY W. FOX.

TO THE REV. R. T. NOBLE, MASULIPATAM.

Steamer "Ripon," near Gibraltar, March 23, 1848.

MY DEAR ROBERT:

I wrote to Sharkey by the returning Precursor, and we have not since then had any opportunity of writing to India. * * I am just now emerging from the dream or cloud in which I have been bodily and mentally these last six months: for, during the last four or five days, I have begun, for the first time, to regain a little energy and vigour, as my bodily health began decidedly to improve. Up till then, the voyage has been to me, like the time on shore, full of discomfort, as distracting as pain, though not so hard to bear, and altogether prostrating every energy. The prostration of mind and heart has been as great as that of body, and much more distressing. I have been quite unable to write, or to read any but the most trifling books; the Bible has been generally a closed book to me, and my mind has wandered as I tried to read it. But now, thanks to God, I seem to be restored somewhat. * * I had expected a much more speedy improvement; indeed, during the last few weeks at Madras, I was looking forward with an intense longing to the day of starting, hoping that I should feel immediate benefit as soon as I embarked: but it seems as if my constitution had got too low to be resuscitated at once, and, till I reached Egypt, I continued better and worse, but still very poorly. The change on landing at Suez was surprising; it had not been hot in the Red Sea, but nothing of chilliness had been felt, until we had got into the little boat which took us from the ship, just at sunrise; and then the air was as sharp as on an English spring morning. The whole time we were in Egypt the wind blew from the north, and was very cold and keen, and, consequently, we most of us caught colds, had red noses, and chapped lips. The change at first was very beneficial to me, but just before we left Alexandria, (having been detained there four days,) I caught an internal cold, which brought on my dysentery symptoms again, and reduced me very low. I am thankful to say, that the means employed stayed the disease in two or three days after I embarked again; and I have been daily regaining strength,—the weather has been delightful; a soft, but fresh S. W. wind has blown in our faces, with a blue sky and hazy horizon, and reminded me much of those occasional lovely days at Brighton, which occur during the winter months. I do feel it to be a great gift and mercy, that God is restoring to me my health, and with it his presence; for I am now again able to pray, and to rejoice in him:—during my weakness, I have been in a cloud far from him, neither humbled nor prayerful, but altogether listless. What poor creatures we are, and how vile are our bodies! and yet it has been a comfort and encouragement to me many times, that vile as my body is, and I have felt it to be, yet Christ Jesus has redeemed it, and counts it precious. Certainly the truth of the resurrection of the body is a very precious one during sickness. In crossing the desert I suffered very severely: it still remains to me like a horrible dream, and I scarcely think I could muster courage to go through the trial again, under similar circumstances: it was curious, how differently the very same thing affected a healthy body and a weak one. When I crossed in 1846, I reached Suez after twenty-four hours of jolting, quite fresh, having greatly enjoyed the amusement of the transit, but now I scarcely know how to sit or lie;—pained, and exhausted, and faint, I at one time felt desirous of being rather left alone in the desert than of going forward; but here, God, who allowed the suffering, would not let it go too far, and I was able to feel confident, that as I trusted in him he would carry me through; and he did so, so that I was not materially the worse for it, and had only to lie-up the next day, during which we remained quietly at Cairo. Indeed, all through he has been showing to me his wonderful providences and mercies; and when I think of the tranquil passage we have enjoyed, and the numerous comforts I have had, I see a Father's hand in it all. * *

Your affectionate brother in Christ,
HENRY W. FOX.

REV. R. T. NOBLE, MASULIPATAM.

Durham, April 17th, 1848.

MY DEAR BROTHER,

This first letter to you from me in England, opens again the wounds of separation: I daily feel more and more, instead of decreasingly, the sorrow of having left you all, and having been separated from the work of a missionary. It is no satisfaction to be told by friends that there is much want of the labours of Christ's ministers in England; for this last reminds me how much greater is the want of such in India, and in all the rest of the heathen world, which want is increased by my return. I have however found something to rest on, in what has been suggested by two or three. "He who has brought you back from your own work in India, will have provided some sphere in England, in which you may glorify him." It is not my part to dictate how or where I shall do God's work, and it is my resistance to his will on this point that makes the sacrifice a hard one. * * *

Your affectionate brother in Christ,
HENRY W. FOX.

REV. J. SHARKEY, MASULIPATAM.

Clifton, Bristol, May 9th, 1848.

MY DEAR SHARKEY,

Unless I write to you at intervals, just as I can snatch a little time, I shall not be able to write to you at all by this mail. * * * The weather and scenery are indeed lovely. I cannot convey the idea of them adequately to you, because they are so unlike any thing in India. The trees, which have been bare of leaves for six months, have just burst out into their full covering of bright green and soft leaves; some are in blossom, the fields are full of rich long grass, and enamelled with wild flowers; the whole country looks like a well-kept garden. For a fortnight past we have scarcely had a cloud to speck the blue sky, and *this* we greatly enjoy; for though it is a little warm when we walk in the sun at mid-day, yet the temperature in the shade is delightfully fresh, without being cold. I am well enough and strong enough to enjoy very greatly all these beautiful works of God, and *almost* with the same delight as I used to possess in earlier days; though I feel that there has passed away a brightness from the earth since the days when I used to lie lazily in the woods, or beside some running stream, surrendering myself to the influences around me. Still

I do enjoy it greatly; and if with a chastened, yet, I hope also with a hallowed pleasure: but not for one moment can these enjoyments compete with thoughts and regrets of India: there is nothing so joyful or so glorious as a missionary sphere. There are some respects in which *you* are a gainer by being a missionary in your native land, as, for instance, you are spared all the trial of a continued absence from the friends, scenes, habits, climate, and land of your childhood and boyhood. India presents nothing which is disagreeably *strange* to you; the hot land-wind, uncomfortable as it may be, is not unnatural or foreign, so you have not the suffering which we, who come from England, have; but, on the other hand, you are in the same matter a decided loser, exactly because you have not the suffering. God may be pleased to make up to you the loss by some other sorrows equally precious and useful: but, believe me, it is a choice gift of his to keep us, while at work in that *dangerous* field of missions, in a continued though not acute state of suffering. I refer to this subject in order to append to it a line or two of advice or exhortation; viz. that as you are without this spiritual blessing, as a continued stream commingling with the stream of your life, you have the greater necessity for watchfulness, lest Satan draw you into a state of dulness, and absence of spiritual-mindedness. And there is the more need of caution, because your continued occupation all day long acts as a temptation to be negligent in prayer and reading. Forgive my word of advice: I do very earnestly yearn for you all, that you may be men and women mighty in prayer and in faith, and abounding in every Christian grace. The more that I reflect on my low estate in this respect, both now and while in India, the more do I desire and pray that every one of you may be lifted up toward God, and be filled abundantly with his Spirit. As yet in England the real active interest in missions is very low: there is abundance of material on which to work, that is, there are vast numbers of truly religious men and women who acknowledge the duty, and feel *some* interest in missions, but they have not as yet been more than very partially worked. I am going down to Oxford in a few days, to endeavour to work the young men there, but "not by power nor by might, but by my Spirit, saith the Lord." I hear of no movement either there or at Cambridge, or among our clergy. It may be many years before men are sent forth abundantly, and before you receive help to enable you to spread the gospel far and wide; but it is nevertheless a glorious privilege to be allowed to be digging the foundations, or hewing the stones, which others shall build up. I was very glad to hear that you and Darling had been out in the villages again, and the latter by himself on one occasion; for this shows that he is feeling himself at home in the language. His village work will form a valuable antidote to the disease of sinking down to be a stagnant missionary, with a vernacular school or two to look after, and a little congregation to speak to. The village work stirs up to greater activity in town work. How goes on your preaching in Robertson's pettah? My heart goes along with you there most thoroughly. May the Lord bless you in your work, and especially in your own soul!

Believe me very affectionately your's in Christ,

HENRY W. FOX.

Wadham College, Oxon, May 30, 1848.

MY DEAREST SISTER,

My heart is so disturbed and so full, that I long to write to you to relieve it. My return here is as painful, and more so than it is pleasant. It is not that my time here was more happy than present times, for I could not so belie the grace of God which has been given me these eight years past; but every scene and sound is recalling thoughts and feelings which have slumbered for long, and is reminding me that much has passed away which I never can have again in this life—much elasticity, much joyousness, much brightness. This does not make me melancholy, for I have received things which are much better; but it greatly disturbs me, and I cannot enjoy myself in beautiful Oxford in May; this perturbation will, I know, subside after a while. All these scenes carry me back beyond the happiest days which I have yet known: and so they cause painful feelings to arise; for they make me think of all that has passed since, my five years with dear Elizabeth, and my missionary life in India; and till I go down to the grave myself, and till I am called away from all work on earth, these two recollections cannot but contain much that is bitter. My cessation from missionary work is still a fresh grief, and at times it is very hard to bear; I knew it would be a trial, but I did not know how great a one, and sometimes I begin to think of going back again, but am checked by the strong assurance that I have, that I should return to India—but not to active work. How little do men know the real state of the case, when they think that the trial consists in *going* to be a missionary; for with all its palliations of returning to England, to home, friends, family, and children, it is the *coming* from being a missionary which is the real sorrow; and beautiful as are our green field sand hedge-rows, they make me sigh to be back at dear Bunder, even in the midst of this burning May. You will see, as I do, that in these feelings there is very much of the natural heart, and that they do not altogether spring from a desire to advance Christ's kingdom: for if I had his glory more truly at heart, I should more cheerfully submit to his manifest will that I should no longer remain in India. * * *

Your affectionate brother,

HENRY W. FOX.

It was a great satisfaction to his friends, to find that though my brother's constitution could not stand the climate of India, it seemed to rally rapidly in his native air: the voyage had done him much good, and as the summer drew on he seemed so much restored to his usual state of health, that he began to consider in what sphere of useful labour he should engage at home. At one time he thought he would like to undertake the charge of some populous parish in our crowded manufacturing districts, as having a population that in some respects resembled the heathen. During the summer, however, the Church Missionary Society proposed to him the office of Assistant Secretary: this was so congenial to his feelings, and seemed to hold out so promising a prospect of future usefulness in that cause which was nearest his heart, that after mature consideration he gladly accepted the offer and at once entered on its duties.

TO H. STOKES, ESQ., GUNTOOR.

Church Missionary House, Salisbury Square, July 7, 1848.

MY VERY DEAR FRIEND,

My thoughts have very often been at Guntoor, since my return to England; and I was greatly rejoiced to see a good account of yourself and your family in a late letter from you to Mr. Tucker. With all the heat of India, and your hard, anxious work as collector, I should envy your position if I might; for to be permitted to live in India appears to be a great privilege, and to be removed from it and from missionary work, while it is a most righteous act of a loving Father, is to me, I am sure, one of chastisement and warning. With my returning health, my desires for, and love of India, have returned: as long as I was suffering from disease, the lowness of my spirits and an intense physical shrinking from the very idea of an Indian sun, made my separation from India a light matter; but I have had many sorrowful seasons since then. It was to me a very great comfort to see in your letter a good account of our dear brother Noble; that he is still permitted to go on without failing or fainting. I have been very mercifully dealt with; for my bodily health is all but entirely restored, and my strength very much so; and though I may not preach to the Teloogoo villagers, I am permitted in an indirect way to have a share in the great work of missions, for I am associated as Assistant Secretary with Mr. Venn and Mr. Tucker in the Church Missionary House; and unworthy as I am of so great an honour, I feel it a great happiness to be thus employed. I have but just commenced my work; but I see great privileges in it; first, I am led to become intimately acquainted with the details of all the Society's missions in the four quarters of the world; then I am an agent in the Society commenced by Simeon, John Venn, and other holy men of the last generation; and our committee-meetings are indeed those of Christian men. Then I am brought into contact with many of the eminently good men of London and its neighbourhood: and, not least, I am allowed the affectionate friendship and intercourse with two such men as Mr. Venn and Mr. Tucker. When I magnify my office, then I lower myself; for who am I, to be thus blessed and set in so privileged a position? Dear friend, pray for us here at head-quarters, as well as for the missionaries in the field; it is not only wisdom and prudence that we need, but holiness and a deep knowledge of God. The Society, which for fifty years has been kept in the truth, and in a pure and earnest faith, is as holy (I had almost said) as the ark of the Lord: and it seems wellnigh a profanity to touch it with such hands as mine. I know of no immediate prospect of a missionary for Bunder; our Universities are still asleep. I visited Oxford for a fortnight, and though a little advanced in missionary interest since I was there two years ago, it is still barely above freezing-point. We have numerous offers of men for the Church Missionary Institution, some of whom are very promising; but the Finance Committee are shy of allowing any fresh expenditure, while the general funds are in so low a state. However, the accumulated subscriptions to the Teloogoo mission justify the appointment of a missionary to Bunder, if we can find one, and I trust the Lord will guide us in the search and bring the right man to us.

Your affectionate, but unworthy, brother in Christ,

HENRY W. FOX.

TO THE REV. R. T. NOBLE, MASULIPATAM.

Hampstead July 16, 1848.

My beloved Brother,

I may well occupy a few minutes of the evening of this day of rest and of preaching the gospel, in writing to you. Never a day passes, without you and all our dear brothers and sisters at Masulipatam being in my thoughts, and seldom do I forget to pray for you; but on Sunday I remember you most;—though by the time I am going to church your afternoon is well advanced, yet I think of you, with that little feeble flock around you; and never do I read the commencement of the Liturgy, but my heart is brimful with the recollections of the Monday evenings which just a year ago we used to spend in trying to prepare a version; happy are you to be allowed to go on with this work; not in wrath, but in loving chastisement and wise discipline for my sinning soul, has God removed me from the glad work. The Lord's prayer raises up many recollections of the Sunday afternoon, when I used to break it up for my poor servants, and the ten commandments carry me away into the streets and lanes of Buttayah, and Sarakilly, and Páta, Ramanah pettahs. May the Lord give you to see the fruits of your work! One soul may be an inestimable treasure, and as Isaac to Abraham, may make you the father of a great nation.

I long and yearn over the dear youths in the school, and I greatly desire to hear that some of them have been strengthened by the Spirit of God, to leave all for Christ. Venkatachillapati, and the Venkatachellums, and Foorshotum, and Rangashai, how do they go on? The sound of their songs on the morning of November 9th still rings in my ears.

And Mr. Sharkey's little girls; we must perhaps wait longer to see fruits in them, but sooner or later, and exactly at the right moment, the desert of Bunder shall blossom as the rose, and our dear Lord shall be glorified in his new children. But I like to look even farther still, to that joyous day, when he shall come to take us home, free from sin, with nothing to make us weary of loving him—nothing to lead us to grieve him. What a prospect! I long to be out of the power of sin, though it does not any longer *rule* in me; it has yet a wonderful power of warping me, and leading me to dishonour my Saviour. I could say that, if I was always victorious, I should not care for the length of the battle, but I grow weary of struggling, and being buffeted, and often taken prisoner. What astonishing long-suffering does God show toward us! and what infinite love that of Christ to us must be, which led him to die for us, though all the while he foreknew what poor, wretched Christians we should be! But we shall have an eternity to praise and admire him, and to recount to each the tales of his goodness.

Your affectionate, unworthy brother,
HENRY W. FOX.

TO MAJOR WOODFALL, 47TH NATIVE INFANTRY.

Hampstead, Aug. 29, 1848.

MY DEAR FRIEND,

I cannot refrain from writing to you to-night, (as indeed I have been long purposing to do,) inasmuch as this is the first anniversary of the Sunday which I spent with you at Ellore. I have again to-day joined in administering the Lord's Supper, and accidentally I took as my subject for my afternoon sermon, the same text, the Pharisee and Publican, on which I preached at Ellore, during the thunder-storm. My memory is almost ceaselessly engaged in retracing the days I have spent in India, and *very often* returns to my last month of missionary work in August and September, toward the close of which I spent those happy days with you, and our other brethren in the Lord at Ellore. Since then, both you and I have had to go through deep waters. I heard of your severe illness, from dear young P——, who kindly called on me after he reached London, to tell me the news about Bunder and Ellore. We have both now experienced what it is to have gone some distance into the dark valley, and I trust that we have been led so far, that when the time comes that we must go right through it, we may prove to be somewhat practised in dying, and to have our confidence strengthened in our Shepherd, who was with us in our first adventure so far, and who will not fail us in our last journey. Perhaps, also, God is intending to make us more fitted during our few remaining years of life, for waiting on the dying beds of others. I have already found my own experience of use, when a few days ago I was called upon to visit an old woman, an aged servant of Christ, who seemed to be almost at the last gasp of life, but who has been raised up again; her case did not seem so strange to me, as it would have been had I not been myself in it, and so I hope I was able to speak more to the point. * * * I rejoice exceedingly in your regiment, and I often adduce it as an evidence of the goodness of God in providing so large a work in a short time; you must remember me, with my affectionate regards, to all the brethren in Christ who are in it. Though I shall probably never see you all again in this world, my interest in you all, and affection for you, is not the less. For I am able—at least, at times—to look forward to the day, when the graves shall be broken, and all the beloved saints of God shall be united in one vast multitude, to be ever with the Lord; and we shall be *like him*, especially we shall be free from that hateful tyrant and disease—Sin. * * *

Believe me,

Your very affectionate friend,

HENRY W. FOX.

TO THE REV. J. RAGLAND, MADRAS.

August, 1848.

MY VERY DEAR FRIEND,

This is ——'s wedding-day, and the fact has reminded me that I must write a few lines to you, as he perhaps has not found time to write to you by this mail. It is doubtless a joyful day for him, but yet it is more joyful to be married unto the Lamb, and our glad bridal-day will be when He comes to take us home. I have come up to town from Clifton for a fortnight, preparatory to spending a fortnight at Oxford to see young men. Since I wrote to you last I have lost my dear father. I was just able to see and speak with him the last day of sensibility; but he has only gone before, and my mother and my brothers and sister and I shall soon follow him, to join the other dear ones laid up in Christ's treasury. Yesterday there was a large Committee at Salisbury Square, to make arrangements about the Jubilee. A fund is proposed to be raised for the disabled missionaries' fund, for school and church building, for education of missionaries' children, and for endowment of native congregations. It is to be a year of humiliation for *our* neglect, and of praise for God's wonderful works. November 1, All Saints' Day, is the day chosen for all missionary friends of our Church, both in Great Britain and abroad, to unite in worshipping and glorifying God. Come what will, that is a sure day for us: if we are here, we will join with the living saints; if we have crossed the flood, it will be only one day out of our ceaseless worship. * * *

Your very affectionate brother in Christ,

HENRY W. FOX.

It was but a few months, in the providence of God, that he was permitted to prosecute his new duties, but he was so fully absorbed in them, and threw so much of his heart into the work, as at least to give all that he had to bestow in carrying on at home the plans of the Church Missionary Society.

The testimony of Mr. Venn on this point is as follows:—"He entered upon the duties of his office in July; and with so much efficiency, and in such a spirit, that his seniors in the office rejoiced in the hope that he was destined to carry forward the work with youthful energy, and to continue his beneficial aid after they should cease from their labours."

The period at which he entered upon his duties, as Secretary of the Church Missionary Society, was a crisis of peculiar interest in the history of modern missions—it was the Jubilee year, and preparations were making to celebrate that interesting event, the Fiftieth Anniversary of the Church Missionary Society, on the 1st of November.

It was with feelings of deep and lively interest that my brother entered into all the plans of the

Society in reference to this great event, and he looked forward with hope and joy to its commemoration, little supposing that when the 1st of November arrived, he should be celebrating a more glorious jubilee in the courts above.

The following lines were written by him as a Jubilee Hymn, which have since been set to music by the Rev. Peter Maurice, D. D., of New College, Oxford:—

I.

I hear ten thousand voices singing
  Their praises to the Lord on high:
Far distant hills and shores are ringing
  With anthems of their nation's joy.
"Praise ye the Lord! for he has given
  To lands in darkness hid, his light:
As morning rays light up the heaven,
  His Word has chased away our night!"

II.

On China's shore I hear his praises
  From lips which once kiss'd idol-stones:
Soon as his banner he upraises,
  The Spirit moves the breathless bones—
"Speed, speed his Word o'er land and ocean,
  The Lord in triumph has gone forth:
The nations heave with strange emotion,
  From east to west, from south to north."

III.

The song has sounded o'er the waters,
  And India's plains re-echo joy:
Beneath the moon sit India's daughters,
  Soft singing, as the wheel they ply—
"Thanks to thee, Lord! for hopes of glory,
  For peace on earth to us reveal'd:
Our cherish'd idols fall before thee,
  Thy Spirit has our pardon seal'd."

IV.

On Afric's sunny shore glad voices
  Wake up the morn of Jubilee;
The Negro, once a slave, rejoices:
  Who's freed by Christ is doubly free—
"Sing, brothers, sing! yet many a nation
  Shall hear the voice of God, and live:
E'en we are heralds of salvation:
  The Word he gave, we'll freely give."

V.

The sun on Essequibo's river
  Shines bright mid pendent woods and flowers;
And He who came man to deliver
  Is worshipp'd in those leafy bowers—
"O Lord! once we, by Satan captured,
  Were slaves of sin and misery;
But now, by thy sweet love enraptured,
  We sing our song of Jubilee."

VI.

Fair are New Zealand's wooded mountains,
  Deep glens, blue lakes, and dizzy steeps;
But sweeter than the murmuring fountains
  Rises the song from holy lips—
"By blood did Jesus come to save us,
  So deeply stain'd with brother's blood:
Our hearts we'll give to him who gave us
  Deliv'rance from the fiery flood."

VII.

O'er prairies wild the song is spreading,
  Where once the war-cry sounded loud;
But now the evening sun is shedding
  His rays upon a praying crowd—
"Lord of all worlds, Eternal Spirit!
  Thy light upon our darkness shed;
For thy dear love, for Jesus' merit,
  From joyful hearts be worship paid."

VIII.

Hark! hark! a louder sound is booming
  O'er heaven and earth, o'er land and sea;

The angel's trump proclaims *His* coming,
  Our day of endless Jubilee—
"Hail to thee, Lord! thy people praise thee:
  In every land thy name we sing:
On heaven's eternal throne upraise thee,
  Take thou thy power, thou glorious King!"

CHAPTER IX.

ILLNESS AND DEATH.

Although my brother was not permitted to be present at the celebration of the Jubilee of the Church Missionary Society, having been already removed to take part in choral strains of a more exalted character in the courts above—yet his anticipations were more than fully realized when the day came round.

The 1st of November, 1848, was a day much to be remembered for the time to come, as one on which the blessing of God was freely bestowed, as one which did much toward enlarging the hearts of men at home, and laying deeper the foundations of the missionary cause among us; many groundless prejudices were removed; many ears listened for the first time to the claims of the heathen upon our church and nation, many a church and parish was opened for the first time to the Church Missionary Society; while not a few of our cathedrals had their time-honoured walls consecrated, as it were afresh, by this sacred cause; for well may it be asked, How could those splendid piles, with their massive pillars, vaulted roofs, and fretted windows, be more

Grave of the Rev. H. W. Fox, St. Mary's in the South Bailey, Durham, Eng. p. 262.

highly honoured, or converted to better use, than when within their walls were celebrated the high notes of jubilee praise; and the glory of God, the advancement of our Redeemer's kingdom, the conversion of the world, formed the noble theme of the preacher's discourse?

But the energy of his mind was too great for his bodily strength, and he was tempted by the ardour which he felt for the work in which he was engaged, to exert himself beyond the bounds of prudence. This brought on a relapse of his Indian complaint, which considerably reduced his strength. In the month of September he visited Durham, intending to take a few weeks of recreation and rest: he reached home on the 14th, in a very feeble condition. The record of his few remaining days is fully detailed by one who watched with unwearied assiduity over him during his last illness, and having been committed to paper while the events were fresh in her memory, will impart a more lively and interesting impression of those closing scenes than could be otherwise given.

MY DEAR GEORGE,

According to your wish, I send you a few particulars respecting the last days of our beloved brother Henry; having had, from being almost constantly with him during the last three weeks of his life, more opportunity of witnessing his faith and patience to the end than any one else. After attending one of the committee-meetings of the Church Missionary Society, on Monday, the 11th of September, in London, he imprudently started for the North by a night-train, being anxious to make the most of a short absence from his usual routine of labour, during which, besides visiting his own family in Durham, he intended in the pulpit and on the platform, in various places, to advocate the missionary cause.

After spending a day with the family of his much-loved and revered master, the late Dr. Arnold, at Fox How, he reached Durham on the middle of Thursday, the 14th of September. We met him at the station, and I was painfully struck by his worn and debilitated appearance. He confessed himself extremely unwell, and willingly allowed us, upon reaching home, to send for medical advice. He was pronounced to be exceedingly unwell, suffering from diarrhœa, which had been upon him several weeks, and very unfit for the work before him. Still it was not imagined that by going through it he would endanger his life. His name was advertised for two sermons to be preached at South Shields, and four consecutive meetings at different places on the four following days. We hoped that the two days' rest before him would restore him in some measure, especially as in part he was suffering from cold caught on the journey.

On Saturday, the 16th, he was sent in my mother's carriage to Shields in preparation for the Sunday's duty. In a letter he wrote to quiet our anxiety about him, he told us he had felt so ill, during the previous service, he feared he should have been quite unable to acquit himself in the pulpit, either morning or evening, but that God had wonderfully helped him.

Next day he addressed a very large and crowded meeting at Bishop Wearmouth, and the following morning the Sunday-school teachers, assembled at the house of the rector; after which he returned to Durham, in preparation for the meeting to be held that evening. I was grieved to the heart to see him arrive, at four o'clock, exhausted to a degree. He went to bed, and got up only to attend the meeting, where it was arranged that he should speak first, and then retire immediately, which he did. Most touching was his appearance, "thrown aside as a useless wreck," as he himself feelingly said; pale and languid, he yet spoke with his usual simple earnestness and energy, his countenance beaming with that peculiar expression of love to God and man, for which it was so remarkable. * * *

He returned home, and every attention was paid to his health, which, anxious as we felt, we had no idea but rest and proper measures would speedily restore. The next two days he kept his room, after which he never left his bed, the disease gaining ground rapidly, and laying such firm hold of his constitution as baffled all efforts to overcome it.

During these days I had scarcely any intercourse with him, besides seeing that his comfort was attended to, he being ordered to be left perfectly quiet, and unexcited by conversation or reading. His weakness was very great, so much so that upon asking him if he would like a little prayer one night, he said it must be very short—he was so weak. The following evening on my commencing, he put his hand on mine, saying, "I am too ill, I cannot bear it." Still our fears only arose slowly and gradually.

After some days he asked me if the doctors thought him in danger. I truly replied, not so,—but that his state was certainly critical. He then made me promise I would tell him in case they thought worse of him. At this period of his illness he expressed a desire to recover, that he would rather recover and labour in God's service. I asked him if he were willing to depart? "Oh yes, willing, I hope, if it be God's will, which is best; only, if he sees well, I should prefer remaining."

Another time he said, "For *me*, it is far better to depart; but I am only a young man yet, and I might work in God's service if he raised me up. Yet when I think of my own deceitful heart, and the power of the world, I tremble, lest I should not stand firm." I said, we must trust God for life as well as death. He who had begun the good work could finish it. "Yes," he replied, "and then we have the promise of the Holy Ghost to uphold us, and sanctify us—yes, to sanctify us."

Upon my remarking, while giving him some food, "What an aggravation to sickness poverty must be, where there can be none of those alleviations you have;" he replied, "Oh, God is merciful, very merciful, and full of love, more than we can count up." I added—"How dreadful it must be to endure sufferings caused by sin, such as intemperance." He added, "All suffering is from sin; mine is from sin, perhaps some particular sin; I don't quite see what." He wondered how those who had not the consolations of the gospel could endure suffering.

About the same time I believe he expressed to you very humbling views of himself; how, with great privileges, he had been only a very ordinary Christian, and lived far beneath the standard he ought.

He also said to me, "I have not worked enough by faith. I have overworked myself, and made myself ill. God has punished me by this sickness." He meant he had not sufficiently trusted God to do his own work, in his own way, independent of his personal exertions, thinking, if he did it not, it would be left undone. He firmly resolved to amend in this point, if God raised him up, and not again to labour beyond the strength given him.

Except once, he scarcely after the first week of his illness alluded to himself, except in connection with Christ's wonderful love to him. It made me think of the promise, "He that humbleth himself shall be exalted."

During the days on which he made the remarks already noted, he mingled much of praise and thanksgiving, together with such expressions of love to God his Saviour, as made me again and again feel as if I had never loved Christ at all. In fact, the one great striking feature of his illness, as of his life, I may truly say, was his abounding love to his Saviour. It literally filled his heart, and nothing came in competition with it; "Him first, Him last;" He was indeed the Alpha and Omega with him. In his weakest and most tried moments the name of Jesus would bring a smile of happiness across his worn and suffering features. I wish that thousands could have partaken of the privilege I enjoyed of being an eye-witness of his faith and love. Words cannot describe it. A few disjointed expressions of his own cannot picture it. It was the whole tone and bearing of his mind, his conduct, and his looks, which bore such striking witness to the Spirit of Christ which was in him. It was beautiful beyond description.

But his habitual tone of mind was shown very affectingly in the wanderings of mind caused by fever; proving that he had indeed put on Christ, and that the mind which was in Christ was in him. And here I may remark, that as in his sober moments, so in these wanderings caused by disease, there was a remarkable absence of excitement; the mind was occupied with unrealities, but still there was a striking calmness and quietness of tone. In fact, he was remarkable for a deep, steady earnestness of character, which is opposed to the flickerings of excitement. It always struck me that he "spoke because he believed," that he acted on conviction and the exercise of a sound judgment. All that knew him must remember the peculiar calmness, gentleness, and I may say repose of his manner. This continued throughout his illness.

To give an instance of how his soul was filled with love to God and man, even when wandering, I will mention the following. He asked the servant, who was at the time in the room, if she saw "that sheet of white paper on the bed." There was nothing. "That," said he, "is the plan of salvation, laid out all plain and clear for the heathen; there is no crease or rumple on it to prevent their taking it, and it is offered to them." Then, in a sad tone, after a pause: "But alas! alas! I see none coming to lay hold on it."

But to return to my narrative. He was too weak, during the whole of his illness, to bear continuous reading or praying. One or two verses of Scripture at a time, however, and an ejaculatory prayer to meet his wants, were great comforts to him; and in this way I repeated to him a great portion of the promises of the Bible; some of them many times over: and most affectingly now are they associated in my memory with him, as having raised the eye of faith, and brought many a smile of angelic happiness across his countenance. Early in his illness, upon repeating from John iii. 36, "He that believeth in him hath everlasting life," he said with a solemnity of tone and look I shall never forget, "I *have* believed, I *do* believe." This was the secret of his strength and comfort throughout his illness, and it was striking that he should have said this to show it at the very commencement.

The second Sunday before he died, upon my remarking, "It was the close of the Sabbath, and there remaineth a Sabbath (rest) for the people of God," he said, "And what a Sabbath! perfect rest! when shall I get there? It is that little stream which divides us and makes us shrink. Earth has such hold of us."

This was on his thirty-first birthday, the first of October. He had felt too ill for several days to see his children, but now begged they might come. They came, bringing him nosegays of flowers, gathered from their own little gardens, wishing him, in child-like glee, "Many happy returns of the day." "Perhaps," said he, "it will be the last." I did not think it then: hope still predominated with us. After the children left him, (and he could only bear their presence a few minutes,) he said, "Dear little things, how they wind themselves round one's heart!" His affection for his children was very deep and tender, which made his readiness to leave them and commit them with faith to the God of the fatherless, more striking.

Reading to him a portion out of the Book of Revelation, he said, "The second and third chapters are so full of rebuke and exhortation, full of beautiful passages. I read them with R. just before I left Madras. I never met with any one of my own age so full of Christian experience as he is. He did not talk *about* religion, he talked *Christ*. We do not speak enough about Christ. It is because our hearts are not full enough of him."

Reading to him Jer. xxxi. 3, he repeated, "An everlasting love. 'I have drawn thee.' Yes, *drawn*—against our wills."

One morning, upon the medical man reminding him of the many mercies he enjoyed in his present illness, compared with what he had had in India, he said, "Yes, God is indeed good to me. He sends me innumerable mercies. His love is indeed wonderful! wonderful! wonderful! To send his Son to die for such creatures as we are! Surpassing love!" Then, in a low tone, his eyes shut, and a pause between each word, he repeated, "Love! Love! Love!"

This is a specimen, I may say, of his general tone of mind. Innumerable times did he express himself in a similar manner respecting the love of God, and his great goodness to himself and to all men. His heart seemed literally *filled* with the love of God shed *abroad* in it by the Holy Ghost. I now regret I was unable to note down more of his sweet expressions of love and faith; those I give you, I put down at the time, and are his own words. On my saying, "We shall see him as he is," he said, "See Him! See Him! Oh! it will be glorious!" He then went on to speak of the blessedness of heaven: "No crying, no death, no curse, no sin." We then spoke of the happiness of being there. Surely, even then, he had a foretaste of its glory! His heart seemed filled with joyful anticipations, and the poor suffering body could not keep it from mounting into the third heaven, into which he almost seemed to carry me along with him.

A doubt of his interest in Christ never arose, nor

did a cloud for a moment ever come between him and his clear view of his Saviour. I had in my own mind, fears, whether in the hours of nature's greatest weakness, Satan might not be allowed to try him, as he often does God's children;—but no, blessed be God! all was bright to the end. Once, when he seemed much distressed, and oppressed by suffering and weakness, I said, "In going through the dark valley, Satan often distresses God's people." He quickly replied: "Thank God, he has never been allowed to distress me."

This was the day before he died, and I feel assured the same peace continued to the end. Do not imagine, however, there was not conflict; this, I believe, will only cease when we put off this corruptible, and put on the incorruptible. His faith was never shaken, but it was tried. Deeply did he feel those seasons, when from extreme weakness he could hold no sensible communion with God. He seemed to reckon his nights bad or good in proportion to the degree in which he enjoyed the light of God's countenance. He generally answered my inquiries by, "I have not been able almost to pray. I could not break through; I was too ill." Once he said, "Sometimes I can lift up my heart to God, at other times it is so dead. To look to Christ on the cross, *that* is the way to get comfort and help from the Saviour of sinners."

The taking to pieces the earthly tabernacle was, as I imagine it always is when taken down gradually, very painful. Once, on my repeating, "Oh Lord, I am oppressed, undertake for me:" he repeated in a tone of deep feeling, "Lord, *I am* oppressed, *I am* oppressed, undertake for me, undertake for me!"

At such seasons the texts—"The eternal God is thy refuge, and underneath are the everlasting arms"—"Yea, though I walk through the valley of the shadow of death, I will fear no evil, for thou art with me, thy rod and thy staff, they comfort me"—were full of comfort to him. Sometimes he said to me, "Read me some strong passages." Another time, "Read me something about going through." I repeated from Isaiah xliii. 2, "When thou passest through the waters, I will be with thee; and through the rivers, they shall not overflow thee: when thou walkest through the fire, thou shalt not be burned, neither shall the flame kindle upon thee. For I am the Lord thy God, the Holy One of Israel, thy Saviour." This text, and many others from Isaiah, were of great comfort to him, and I often repeated them to him. Once or twice he said, "Oh, it is *very* painful, *very* painful,"—but he never expressed any sense of suffering or unrest, without adding either "God's will be done," or "God's will is best." Frequently did we hear him in low and earnest tones calling upon Jesus. At the commencement of his illness he seemed to be peculiarly sensitive to the fear of sinning by impatience. Many times he said to us, "Pray that my patience fail not," and most fully was the prayer answered.

Never was there a word, or sign, or look, which betrayed a failing of perfect patience. We felt from his words and conduct that God's will was indeed sweeter to him than his own ease or comfort. Neither was he passing through these trying days without profit. He said to me, "I do feel thankful, the last fortnight I have gained so much more knowledge of Christ. I could not have believed illness would have done so much for me. You know I used to say I felt illness unprofitable." He at other times told me how he had gained deeper views of the love of Christ since laid on his sick-bed. He seemed to have a constant sense of his less, as well as greater mercies. While bathing his hands, I remarked, "You see, God sends many alleviations to your sufferings." "Oh yes! tender mercies, wonderful mercies. He makes all my bed in my sickness. He just gives me all the comforts I need." Another time:—"I never wake, but I think of fresh mercies—God's mercies are innumerable." If you had seen the happy, grateful, heavenly countenance with which he uttered all his praiseful, grateful sentences, it would have engraven them on your very soul.

Although he had not yet given up hope, his illness was assuming a more and more serious aspect, while he who was the subject of it seemed daily nearing heaven. His mind increasingly dwelt with holy joy on the probable prospect of soon being with his Saviour.

He literally was without carefulness. After reading to him the concluding portion of 1 Cor. xv., ending, "Thanks be to God, who giveth us the victory!" he exclaimed: "Victory! yes, victory. Oh that it might be to-night." It was the first time he had expressed a decided wish to go, and I said, "Do you wish to go?" He turned his face toward me, and replied with an angelic smile:—"Oh yes, it would be so much better to be with Christ;" adding, however, that he thought God would raise him up, so many friends were praying for him, and instancing God's answering prayer in the release of Peter from prison. It was a great gratification to him to know that he was prayed for by many friends and congregations on his last Sunday, at Durham, Shields, Clifton, Brighton, Hampstead, and Edinburgh. He generally left the choice of portions of Scripture to me, though he sometimes named the subject he desired, according to his need:—but once he asked me to read him the two first verses of the 3d of 1 John, after which he repeated, "Sons of God,—let me dwell on that, *I* am a son of God, yes, a son of God!" He looked up as he said it, and seemed lost in happy contemplation.

At another time, speaking of the conclusion of the 8th of Romans, and that love of Christ from which nothing can separate us, he said, "I seemed to have got deeper into this—this wonderful love of Christ." "This is the one thing God has shown me more of in this illness. This wonderful love of Christ to sinners—such love!" I spoke of the shortness of time, the length of eternity. "Ah, and *such* an eternity *too*," he exclaimed, "and *such* brightness, and such glory—we cannot reach it—we cannot comprehend it now—it will be far, far above our present powers of conception." Such remarks were the more striking from his state being throughout one of much lethargy and physical depression—with a total absence of excitement. A large portion of his illness was passed in unrefreshing, painful sleep.

All I have recorded, was before hope was given up. On Tuesday, October 10, worse symptons appeared, but it was not till the following morning the medical man expressed his decided opinion that he would not recover. It so happened, that this was the only time I missed seeing him during Henry's illness. After he was gone, Henry sent for me, and said :—"George has been with me, and is much cast down about this, he tells me that Mr. J—— thinks me worse, and that I shall not live long; did he say so to you?" I replied,—"I missed seeing him." I confess my heart rather trembled. I feared that now the near and certain approach of death was brought before him, its terrors might at first dismay him, and I was quite unprepared for what followed, when he went on to say: "When he comes again, I wish you particularly to ask him, and if he says the same thing, are you all prepared to join me in praise?" I was overcome, and hid my face;—he continued, "I fear I ask a hard thing of you." I replied, "God has made us *willing* to part with you, He can enable us to praise Him." He went on to say—"Oh, it will be glorious, so glorious."

After this his whole heart seemed fixed upon the joys to which he was going, the prospect looked to him inexpressibly bright. This seemed to him a day of peculiar joy; for as yet the body, though very weak, was not so painfully oppressed as it afterward became.

When I went into his room the next morning, he said to me, "I am very weak, can scarcely speak, but oh! happy! happy! happy!" He now thought his time might be short, and desired to see his children. They got on the bed and kissed him; he said, "That is your last kiss. God bless you; if you wish to see papa again, you must come to heaven, where you will find him and dear mamma and little Johnny; now, good-bye."

He was calm and not overcome. I remembered his deep emotion when he parted from them to return to India, two years before. The struggle—and it was a bitter one—was gone through at that time; the sacrifice had been made, and God spared him the pain of a second.

One of the servants told me that while sitting up with him one night, he began to repeat from the Revelation, "What are these which are arrayed in white robes, and whence came they?" then pausing, as if memory failed him, she concluded the passage, "These are they which came out of great tribulation, and have washed their robes and made them white in the blood of the Lamb." Then he said, "Ah! there will be many from India, many from the Teloogoo nation." He then spoke of the approaching Jubilee, how he had written for it, preached for it, prayed for it, adding in a joyful tone, "It will be a glorious Jubilee for me."

I may here mention his dying testimony to the cause to which he had sacrificed his life. After reading to him the first three verses of Isaiah xl., I remarked it was a privilege to have been called even in a small measure to "prepare the way of the Lord." He replied, "Yes, there seems a special blessing rests on it; I often thank God that he called me to be a missionary to go abroad." On his mother's asking him whether he repented having giving his life to missionary work, he said, "No, never! if I had to live over again, I would do the same." This he said only a day or two before he died, when he knew he was, humanly speaking, losing his life in consequence of his labours abroad and at home in that cause—a cause so glorious, even the rescuing of immortal souls from sin and Satan, that it was dearer to him than life itself, through love to his Redeemer.

And now his work on earth seemed done, and truly "his soul was in haste to be gone." Every symptom that spoke of the nearness of death was precious to him, and raised a smile of joy. Once he complained that the extra clothing on his feet produced no warmth; then turning his eyes on me with a smile, he asked, "This is a *good* sign, is it not?" Any little thing I could name to him as a sign of approaching dissolution was a pleasure to him. Strange did it seem to be affording him comfort, by telling him of various little signs of the nearness of death; but so it was. Still there was no impatience, but perfect submission to God's will. Once he said, "It matters little, a day or night more or less; God's time is best." He liked me to repeat to him his favourite Baxter's saying, respecting his own death, "When Thou wilt, where Thou wilt, as Thou wilt."

He was detained nearly two days and a night longer than he had been led to suppose. On Saturday morning he said to me, "For half an hour in the night I thought I was just going to be at rest, but I rallied again. God's will be done, God's will be done, God's will is best. I said, "You have *peace* in Jesus?" "Yes, *in Jesus,* he is the dying Saviour?"

On the medical man's saying the same morning when he visited him, "I had hoped to have found you released," he replied, "Mr. J., *perfect* subjection of our wills to God's, *that* is the thing."

He had told Mr. J. the night previous, that the only thing that distressed him was, "seeing your and our dear mother's grief." He said to her once, "Why have you been crying, dear mother? Have they told you I am going? It is right you should know. O mother, it will be so joyous! To meet father and Lizzy, and all who have gone before." In general, however, this happy anticipation of seeing departed relations was swallowed up in the higher joy of seeing that Saviour whom, not having seen, he had so truly loved.

On my reminding him, as a cordial to his bodily suffering and weariness at the moment, "that he would soon see his dear wife," he replied, "To see Him that was pierced for us, that is the thing."

Another time, speaking himself of the happiness of finding so many dear ones whom we had loved on earth, in heaven, after a pause he said, "But we shall there be so taken up with Christ, we shall have little thought for other things." Another time he remarked to me, after speaking of some dear relations now in heaven, "We think much of those few, but there are so many more: such a glorious company of saints to see and be with—St. Paul, St. Peter, Hezekiah, Henry Martyn. It will be so blessed to meet them."

As he grew weaker and weaker, he at times seemed much oppressed, and I said, "You must not faint;" he answered, "I sometimes feel as if I should." I replied, "I do not mean your body, but your spirit must not fail." "There is no fear of that, it is all joy." Another time, when my heart ached for him, more to re-assure myself than for his sake, I asked, "Have you peace?" "Yes, peace; the only anxiety is to be gone; but God's will is best; that is the best thing, perfect submission to his will."

As the outer man decayed, the inner man grew stronger; it was a love and faith made perfect which had cast out fear. To his dear mother he said, "In due time we shall meet in Jesus; we shall see him as he is, very beautiful! very beautiful!"

Once he said, "It is a hard thing to die, to pass through; nothing but the Lord's promises could enable us to do it;" then, in a firm tone, "but they are sure and *steadfast.*" He seemed to lose all sense of time, which seemed often immeasurably lengthened. I said, "Time seems long when suffering. You have scarcely been three weeks confined to bed yet;" he went on, "and by the time these weeks are completed, I shall in all probability be in heaven."

Speaking of Christ, he said, "It would be ten thousand times better to be with him: perhaps I may see him to-morrow." The happy calmness of tone and look with which he expressed himself throughout was striking; it was the result of a firm conviction of the certainty and reality of the truths he believed, and the glory he anticipated. It was as if he was speaking of soon joining a loved parent or brother on earth, only his feelings were holier, higher, more blessed. I may again repeat, I never witnessed any thing like excitement in him; it was the sober certainty of waking bliss, which filled his heart; and there was a reality about it that made me almost feel as if faith were turned into sight.

He was now getting very near putting off this mortal body; his hands were like ice, he begged me to come closer to him, he could not see me. My sight is going—it is coming back."—"It will come back in eternity," I said. For the last two days he could hardly bear me to absent myself from him; and if I left the room, would send for me, and have me sit close to him administering to his bodily and spiritual wants. "How different your hand is to every one else's!" he said, as I bathed his forehead with Cologne water. "Do you like it best?" "Oh" yes. I had left him a few minutes, he sent after me. When I came, "O Isabella, I want some of your comfort." I said, "You mean God's." "Yes, read me some passages." Once previously, I had taken up Clark's Promises, and he said, "Not that little book, the real Bible." Once he remarked with a happy smile, "There, (in heaven,) there will be no Bible." During the last day, he frequently exclaimed, "Lord, why tarriest Thou : come, Lord," —but always adding, "God's will be done," or "God's time is best."

While sitting quietly by him, he exclaimed, "How happy! If it please God I may just sink away thus, it will be a great mercy." At three o'clock of this last day, he said, "O Lord! gracious Lord! loving Jesus! how gracious he is. Oh, let me go to-day! O Lord, thou knowest best! Are there two or three hours yet before God comes! pray that he will come."

And now the last enemy was nearly conquered, for "death," as he himself remarked, "is called an enemy." He had for the last two days and nights frequently seemed near going, so that even now I scarcely knew whether he might not still linger for a while, though my prayers were joined with his, that if it were God's will, his happy soul might speedily be released. I heard him faintly saying to himself, "Jesus, Jesus must be first in the heart." I said, "He is the first in your's." "Yes, he is." They were his last words. I felt his firm grasp of my hand relaxing, his pulse was gone; breathing became slow and more faint. I sent for you and my mother; and, soon after your arrival, he gently ceased to breathe, and was with his Saviour.

"Blessed are the dead which die in the Lord from henceforth: Yea, saith the Spirit, that they may rest from their labours; and their works do follow them."

I did not think I could have praised God under the blow, but he did enable me; and does, and ever will, I trust, enable us all to join in thanksgiving, for that he permitted his servant so to glorify him in life and death, and us to be witnesses of his faith and patience. May we be followers of him as he followed Christ!

THE END.

www.ingramcontent.com/pod-product-compliance
Lightning Source LLC
LaVergne TN
LVHW010225110826
845151LV00004B/1183